Social Control at the Margins

Toward a General Understanding of Deviance

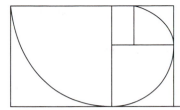

Social Control
at the Margins

Toward a General Understanding
of Deviance

David P. Aday, Jr.

The College of William & Mary

Wadsworth Publishing Company
Belmont, California
A Division of Wadsworth, Inc.

To my parents, David and Virginia, who taught me the value
of hard work and gave me the gift of caring.

Sociology Editor: Serina Beauparlant
Editorial Assistant: Marla Nowick
Production Editor: Michael G. Oates
Interior and Cover Design: Andrew H. Ogus
Print Buyer: Barbara Britton
Copy Editor: Patricia Tompkins
Compositor: Omegatype Typography, Inc., Champaign, Illinois

Printed in the United States of America   19

1 2 3 4 5 6 7 8 9 10 — 94 93 92 91 90

Library of Congress Cataloging in Publication Data

Aday, David P.
    Social control at the margins : toward a general understanding of
deviance / David P. Aday.
        p.   cm. — (Wadsworth series on deviant behavior)
    Bibliography: p.
    Includes index.
    ISBN 0-534-11994-8
    1. Deviant behavior.   I. Title.   II. Series.
HM291.A32   1989
302.5'42—dc20
                                                            89-33456
                                                              CIP

Contents

CHAPTER 9

White-Collar Crime   190

CHAPTER 10

Some Final Thoughts on Social Policy   226

Preface

Social control is a fact of collective life. Even the most "permissive" groups and communities impose limits and exact compliance to standards and expectations. It is nearly impossible to imagine the actual range of human expressions and conduct. We are so accustomed to constraint that we are seldom aware of its presence or consequences—especially in our own society where we glorify individuality and personal freedom. Because social control is an integral part of social life, it is natural that deviance would be found in all groups and communities.

The paradox of control and deviance is the central theme of *Social Control at the Margins*. This is not an attempt to illustrate, discuss, or explain the full range of *deviance* in this or other societies; instead, I focus on methods of sociological description and explanation. How can we define deviance without making value judgments? Is deviance a personal quality, an attribute of certain kinds of behaviors, or a social definition? These questions are raised and considered. I have selected topics to introduce and illustrate a sociological approach to answers. The emphasis is on *doing* sociology—readers are invited to take an active role in efforts to *understand* and *explain* deviance and social control.

Describing and Defining Deviance

Social Control at the Margins begins with the observation that *deviance* is a
sociological concept—that is, it is an idea developed with the hope of capturing
some part of human experience in an accurate and precise way. The words
deviance and deviant are seldom used in ordinary language, and in everyday
affairs they are virtually never used with any clear or precise meaning. Our
concern, then, is to define and specify *sociologically* what we mean by deviance.
The goal is not to expand sociological jargon. Rather, we pursue careful
conceptualization and definition to promote more incisive thinking and more
precise observation. Concepts are among the essential tools of science, and
deviance is a potentially powerful concept for seeing similarities and differences
that otherwise may be obscured.

Sociologists long have suspected that deviance is more than the violation
of some norm, rule, or law. At the same time, we know that it is not just an
arbitrary definition imposed by people with power. Deviance usually involves
norm violation; however, sometimes it does not. Deviance always involves
sanctions—either applied or threatened. And, deviance and social control are
linked inseparably. I will argue, as others have, that deviance and social control
are integral parts of social life.

Norms and their violation are not random or arbitrary. Instead, they reflect
the organization of society. Likewise, reactions to norm violations are not
arbitrary or simply the result of oppressive political power. They, too, reflect
and reveal the organization of the society. The problems of defining deviance
are discussed in the first two chapters, and an explicit definition of deviance
is introduced in Chapter 3. The conception is different from those that currently
prevail. It is explicit, and it asserts the importance of norms and their violation
and reaction to violations.

How, exactly, are deviance and social organization related? Under what
conditions does deviance increase or decrease? These questions concern deviant events and activities considered collectively; they have to do with *patterns*
and *rates*. It is not hard to imagine that rates and patterns of deviance change
as societies change. Current drug use patterns are different from those seen at
the turn of this century, rates of prostitution increase and decrease, and
methods of enforcement and control develop and change over time. Contemporary Americans are keenly aware of rapid social change and changing standards of conduct. What forces, if any, lie behind these patterns?

If patterns and rates of deviance can be explained, it may be possible to
identify the *sources* of deviance. Most 20th century sociological explanations
have been concerned with causes. Some contemporary theorists believe that
we are close to an *integrated* causal theory. They propose to find links among

the current theories and develop an explanation through "synthesis".* This text suggests an alternative and gives students the foundation for analyzing theories to discover answers of their own.

Organization of the Text

Social Control at the Margins is divided into two parts: "The Elusive Reality of Deviance" and "Deviance: Social Organization, Niches, and Actions." Part One, which contains Chapters 1–5, provides the information and conceptual foundation for explaining deviance sociologically—that is, objectively, analytically, and empirically.

The first chapter introduces the social reality of deviance and attempts to maximize readers' understandings from personal experiences. The use of formal concepts is kept to a minimum and examples are presented in everyday language. Issues that have troubled sociologists and other researchers are raised and considered, but the extensive and informative research literature on these issues is cited in the endnotes rather than reviewed in detail. Those who are intrigued and want to explore these matters more fully will find key sources—and an exciting history of thoughtful and controversial discussions—identified in the bibliography.

Because deviance and social organization are linked inextricably, an explanation of one requires an understanding of the other. There are no more compelling discussions of social organization than those found in the works of the founders of sociology: Emile Durkheim, Karl Marx, and Max Weber. The second chapter offers a brief review of these classical explanations of social organization and social control. The ideas discussed in this chapter form the foundation of a general explanation of deviance called *convergence theory*. The ideas are abstract, and they may be unfamiliar to those who have little background in sociology, but they are carefully illustrated. The examples center on prostitution and homosexuality. The discussions and illustrations suggest broad outlines of the approach that will be developed and applied in later chapters.

---

* A conference was held at the State University of New York, Albany, in the spring of 1987. The purpose of the conference was to advance the prospects for developing an integrated theory of crime and deviance. Invited speakers discussed different aspects of the process of integrating, and most seem to share some hope that an encompassing theory could be developed by finding the linkages among existing theories. (See Messner, Steven, Marvin Krohn, and Alan Liska. Forthcoming. *Theoretical Integration in the Study of Deviance and Crime: Problems and Prospects.* Albany: State University of New York Press.) I am convinced that we must be concerned first and foremost with the empirical realities that we seek to understand.

Chapter 3 introduces a basic set of concepts that will be used to describe *social arrangements* and the relationship between social organization and deviance. Research and theories from Durkheim, Marx, and Weber are used to describe this relationship. Drawing directly from these discussions, the first part of the general (convergence) theory of deviance is introduced. It is an *epidemiological* theory—that is, one concerned with explaining patterns and rates and their relationship to characteristics of the society. Examples are drawn from education (success and failure), prostitution, drinking, and changes surrounding industrialization in the United States to amplify the central points of the analysis and the proposed explanation.

In Chapter 4, I review current theories of deviance. The focus *is not* on linking them together. Instead, they are treated as information about what various observers have regarded as important in the *realities* of social deviance. The proposed definition of deviance is reconsidered in light of this information. Then, I propose a general *causal* theory.

The first part of the text ends with a discussion of methods and issues of deviance research (Chapter 5). The central concern is to introduce and describe procedures for evaluating deviance explanations. Chapter 5 is not a substitute for a course in sociological research methods. Instead, I introduce the basic issues of research design (validity, reliability, control, and generalizability) and suggest ways to use these standards to assess the viability of proposed explanations. The points are illustrated through research on homosexuality, drug use, delinquency and juvenile justice, and homicide.

It would be possible to skip Part One and go directly to the first substantive topic (Chapter 6: "Heterosexual Deviance"). However, that strategy risks substituting idle curiosity and gawking for sociological research. Obviously, there are sociological approaches other than the one proposed here. But some systematic conceptual foundation and some set of empirical methods are necessary to escape the limitations of personal experience and biases. The success of the proposed approach can be assessed in a limited way through the chapters on specific types of deviance (Chapters 6–9 concern prostitution, mental illness, violent crime, and white-color crime). The general theory is applied to each type of deviance to present a coherent explanation. These more applied discussions should help readers understand the proposed general theory.

Each of the chapters in Part Two includes a discussion of the policy implications of the proposed explanation. The final chapter offers a consideration of the policy implications for the convergence theory of deviance and social control. It is clear that the historical drift in the United States (and, perhaps, in most Western societies) has been toward more law, more law enforcement, and more formal social control generally. Has the result been *more effective social control?* If not, why not?

Evaluation of the Proposed Theory

Does the approach offer a clear and coherent description of the behaviors, events, and arrangement of concern? Have research studies produced data that tend to support the proposed explanation? Does the explanation suggest research questions that are incisive and in line with or beyond previous studies? Ultimately, the viability and usefulness of the proposed theory must be tested through the collection of original and systematic data. Each chapter presents illustrations of the kinds of research that are needed to test the theory. For now, we can at least evaluate the promise of the conception and explanation.

The proposed approach—conception, conceptual framework, theory, and analyses of various types of deviance—is an attempt to build on the diverse and impressive accomplishments of earlier researchers and theorists. In that sense, there is nothing new here. Still, there is the possibility that we do not need to choose among the diverse and seemingly conflicting perspectives and theories that comprise the sociology of deviance. I have no illusion that the theory proposed here is the final explanation. I am certain that my colleagues and their students will find the limitations of this effort. I hope that this effort will encourage others to strive for general explanations. *Social Control at the Margins* details a strategy for developing a general theory: Treat theory and research as sources of information that form a foundation for a more inclusive conception and explanation of deviance.

Acknowledgments

Many people have contributed to the publication of this book. Sheryl Fullerton, executive editor, understood almost from the beginning what I hoped to accomplish in the project. Her support and her willingness to take a risk are greatly appreciated. Serina Beauparlant, sociology editor, took charge and made sure that this text fulfilled the needs of instructors and students. Michael Oates, production editor, provided firm but gentle guidance that resulted in remarkable efficiency. Pat Tompkins did a superb job of copyediting and brought keen insight to the preparation of the final manuscript. And Andrew Ogus's inviting design enhanced the text's readability. The professional staff at Wadsworth has made the publication process a joyful one.

I am grateful to the reviewers who responded to drafts along the way: William Sims Bainbridge, Illinois State University; Dean Bowman, Bemidji State University; Morris A. Forslund, University of Wyoming; Joan Gurney, University of Richmond; Gary Jensen, University of Arizona; Jim Skipper, University of North Carolina at Greensboro; Sol Tannenbaum, University of

Houston; and Joseph G. Weis, University of Washington. Their suggestions may or may not be fully reflected, but their comments were almost universally helpful.

I would also like to thank the many sociologists whose works are quoted, paraphrased, examined, and from whose works many of my conclusions are drawn. A complete list of copyrighted material follows the index.

My debt to family, friends, mentors, and colleagues is great. They have endured my restlessness and impatience while I struggled to articulate ideas that, in the final analysis, are fairly simple. Gary Kreps, colleague and friend, alternately inspires and provokes, but unfailingly supports my efforts. In his own work and in his thoughtful reaction to mine, Gary provides a model of scholarly devotion. Satoshi Ito is a patient listener, a supportive and incisive critic, and a faithful friend. Other colleagues, within and outside of the sociology department, have provided encouragement and support. I want to thank specifically colleagues and administrators who provided support through a college summer research grant and a semester research leave. Graduate and undergraduate students have given me confidence that a coherent explanation of deviance can be communicated and understood. Many have contributed to my efforts as assistants. They have made countless trips to the library, spent hours searching for obscure references, and read multiple drafts hoping to improve the clarity of presentation.

Above all, I appreciate my family and their contributions to my continuing efforts. The life of an academic is a privileged one. My family—Sherry, Derek, and Ryan—make mine a blessed one.

David Aday, Jr.

PART ONE

The Elusive Reality
of Deviance

Experiencing and
Describing Deviance

"Jason" is 21 years old, 6'1", and 170 pounds. He is a college junior who has paid most of his college expenses working part time in two jobs. He works once or twice a month as a chauffeur for a limousine rental agency that serves "VIPs." And several times a month, he works as an escort in a nearby city. Women who use the escort service typically are rising executives with business, government, and nonprofit organizations who travel frequently and attend business-related parties and social occasions. Some of the clients understand that with "tips" they can privately arrange for "additional services" with individual escorts.

Jason is bright, handsome, charming, and well read. He enjoys life as a student, dates frequently, and belongs to a social fraternity. He sometimes worries that his friends and college acquaintances will learn of his job as an escort, but he doesn't think his job is wrong or inappropriate. Instead, he thinks most people are very "narrow minded" and "wouldn't understand."

He recounts an experience in which a woman called the service and asked that a young, good-looking man come to her home in *brief* athletic attire. When he arrived, the woman (in her mid-50s) asked him to jog with her around her neighborhood. As they ran, she explained that her husband had died recently and all of her busy-body neighbors were trying to fix her up with "dowdy old bachelors." She hoped that this maneuver would slow them down for a while.[1]

Is Jason deviant? Is it deviant to be a male escort? How do we determine whether something is or is not deviant? Are there universal criteria that distinguish *deviant* from *acceptable*? If so, what are they? Where do they come from? The brief case study of Jason and the questions it generates illustrate fascinating and compelling issues. Researchers, politicians, psychiatrists, social workers, police officers, and students have wrestled with these issues in one form or another for years. Some have regarded deviance as a quality that is a part of the "thing" (for example, a person, act, event, trait) and have tried to understand deviance in terms of this thing's characteristics. Explanations have been sought in the properties, characteristics, or traits of those who engage in the behavior. A typical explanation might suggest that Jason and those like him have developed insecurities from unmet needs. The explanation might suggest that they engage in "unnatural" behavior because they seek attention or gratification of needs that are not met in usual and appropriate ways.

Others have regarded deviance as nothing more than an opinion, a definition, or a label. Something is or is not deviant, then, depending on who gets to decide and what is decided at any moment, within any situation. Explanations developed from this point of view focus on the definitions, those who make them, and the ways in which they are made. They suggest that "deviants" are simply people who have been identified through more or less arbitrary decisions and who are treated differently as a result. A typical theory might contend that Jason's so-called deviance is a result of discriminatory sexual norms that condemn certain practices, such as women buying sexual services. Proponents might note that the same norms are tolerant of other similar practices, such as women using their sexual traits to promote business. They might argue further that these norms operate to maintain social arrangements that benefit some members of the group or society.

So, Jason *is* deviant, according to one point of view, because he and his behavior are "obviously," "naturally," and "inherently" bad, immoral, or inappropriate. From the other vantage point, Jason *may be defined* as deviant. If he is, then the deviance simply reflects the interests, values, and biases of those who do the defining. Viewed in this way, Jason's deviance is a matter of chance that depends mostly on the characteristics of the audience—that is, the *definers*.

In the discussions that follow, we will consider these alternative approaches. Neither is correct or adequate, and both are right—as far as they go.[2] A third point of view suggests that deviance is best understood as something that is both very real and very much a matter of definition.

A Sociological Conception of Deviance

Deviance is a *sociological concept*. As such, it is an idea developed and introduced to promote careful and precise thinking about and observation of part of the real world of human experience. The value of any concept can be determined only as it is used. If it is a good concept, then it will facilitate efforts to understand and explain.

Are Some Things Inherently Deviant?

Consider the "deviance" of nakedness. When is it appropriate, acceptable, or permissible to be naked? In our culture, it is generally okay to be without clothes while bathing, in various private places (such as one's home or bedroom), and during military physical examinations. Note, however, that this appropriateness depends on social definitions. To be naked in our society usually means to be entirely without clothing, and there are times and places where that is permissible. But on Inis Beag (a small island off the coast of Ireland), there is virtually no circumstance in which nakedness is appropriate or tolerable. Even bathing is accomplished by sponging off certain important areas—without undressing, or removing as few clothes as possible. And being naked includes being fully dressed but without shoes (Messenger, 1971.)

In our culture, being naked is acceptable if it's hot, the nudist is under the age of two, and the episode doesn't last too long. In the early 1970s, nudity was tolerated if the person without clothes was a college student who ran through some public gathering. In this case, the event involved "streaking," which was somehow different from being naked in public!

Is nakedness deviant? The best answer is that it depends. It depends on the culture, the characteristics of those involved, and other matters such as historical fads and fashions. Does it follow that deviance is simply a matter of definition and opinion? No. Informal observations and more systematic research studies suggest that something identifiable as nakedness is regarded as wrong in most cultures and at most times throughout recorded history. Even in nudist camps and colonies, for example, certain kinds of nakedness are considered bad and unacceptable. Highlighting genital areas in any way, sitting in certain "revealing" postures, and strategically concealing body parts are all regarded as wrong—and maybe perverse (Weinberg, 1978). This suggests some consistent tendency to treat certain matters of body exposure as wrong. To the extent that this is true, nakedness may have objective properties, some of which provoke negative reactions.

The analysis and discussion to this point are not intended as arguments for a philosophy of cultural relativism. The conclusion is not that there is no right or wrong in the world. Instead, one implication is that even if moral imperatives exist, they do not determine practically how human affairs will be treated or understood. A second implication is that some things may be treated consistently as deviant in different cultures or in different time periods (or both) because they are, in some sense, consistently deviant. Are some things naturally deviant? Murder, for example, surely must be abhorred by all reasonable people at all times. How could it be otherwise?

To answer the question, we must define *murder.* If it refers to taking a human life, the following commonly recognized acts would qualify: first-degree murder, execution (for a capital crime), euthanasia, war, and abortion. Are these treated the same in our society? Clearly, execution and first-degree murder are treated differently. Both involve taking a life, but one is accepted and approved (at least sometimes), while the other usually is condemned categorically. The act of taking the life of an enemy soldier is an integral and relatively routine part of battle. Euthanasia raises even thornier problems. It refers generally to "mercy killing," but what is merciful and what is legal are controversial and difficult judgments. The case of Roswell Gilbert provides an example.

> **Fort Lauderdale, Florida, Spring 1986: Roswell Gilbert (age 75) has been convicted of killing his wife of 51 years and was sentenced to life imprisonment with a mandatory prison term of 25 years. Gilbert's wife, Emily, was 73 and suffered from Alzheimer's disease, brain degeneration, and osteoporosis, a painful disintegration of bone. Witnesses testified that Mrs. Gilbert begged for death to end her suffering. Mr. Gilbert testified that he shot his wife twice in the head out of compassion. He called the police immediately after the shooting and surrendered himself to them when they arrived [author's files].**

The Gilbert case suggests that it is not true that "murder is murder is murder." Many regarded Mr. Gilbert's behavior as euthanasia—even though the judge found him guilty of murder and sentenced him accordingly. Taking a life may or may not be considered deviant. Recall the question: Are some things universally deviant? To answer that, we must ask about behaviors and events in their most generic form. *Murder* is not a generic description of human behavior. It is not just the act of taking a life. Instead, the term incorporates certain presumptions and distinctions. We can rephrase the question raised earlier: Is taking a life deviant? Again, the best answer seems to be: It depends.

It depends—but deviance is not entirely a matter of judgment. How are instances of deviance to be identified? Are there *objective* criteria that differentiate deviant from nondeviant?

Objective Properties of Deviance: Expectations and Violations

Common sense suggests that certain things are *objectively* deviant—that is, "naturally," "always and everywhere" wrong and unacceptable. However, the criteria of such "universal" beliefs are highly elusive—if, in fact, such things exist. Consider, for example, two characteristics that seem to distinguish deviance: (1) harmfulness and (2) extent of violation. People often believe that things are deviant to the extent that they cause harm. Are harmful things treated consistently as deviant? Consider the "harmfulness" of selected drugs as described in Table 1.1.

In Table 1.1, harmfulness is measured roughly by the number and percent of emergency room episodes and fatal overdoses. Taking aspirin is not usually regarded as deviant in our society, but it resulted in over 6,000 emergency room visits—more visits than were caused by use of marijuana, cocaine, amphetamines, PCP, or LSD. Using heroin usually is regarded as deviant in the United States, but it was "less harmful" than using minor tranquilizers (in 1981–1982, as indicated by the data on emergency room episodes).[3] Many drugs are dangerous (harmful), but only a few become matters of social control.

The issue of harmfulness can be considered in a different way. The U.S. Department of Health, Education, and Welfare (1981) lists the following as America's "leading causes of death" in order: heart disease, cancer, strokes, accidents, pneumonia, diabetes, cirrhosis of the liver, suicide, homicide, and emphysema. Some of these causes of death might be regarded as deviant. Most Americans would agree that suicide and homicide are deviant, for example. Some would include cirrhosis of the liver and emphysema, reasoning that these diseases result from the deviant practices of drinking alcohol and smoking, respectively. Few people regard as deviant the top three killers. Heart disease, for example, is very harmful and unfortunate, but it is not ordinarily regarded as deviant. Perhaps the things on this list are harmful but differ on some other basis.

The earlier discussion of taking a life may provide a clue. Murder involves harm. It also involves the intention to cause harm. Perhaps harmfulness and the intention to harm identify a class of things that are treated consistently as deviant. Our laws distinguish between *involuntary* manslaughter and criminal, or *willful*, homicide, and suggest that the difference is real and meaningful (see U.S. Department of Justice, 1981:63–64). However, some acts of life taking involve intention, but they clearly are *not* regarded as deviant. Capital punishment and war involve intention and killing, but both are justified by

T A B L E   1 . 1

Emergency Room Episodes
and Fatal Drug Overdoses by Drug or Drug Type, 1981–1982

	Emergency Room Episodes		Fatal Overdoses	
	Number	Percent	Number	Percent
Minor tranquilizers	21,413	15	480	9
Methaqualone	3,921	3	121	2
Other nonbarbiturate sedatives	10,398	7	317	6
Barbiturates	7,112	5	648	12
Heroin	11,538	8	771	14
Methadone	2,246	2	137	2
Other narcotics	5,222	4	631	11
Aspirin	6,291	4	104	2
Other nonnarcotic analgesics	9,274	6	224	4
Antidepressants	8,768	6	651	12
Antipsychotics (major tranquilizers)	8,050	6	101	2
Amphetamines	5,013	3	73	1
PCP	3,857	3	112	2
LSD	1,464	1	1	*
Alcohol-in-combination	27,928	19	952	17
Marijuana	5,123	4	4	*
Cocaine	5,830	4	198	4
Inhalants	486	*	31	1

*Less than one-half of 1 percent. Source: Drug Abuse Warning Network (1983:11) cited in Goode (1984b:44).

some social arrangement such as law or custom. War involves killing that has been justified by ideology. Thus, harm and the intention to harm *do not* seem to identify things that are treated consistently as deviant.

Consider the other side of the issue. Some things are deviant but not apparently harmful. None of the following is obviously harmful: drinking beer at the age of 20 when the legal age is 21, smoking marijuana, engaging in sex outside of marriage, oral sex between a husband and wife, men wearing earrings, men or women growing their hair long—or cutting it short. Nonetheless, all of these have been identified as deviant at one time or another in our society.

"Degree of departure" is another criterion that often is thought to identify things that are *objectively* and obviously deviant. So far, however, the standard does not seem workable. Cannibalism, for example, is an extreme and rare behavior. Yet, it is not regarded as deviant always and everywhere. Some cultures practice limited forms of cannibalism, and under some circumstances, it has been condoned as necessary for survival (for example, in the plane crash of the Uruguayan rugby team in the Andes in 1972).

No criterion, including harm and degree of departure, has been found that distinguishes things that are necessarily deviant from those that are not. But *deviance is objectively real.* It is not simply a matter of individual judgment or opinion. To understand deviance, we must identify its component parts: *violation, expectations*, and some punitive or condemning *reaction.*

Violation is an objective property of behaviors, traits, events, and characteristics (Gibbs, 1966). It is inherently relative because it refers to some expectation (Gibbs, 1972). Violation is departure from some norm, rule, or law. Expectations vary from society to society, but all societies have them. And these expectations probably are not arbitrary. Some norms or laws may be necessary for the survival of social organization (see Davis, 1959; Campbell, 1969; and Faia, 1986.) Moreover, both expectations and violations appear to be necessary parts of social organization. These assertions will be examined in detail in Chapter 2.

Violation requires a referent: some expectation or law. Such expectations are objective, real, and observable. The following case provides a description of expectations and violations.

Two teenage boys have been referred to the local juvenile court. The police report indicates that the juveniles were apprehended after "throwing missiles at a moving vehicle." The police report is reviewed at a meeting of the staff of the local juvenile court services agency. An intake officer who spoke with the arresting officers reports that the incident involved throwing water balloons (not mentioned in the police report) at a car. The police report characterized the event as "felonious damage to property." Court services staff discussions (lasting approximately 20 minutes) center on recreating the event and trying to understand how a water balloon can break a windshield. At one point, it appears that a formal petition will be filed charging the juveniles with a delinquent act. Further discussion produces the conclusion that the water balloons would not have broken the windshield if it had not been cracked. No one present knows of any previous court contact with the juveniles. The decision is made to handle the case informally and to try to make arrangements for the youngsters to pay for the damages [Aday, 1977, pp. 91–94].

What happened? Did the event involve a serious crime or relatively harmless mischief? The police report indicates that local juveniles committed a felony offense (violation of a criminal law). The court services report describes an event that involved a minor youthful misbehavior. No formal charges were filed.

The case illustrates a range and a variety of expectations—for example, about the proper conduct of youth and respect for property and human safety—and assorted real and alleged violations of those expectations. The event was described through information communicated from the police to the court services counselor. The situation involves matters of fact, at least partly. There are expectations and violations. Descriptions of the event were more or less correct, but the event is objectively real. The facts influenced the handling and outcome of the event (that is, the informal probation). The entire matter reflects outlines of the community and society: Property rights were violated, representatives of the state responded, offenders were treated in terms of their special status as juveniles, and the peculiar role of the juvenile court was reflected in the final outcome.

The water balloon episode has become part of the community's history and efforts to control human behavior and human relationships. It is described in police reports, juvenile court case files, and statistical summaries. Deviance as an objective reality exists: The norms and laws have been recognized; a violation has been identified and handled. The expectations and the violation are not arbitrary. Both are parts of the organization of social life and the ongoing community. Note, however, that different information could have been selected and considered at any point in the unfolding case. That is, different "facts" could have been selected (discovered, recognized, or created). For example, the incident in fact involved throwing a water balloon at a police car. The boys had been arrested and referred to court for a previous offense. And the windshield was not cracked before the incident. Thus, the episode might have been described and treated as a malicious attack on authority and a felony assault on a police officer. And that description could have emerged even if the same actors were involved. Deviance clearly involves more than expectations and violations—more than objective facts.

Subjective Properties of Deviance: Reactions and Outcomes

The preceding discussion suggests that objective facts do not determine reactions to violations or the outcomes of such events. Instead, *reaction* is a critically important variable that gives character and form to violation and shapes the *outcome* of violating events. The police and the court services staff reached conclusions on the basis of selected facts and interpretations. The conclusions represent deviance. Indeed, "deviance results" *without violation* are possible.[4] And violations do not ensure that something will be identified as deviant. Return to the example of the male escort and consider the possibilities:

> Jason is a college student who works occasionally as a male escort. He does *not* provide "extra services," but his co-workers, some of the agency's clients, and his supervisors assume that he does. An investigative reporter learns of the agency and its activities and publishes an exposé in which Jason and some of his co-workers are identified by name. The news story does not distinguish between escorts who do and those who don't engage in sex with their clients.

Jason has been identified as a deviant. The news story implies that Jason is a male prostitute in spite of, or regardless of, the facts. Jason may experience the consequences of his "deviance." College friends and acquaintances may shun him. He may be the object of ridicule or of uninvited sexual attention. The fact that Jason does not engage in the accused deviance may be completely irrelevant to his identification and treatment as deviant.

It could have gone the other way. Jason might have provided sexual services on a regular basis. His co-workers and supervisors might have assumed that he didn't. The agency might never have been noticed by any reporter or the general public. Assuming that none of his friends ever learned of his sexual involvements, Jason might never have experienced any consequence of his violating behavior. There would have been *violation without deviance.*

Is something deviant if no one knows except the person who violates a norm? That is an interesting question, but for our purposes its answer has little value. We can say with some confidence that violation is violation whether or not anyone else knows—and it is an instance of *potential deviance.* For our purposes, however, the focus is on instances of deviance that can be identified (seen, experienced) empirically. Deviance is most easily identified by observing the reactions of others. Whether we are participants in everyday affairs or sociological observers, we are most certain of what deviance is when we see social control imposed: people arrested, friends deserted, rumors circulated, and so on. The implications are important: We can "see" deviance *without* violation and violation occurs without deviance—that is, without social control reactions. The presence of a negative sanction (whether arrest, scorn, or punishment) is a better indicator of deviance than is violation of norms.

Deviance is shaped partly by shared understandings. In the earlier example, it was not relevant that the water balloon broke the windshield of a police car or that the boys had previous records. And it was not relevant whether or not Jason provided sexual services. The reality of deviance results emerges partly from interpretations (Kitsuse, 1962; Erickson, 1962; Becker, 1963). Said simply, deviance is an outcome. More specifically, it is a *negotiated outcome*. Such outcomes will be explained more fully in subsequent chapters. For now, the central point is this: Deviance is not simply the violation of expectations.

Toward a Scientific Definition of Deviance

Deviance involves shared expectations, violations, and reactions. The expectations may be more or less explicit, more or less formal, and more or less widely shared. The violations may be real or alleged. The matter of allegation is complicated but important. Deviance results may occur when nothing more than an allegation exists—whether the allegation is true or false and regardless of the evidence. The reactions may accurately reflect the facts, or they may be interpretations that bear little resemblance to the facts. The appropriateness of the reactions always will be subject to dispute. Interpretations often reflect selective attention to so-called facts and just as often involve conclusions that cannot be derived from the facts. Information may be truncated, elaborated, and overgeneralized. Moreover, what information is provided, what pieces are considered as relevant, and the implications of the facts are determined within the ongoing interactions. These interactions and the negotiated outcomes are shaped by the characteristics of the events, settings, and participants.

Deviance is both an *objective* and a *subjective* reality. Objectively, deviance is a matter of expectations and violations. We can directly observe the presence or absence of expectations and violations. Is there a norm, law, or other shared expectation? Does the behavior, trait, or event violate or depart from the expectation? We can also observe reactions. Someone responds to a real or alleged violation by imposing or attempting to impose some sanction: That person makes an arrest, scowls, scolds, or otherwise invokes some penalty. Subjectively, the reaction reflects an interpretation or subjective judgment, and it produces a result. Deviance is thus a matter of objective facts and subjective definitions.

Consider the logic of this conception of deviance:

If something happens that is a violation of some norm, and

if some interpretation of deviance is offered as a definition of what happened,

then a deviance outcome *may* result.

Whether or not deviance *is* the outcome depends in part on what happened, what participants can do about it, and the ongoing or emerging relationships among those involved. From this point of view, several things are necessary to understand deviance. We must:

1. observe and describe generically and factually instances of human behavior or traits

2. observe and describe the facts and interpretations that emerge

3. observe and describe reactions to these instances

4. observe and describe negotiations and outcomes

5. identify events and reactions that result in deviance outcomes

6. account for differences in events and reactions that result in deviance and those that do not

Note that the outlined tasks for understanding deviance do *not* include asking or finding out *what is wrong with someone*. Our common sense often suggests that this question is the central problem for understanding and explaining deviance. What is wrong with this man that made him kill his wife? What is wrong with this woman that made her sexually attracted to other women? What is wrong with this kid that made him delinquent? What is wrong with people who want to run around naked?

Deviance is a negotiated outcome. Note, however, that the idea of negotiation does not mean that the people involved are aware of the process or how it works. Participants seldom have any sense that they are engaged in bargaining facts or interpretations. They may be more aware that the outcome is problematic and subject to dispute. However, most people believe that there are rules and that these are widely shared. As a result, common sense allows us to predict and estimate outcomes of deviance and other actions. For scientific purposes, however, we must observe and describe what happens, not what we assume will or should happen.

To understand deviance scientifically, we need accurate and reliable information about human activities and events and about the reactions to and interpretations of those activities and events. The accuracy and reliability of information is largely determined by the extent to which it comes from direct *empirical* experience: something seen, smelled, heard, touched, or tasted by someone who can report the experience carefully.

Describing Deviance: Information

Deviance is elusive in part because information is problematic. In our common sense world, things are obvious or, if not, we recognize their fuzzy edges and make choices accordingly, in spite of the lack of clarity. If we tried to define and specify our everyday world, we would quickly become frustrated—and maybe even immobilized. But in our scientific efforts to understand, we must be systematic and precise. Assumptions in our ordinary lives must be questioned and specified. Often things are not what they seem. (Eitzen [1982:6–7] presents an interesting discussion of this problem as it relates to the sociological perspective; see also Berger [1963:31].)

Consider an example. In 1986, President Reagan declared a war on drugs. He is not the first American president to attempt such a campaign. In the United States, systematic and sustained efforts to control drugs and their use through law and other political tactics date to 1842, when a tax was levied on imported crude opium (Ray, 1983). The Pure Food and Drugs Act of 1906 and the Harrison Act of 1914 are more important milestones in the effort to control drug use politically (Goode, 1984b:217–223). The drugs of major concern today are heroin and cocaine. Concern about heroin and other opiates has a long history, but critical concern about cocaine is relatively new. (However, there was a flurry of concern about "negro cocaine use" at the turn of the century; see Ashley [1975] and Grinspoon and Bakalar [1976].)

Consider the "heroin problem." Most of us know about and are troubled by this drug problem. We know that users are disproportionately members of minorities (especially blacks), urban, poor, young, and marginally educated. We know that users frequently engage in crime to support their habit and that they represent a danger to our personal safety. We know that heroin is extremely dangerous and highly addictive. Finally, we know that we have not been successful in treating addicts. Many suspect that the only solution is intensive (and expensive) law enforcement to make drug trafficking dangerous and costly.

The problem with what we know about this drug problem is that much of it is false or only partially true. And the partial truths do not support many of our conclusions. For example, heroin is used very infrequently in our society. If we include other opium derivatives, such as morphine, and other narcotics, such as Dilaudid, it is still true that only a very small proportion of Americans have ever tried these drugs. Of the drugs of popular concern, such as marijuana, LSD, and alcohol, heroin is used the least frequently and by the smallest percentage of people (Goode, 1984a:105). Fewer than 1 percent of our contemporary population have ever tried heroin (Miller, 1983).

Many Americans share a belief that heroin use has reached epidemic proportions. But addiction to morphine (from which heroin is derived) may have been more pervasive a century ago than heroin use is today. Morphine was used widely during the Civil War because it is an effective analgesic, or painkiller. Addiction came to be known as "soldiers' disease" or the "Army disease" (Goode, 1984b:217). Ray (1983:332) reports that morphine "was administered regularly in large doses to many soldiers for the reduction of pain and relief from dysentery." By the early 1900s, patent medicines containing morphine, opium, and other opiates (as well as tranquilizers and sedatives) were so widely used that authorities have estimated that at least 1 percent of Americans were addicted to opium or its derivatives (see Kebler, 1910; Edwards, 1980).

The typical addict of that period was not black, poor, urban, young, or marginally educated. Instead, *she* was a white, middle-aged housewife who bought opium or morphine legally at the store or ordered it through the Sears, Roebuck mail-order catalog (Ray, 1983:334). Those who had the "habit" were pitied—but they were not singled out for special treatment or contempt (Lindesmith, 1968). They lived ordinary lives and met their obligations as wives and mothers. They were not a special group or subculture and were not disproportionately involved in crime.

Heroin and the other opium derivatives are addictive and dangerous. But regular unaddicted heroin users outnumber addicts four to one, and most people who try heroin discontinue use without becoming addicted (O'Donnell et al., 1976; Abelson and Atkinson 1975). Approximately 1 percent of all heroin addicts die each year. But Goode (1984b:228–230) observed that most heroin deaths in our society result from the drug's illegality—not from its chemical toxicity. Many users (especially addicts) suffer from hepatitis, tetanus, nutritional deficiencies, and overdoses. None of these results directly from the drug or its properties. Overdosing provides an example of the effects of heroin's illegality. Users almost never know the potency of the heroin they buy. Heroin bought in Hong Kong may be 80 percent pure, but it reaches American users only after being adulterated ("cut") to 3 to 5 percent purity. Because the difference between an effective dose and a lethal dose is small, the great variation in the potency of illegal heroin makes overdosing a real and persistent danger.

A comparison with a different group of narcotics users is instructive. Physicians use narcotics (principally Demerol, but also Dilaudid and morphine) at a rate much higher than does the general population. Physician addicts almost never suffer any of the physical ailments that street junkies experience almost routinely. Goode (1984b:230) explains that doctors avoid these problems because the dosage of their drugs is standardized in strength and purity, they use sterile needles, they compensate for nutritional deficiencies, and they obtain the drugs without intensive involvement in criminal activities. (Ball and Urbaitis [1970] summarize the effects of heroin compared to the effects of the life-style of the street junkie.)

Intensive and expensive law enforcement efforts have not stopped or even slowed the rate of illegal drug trafficking in the United States. Instead, the profit from the illegal market has increased steadily. Fortunes are made daily and law enforcement and the drugs' illegal status only ensure incredible profits (Bunker, 1979; Branch, 1988). Brinkley (1986:A1) described the South Florida Task Force as "the most ambitious and expensive drug enforcement operation in the nation's history." Federal officials responsible for the program have concluded that it failed: "Officials say they have had almost no success in penetrating the principal drug smuggling organizations and in most cases do not even know who the major traffickers are."

However, the prospects of recovery from addiction may be fairly good. Goode (1984b:242) reports on research on Vietnam War veterans who returned to the United States with some pattern of use or addiction. Most of them had stopped drug use entirely or used it only sporadically when interviewed 8 to 12 months after their return. Physician treatment programs and recent studies of former heroin addicts also offer encouraging signs (Ray, 1983:358–367; Alcohol, Drug Abuse, and Mental Health Administration, 1981).

So what do we know about the deviance of drug use? The brief analysis of the heroin problem sharply differs from the original common sense characterization. There are several reasons for that difference. Most importantly, we do not ask much of our common sense understandings. We typically do not carefully distinguish between facts and opinions, and we seldom verify information that we treat as factual.

In our everyday world, we do not worry much about such matters, and our values and beliefs may guide decisions and actions regardless of facts. If we were to stop and make demands on all or most of the information we receive and use, then we might live in a world that is vastly different from the one we know. Instead, our lives go humming along, in spite of limited or faulty information and judgments based on such information.

The scientific understanding of deviance requires solutions to "information problems," some of which were suggested in the example of illegal drugs:

1. *"Common sense facts" are often minimal.* For example, the "drug problem" was seen in terms of one use pattern (inner-city heroin junkies), ignoring relevant comparisons such as morphine use in the early 1900s and physicians' use of Dilaudid.

2. *The reliability and accuracy of the "facts" are not tested or questioned seriously.* Popular understandings suggest that a single "fix" of heroin is sufficient to produce addiction, with death and disease as normal consequences of heroin use. But evidence on the physiological hazards of heroin use is equivocal, and most people who have tried heroin never become addicted.

3. *No distinction is made between facts and interpretations.* Popular images view heroin users as evil or sick junkies who live crime-ridden and horrible lives.

4. *Social control policies are developed and pursued without careful consideration of relevant and accurate facts and interpretations.* The various "wars" on drugs and "dealers of death" have not reduced the major prob-

lems associated with heroin use: poverty, crimes against property, and public fear of an "epidemic" of disease and "immorality." Still, we persist in our law enforcement efforts and campaigns to conquer "the drug problem."[5]

In Chapter 2, the idea of deviance as a negotiated outcome is developed and compared to other conceptions of deviance. This chapter ends with brief answers to some of the critical questions posed:

Q: What is deviance?

A: Deviance is a negotiated outcome. It involves some "thing" (behavior or trait) and some reaction that treats the thing as a departure from the expected.

Q: Is deviance objectively real?

A: Yes. It involves expectations and violations. Deviance is a part of ongoing social reality.

Q: Is deviance subjective and a matter of definition?

A: Yes. Information about violations and definitions of "what happened" contribute to interpretations that produce outcomes, or deviance results.

Q: How are instances of deviance identified?

A: Reactions that condemn or punish are the best indicators, especially because some violations are not treated as deviant and some things that are treated as deviant do not involve violations.

Implications of the Proposed Definition

The discussions in this chapter suggest that the concept of deviance does not refer to some evil force, diseaselike pathology, or malady that infects a community or society. Yet the things that are identified as deviant—through the application of social controls—concern or trouble many people. If deviance is best understood as a negotiated outcome, can we do anything to reduce it or to manage troublesome or problematic consequences? For example, could we reduce the amount of injury, death, or property loss from heroin use? Or, as another example, could we reduce sexual exploitation in our society?

The answer is yes. Social control and social change are possible. But we cannot expect to control or change things if we misrepresent them, think about them in ways that distort reality, or develop programs based on false assumptions or bad information. We often talk about deviance as if it were a disease.

We refer to "epidemics" of crime, child abuse, and rape, for example. But deviance is *not* a disease. It involves some action (real or alleged violation) and some reaction (threatened or actual sanction). Reactions shape and influence the objects of concern. Laws can transform troublesome behavior into crime and people who are nuisances into criminals. Whether oriented to so-called treatment, correction, rehabilitation, or punishment, our efforts will identify, define, and shape the "deviance" of concern. These issues are discussed more fully in the following chapters. The central premise is this: Deviance can be understood only to the extent that social control is understood. The reverse is also true.

CHAPTER 2

Deviance, Society, and Human Experience

When Ernenek raised his head from the sleeping bag his thoughts usually ran at once to the heap of fish and meat rotting into tenderness behind the seal oil lamp.

But not today.

Today, seeing Siksik bent over her husband's bearskins in a corner of the little igloo, he made a sudden resolution before lending an ear to the demands of his stomach. Since he contributed more than his share to the sustenance of the little household he was going to demand a full share in Anarvik's marital rights also, so that he no longer would have to ask permission each time he felt like laughing a little with Siksik, or when he needed new mittens sewn or his boots mended. He would at last have a wife of his own to order around—something he had not known, because he was young, and because here in the farthest North, woman was as scarce as bear was plentiful. But Ernenek knew the importance of a wife of one's own—to scrape one's skins and sew one's garments and to listen to one's jokes during the night.

Especially when the night lasts six months.

Even now he would have liked exchanging a little laughter with Siksik before leaving for the hunt. But he knew right from wrong as well as any man, and so he knew it would be most improper to avail oneself of another man's wife without first asking the husband's permission.

And Ernenek seldom did anything improper.

But he was tired of asking. Not that Anarvik ever refused: refusing the loan of a wife or a knife was a sign of intolerable meanness [Ruesch, 1951:1–2].

The life of Ernenek, Siksik, and Anarvik is not ordinary—or even imaginable—to most of us. But it is orderly, routine, and, within limits, predictable. The orderliness comes from and is reflected in unwritten rules that are shared and understood: It is okay to "laugh" with another man's wife as long as the husband's permission has been sought; it is wrong (and mean) to refuse the loan of a wife or a knife. The rules are unfamiliar to us, but they constitute central understandings among the Innuits, whom we call "Eskimos." Our life would seem as unusual to Ernenek and his friends, although we see it as perfectly normal.

Social reality has that quality. Our way of living seems natural, even though we know that other people around the world live very differently. Most of the time we take our ways for granted. We seldom question expectations and laws—constraints that are not necessarily our preference or in our best interests. We refer to these patterned, routine, "ordinary" ways of doing things as "society" or, more accurately, the *social order.* (For an excellent discussion of the reality of society, see Warriner, 1956, 1970.) Our common experiences tell us that there is such a thing, but we seldom think carefully or systematically about its character or consequences. We are most accutely aware of its existence when it is violated, or when some violation is perceived or alleged. Ethnomethodologists who study this order by disrupting it experimentally to observe the consequences have demonstrated the importance of this taken-for-granted reality (Garfinkel, 1967). Deviance refers to a social reality that derives from the social order. And so the social order, whatever it is and however we know about it, is critically important to our understanding of deviance.

Deviance has been described and defined as a *negotiated outcome.* Part of that negotiation involves the social order and its attendant expectations as one reference point. The real or imagined departure constitutes another reference. In its simplest form, deviance involves some real or alleged violation of the social order that someone other than the accused notices. *Negotiation* refers to the social activities that are focused on the real or alleged violation—for example, accusing, denying, arresting, and gossiping. *Outcome* refers to the results of the negotiating activities. The outcomes may be more or less temporary or permanent, but they reflect and become a part of the social order.

In this chapter, the proposed general theory of deviance, the *convergence theory*, will be developed in greater detail. I will describe some of the connections between this theory and the work of some classical theorists of sociology. Emile Durkheim, Karl Marx, and Max Weber are not just names from the past or founding fathers of sociology. Their work has had lasting value to the discipline because they identified and questioned issues that are critical for understanding social realities. Convergence theory builds on their contributions to our understanding of the organization of society, the social order. It also addresses many of the controversies that have stimulated and troubled contemporary deviance researchers.

Durkheim, Marx, and Weber: Social Order and Deviance

There is a purpose to the order in which we will review the works of Durkheim, Marx, and Weber. Durkheim's view of the social order, deviance, and social control is the starting point because it seems most encompassing. Durkheim saw deviance as a *normal* part of society and as *useful* for maintaining the social organization. Marx also saw deviance and social control as parts of society, but he paid more attention to conflict and the differences in interests and power within societies. Weber's work points to the subjective dimension of society, deviance, and social control. Weber also suggested how social organization shapes and sustains deviance through various forms of authority that legitimize social control. The works of all three men have contributed to the approach proposed here, in part because all three appreciated the complexity and multiple dimensions of the social world.

Durkheim and the Functions of Deviance

Emile Durkheim (writing in the late 1800s and early 1900s) was among the first to suggest that deviance is not a property or characteristic of a behavior, event, or person. He argued that deviance is partly a matter of selection. He observed that crime (which we consider here as a type of deviance) is *not* an "intrinsic quality of a given act" but a definition imposed on an act or person through understandings shared within a community or society (Durkheim, 1966:70). He went on to note that crime is a normal feature of society:

> Crime is present not only in the majority of societies of one particular species but in all societies of all types. There is no society that is not confronted with the problem of criminality. Its form changes; the acts thus

characterized are not the same everywhere; but, everywhere and always, there have been men who have behaved in such a way as to draw upon themselves penal repression [1966:65–66].

Durkheim pointed to an example of a society of saints. Crimes, as we know them, would be absent. But, faults and other departures would occur and would create reactions that would define them as serious and important (like crimes). Examples might include breaking the vow of silence in a monastery, or praying only 8 rather than the expected 10 hours. Not everyone within a community or society will (or can) share equally in what Durkheim called the "collective sentiments" that are a central part of the social order. (Durkheim also called these a "collective conscience" or a "moral consciousness.") As a consequence, the collective sentiments do not control entirely the conduct of all members, and "a society exempt from it [crime] is utterly impossible" (1966:67).

Durkheim's analyses went beyond the conclusion that societies without crime are impossible. He contended that crime is *useful:*

> Crime is, then, necessary; it is bound up with the fundamental conditions of all social life, and by that very fact it is useful, because these conditions of which it is a part are themselves indispensable to the normal evolution of morality and law [1966:70].

What are the "fundamental conditions of all social life" that make crime (deviance) normal and necessary? Among other things, Durkheim implied that societies (social orders) evolve. As they do, they require different arrangements in order to survive in their environments. Why and how do societies evolve, and what does societal evolution have to do with deviance?

Durkheim maintained that the form or character of a society at any time is not a matter of chance. For example, it is *not* an accident that "sharing" a wife is acceptable in the far North, but generally is not in our society. Society is organized. The various patterns, expectations, rules, and laws that we take for granted are related. They emerge over time as solutions to various problems of living. As the patterns persist, they come to seem natural and take on a life of their own. They offer a "healthy resistance" to change, but that resistance cannot be total:

> The collective sentiments at the basis of morality must not be hostile to change, and consequently must have but moderate energy. If they were too strong, they would no longer be plastic. Every pattern is an obstacle to new patterns, to the extent the first pattern is inflexible [1966:70].

SEX AND ORGANIZATION: AN EXAMPLE OF SOCIAL EVOLUTION The practice of limiting sexual intercourse to adults of the opposite sex who are bound together by religious or civil pledges and ceremony is not natural—that is, not given in nature. But marriage and related sexual norms have persisted in certain parts of the world for many centuries. And, in our own society, sex within marriage is treated as mandatory by religious groups and organizations and by civil and criminal law. Mandatory or not, the expectation is violated frequently, but it continues to define what is right and wrong, moral and immoral, legal and illegal, acceptable and deviant.

Durkheim would argue that monogamous, marital sex emerged as a solution to the problem of continuity. If a society is to persist, then members who die or leave must be replaced. Otherwise, the society cannot last beyond a single generation. Note that it is not necessary (or appropriate) to argue that societies "want" to persist or that individuals "want" societies to persist. Durkheim's premise is that those societies that survive do so because the problem of continuity (among other problems) was solved. The matter of wanting, either by society or by any individual, is not relevant.

Nothing in Durkheim's argument suggests that any solution is the best or even preferable to any other. There are potentially many solutions to the problem of continuity: kidnapping members of other groups or societies, continuous conquest, immigration, and selective breeding, to name only a few. To summarize Durkheim's analysis: (1) Patterns of conduct emerge over time, (2) some of these represent solutions to a society's problems of existence, (3) patterns persist largely to the extent that they have some survival value, and (4) the interrelated patterns form an order or organization with properties of its own.

The properties of the organization result from the forms and relationships among the patterns. For example, monogamy is a form and includes certain relationships: married persons to each other, married persons to unmarried persons, and parents to their children. Given the form and these relationships, the social order will have certain properties: Change will occur at a certain pace (for example, across generations), the biological family unit will occupy a position of some importance—at least for a certain time, and gender relationships will be relatively important (salient) in the ordering of activities (men and women will do some things together, while gender will segregate other activities).

The properties of the organization also derive from the survival relevance of the forms and relationships. As a solution to the survival problem of continuity, monogamy imposes certain constraints on the evolving society. For example, the group (tribe, community, society) cannot be continuously mobile or dispersed over too wide an area or else it will limit the capability of members to form monogamous pairs that can reproduce. Neither can the group be too small and isolated or else, in time, the biological effects of in-breeding will destroy the survival value of the monogamy (as a form). Sexual exclusiveness is a typical feature of monogamies—at least under certain environmental conditions. But Eskimo society exists within an environment that is not typical.

Wife sharing within this context has some survival value, or at least Durkheim's argument would lead us to expect that.

Some of you (especially those with an interest in biology) should recognize the form of Durkheim's basic theory. Environmental demands, emerging traits, survival—these ideas are familiar to those who have studied Darwinian evolution. Durkheim proposed to understand societies as members of the genus of social organization. As such, those "species" with certain traits would survive under certain conditions. Traits would change and new traits would evolve with different survival value. Societies are to be understood as organized systems of interrelated parts. These parts are patterns of conduct that persist and become expectations, rules, laws, and other components of social reality.

THE PECULIAR LOGIC OF FUNCTIONALIST THEORY Durkheim's analysis of societal organization (like Darwin's theory of evolution) is an example of *functionalist theory*. The logic of functionalist theory is different from common sense reasoning and may seem strange at first. Used carefully, however, it provides insight and an excellent starting point for understanding deviance. Using functionalist reasoning, we attempt to explain the existence and characteristics of any "thing" by examining its consequences.

For example, we noted that nonmarital sex violates conventional expectations and is subject to some kinds of repression (punishment). But it persists. A common sense understanding of this would suggest that deviant nonmarital sex persists because the punishments are not effective. The functionalist hypothesis would be different: Nonmarital sex continues because its punishment supports the normative patterns of exclusive, monogamous sex.[1] Thus, nonmarital sex is useful—at least indirectly. Social control activities select some departures from accepted patterns, whether these are actual or imagined, real or perceived. *Negotiated outcomes*, or instances of deviance, result. These so-called deviant acts define the acceptable and the unacceptable by example. In the process, the collective sentiments are underscored and reinforced. In this way, deviance supports existing patterns of the social order. And recall that these patterns have some survival value—that is, deviant sex practices support the accepted, existing order. *It does not follow that all types of deviance are functional*. Deviance at some level or in some amount may be nonfunctional, or dysfunctional. These issues are considered at the end of this chapter and will be examined in later chapters.

To repeat, social control activities select some norm violations (real or perceived) and treat something or someone as deviant. This deviance supports the existing order by defining the boundaries of acceptable conduct (among other possibilities). This central theme of a *functionalist* explanation of deviance and social control is straightforward and it seems reasonable. But what does it really mean? The most frequent interpretation is social psychological in character: People "feel" more committed to the rules when violators are punished.

Durkheim and other functionalists may have intended that interpretation (at least in part). But that is not the most useful understanding or the one that best reflects the logic of functionalist theory.

Recall that Durkheim's analysis focuses on the organization of society. Any society at any time is simply a member of the species with certain properties that relate to its capacity to survive. Deviance is understood in terms of these properties and the process of adapting to the environment. Accordingly, the psychological and social psychological experiences of members of the society are not directly pertinent.

Consider an example that focuses instead on *structural* and *organizational* variables. Prostitution, premarital sex, adultery, and homosexuality violate norms that prohibit nonmarital sex. Marriage and family are structural arrangements that contribute to the continuity of our contemporary society. These forms of sexual conduct undermine arrangements that currently operate to replace societal members in an orderly way—that is, the arrangement has survival value. Homosexual conduct is perhaps the most obvious example here. If homosexual conduct were allowed to exist unchallenged and unpunished, then it might in time undermine norms and laws that underpin monogamous marital sex, at least some of which results in the production of offspring to repopulate the society. (This argument may have seemed more compelling when the world's population was smaller.) The punishment of homosexual conduct, from ridicule and discrimination to imprisonment, reinforces expectations about heterosexual and marital sex and defines the boundaries of the society. (See end note 2 for a diagram of the logic of functional analysis borrowed from Stinchcombe, 1968).

Notice that the explanation does not refer to or rely on the wants, wishes, or motives of individual human beings. Some people may want things as they are, or others may not like the existing norms or their enforcement. These preferences do not matter. The relationships among the existing order, violations (real or imagined) of the order, and reactions to the violations are understood in terms of the properties of the system. These properties are independent of people. They operate as they do because of their characteristics and the ways in which they are interrelated.

Consider an example from biology: Some reptiles grew wings. The wings did not result from the wishes or wants of the reptiles. Instead, some members of the reptile species developed wings as a matter of chance mutation. Within a particular environment, having wings created a competitive advantage for survival. Wingless reptiles did not survive in the environment. The structural arrangement of wings supported survival under changed environmental conditions.

This analysis suggests a peculiar relationship between deviance and social order. The structural conditions—norms, arrangements to enforce the norms, and arrangements for punishing violations—*do not eliminate the violations*. Nothing in the analysis suggests that violations can or should be eliminated.

In terms of the monogamous marriage example, nonmarital sex is not eliminated and is not likely to be if the system is operating in terms of this design because the social arrangements that enforce norms and laws have functional consequences. They serve a purpose in maintaining the organization.

Societies and other organizations exist in balance: a dynamic balance, equilibrium, or homeostasis. Structural arrangements prescribe certain things and proscribe other things. The arrangements include provisions for enforcement and punishments for violation. The existing arrangements are reinforced through social control—enforcement of the rules and punishment of violations. Recall Durkheim's analysis of crime: Society without it is impossible; it contributes to the survival of the social order.

At the same time, violations *do not cause* the structural arrangements. Norm violations do not cause the norms and rules, their enforcement, or the punishment of violators. Contrary to popular beliefs, social control programs do not develop because of norm violations, and social control efforts do not increase because deviance increases. Instead, a complex relationship exists between norm violations and structural arrangements. While deviance helps to maintain the existing equilibrium, it also is part of that equilibrium. Durkheim (1964:19) suggested that there is an inverse relationship between the integration of a community or society and the rate of punishment (see also Inverarity, Lauderdale, and Feld, 1983:128–129).

Integration can refer to any social order at any time—that is, a particular equilibrium. The rate of punishment refers to the number of events that structural arrangements select as violations. So when equilibrium is relatively unthreatened by any disturbances, the rate of punishment for any norm violation is relatively low. When the equilibrium is disturbed or threatened, the rate of punishment increases—*even if the rate of violations remains the same.*

The logic of functionalist theory is peculiar, but it provides insight. Consider the kinds of questions that it implies and those it does not suggest:

Implied Questions

How is the community or society organized?

What are the structural arrangements that maintain the organization?

What structural arrangements select events as deviant?

How are events selected?

Under what conditions does deviance increase or decrease?

Questions Not Suggested

What is wrong with deviants?

What personal, psychological, or biological characteristics distinguish deviants?

How can deviants be treated, corrected, or cured?

What is wrong with our community, society, or civilization that it produces deviance?

The questions in the second group are not unimportant. They are some of the questions that students of deviance and political decision makers have asked traditionally—with little detectable success in either understanding or controlling deviance.

Marx: Functions, Power, and Deviance

The following editorial comment appeared in my local paper:

> Suppressing homosexuality at [The College of] William and Mary could have a boomerang effect, eliciting sympathy through publicity.
>
> Yet, if the Gay Student Union gets its constitution approved by the Student Activities Board, it will become eligible for funding from the Board of Student Affairs just like any other qualified campus group.
>
> That would put the college in the dubious position of sanctioning homosexuality as a matter of policy. While it is one thing to sympathize with gays and do nothing to inhibit their right of assembly, it is quite another to encourage it. Imagine the reaction of parents who discover that their son or daughter has become "awakened" through a campus organization they helped subsidize. The idea is fraught with puzzlement, sadness, and anger. It could lead to litigation against the administration ["Campus Gays," 1984].

Whether you agree or disagree with the point of view offered by the editor, he clearly is describing an arrangement in which there are important differences in power among the participants. The organization (the university and its committees and boards) does not need to suppress homosexuality. Denying its constitutional and existential legitimacy is enough. The arrangement at William and Mary reflects, perpetuates, and creates advantages and disadvantages for participants depending on their position within the arrangement.

Durkheim noted that social arrangements tend to persist to the extent that they have survival value. Marx, however, focused on conflict as an essential element of human social life. He offered an incisive view of social organization that is strikingly similar to Durkheim's view. But Marx was more sensitive to the dynamics of power in intergroup relationships and the ordering of human affairs. He agreed that social arrangements must be understood in terms of their properties as social systems, but he saw power and conflict as the critically important properties. At the same time, Marx had a keen appreciation of functionalist logic and its relevance for describing and understanding human social order (compare Stinchcombe, 1968:93–98).

PRODUCTION FOR SURVIVAL AND SOCIAL ORGANIZATION According to Marx, human organization begins in the process of taking a living from the natural environment (see Cohen, 1978). Collections of humans become organized as they strive to take from their surroundings the things they need to live. Accordingly, the demands and resources of the environment set certain limits and encourage certain developments in the unfolding of human societies. For example, people who find themselves in the arctic north (like the Eskimos described earlier) probably will not develop farming or gardening practices or organize themselves into agricultural communities. But these material conditions are only the foundation and point of origin of social organization. Marx did not contend that the environment determines the social order.

Working within their natural environment, humans develop resources that are used to produce the means of living. They fashion tools and develop techniques and skills. Marx called these *forces of production* or, considered collectively, the *mode of production*. Marx left little doubt about the importance of the forces for the development of the social order: "The mode of production in material life determines the general character of the social, political and spiritual processes of life" (in Tucker, 1978:4). Consider the following example, in which I describe some of the important transformations that accompanied industrialization, as a new mode of production, in our recent history:

> **Life in the United States was predominantly rural and organized around farming throughout the nineteenth and early twentieth century. The family farm was a social arrangement that emphasized the economic and social interdependence of family members. Families were large, education was relatively unimportant, and social relationships were stable. Everyday life was dictated largely by tradition: Men (as husbands, fathers, and heads of family farms) made most important decisions, and women and children were expected to comply (willingly and with gratitude). People belonged to churches as families, and decisions about individual activities (work, education, marriage, for example) were constrained by the needs and preferences of the family—as interpreted by adult (usually male) members.**
>
> **By the late 1800s, methods of production and economic activities were undergoing radical change. Technological developments (the mechanization of farming and the ascendance of factory production) introduced radical changes into the lives of turn-of-the-century Americans. The locus of production moved from the home to an increasingly large and impersonal factory work setting. Family size decreased, and individuals and families spent less time together in any mutual economic activity (other than consumption, perhaps). Activities that had been the prov-**

ince of the family, including instruction in religion and citizenship, care of children, the sick, and the old, and help during emergencies, moved outside the home and were assumed by specialized agencies (schools, churches, hospitals, baby-sitting services and day-care centers, nursing homes, and social welfare programs).

The organization of human activity is influenced by how we make a living and produce the materials and services we need (or want). To repeat, the mode of production is the material basis of all social organization, according to Marx (1967). These forces give rise to relationships among people who live in a common location. Who owns or controls what resources? How are skills distributed? Who owns or controls the tools? How are the products divided? These are issues of human social relations, which depend on the material conditions of existence. Consider some of the changes that have accompanied industrialization: work outside the family home; the emergence of "service industries" such as nursing homes, preschools, and insurance companies; commuting; two-career families; decreased birthrates; mandatory public education.

Marx contended that the material *forces of production* and the derived *relations of production* constitute the core of social organization. Political beliefs, laws, definitions of right and wrong, and other social control arrangements constitute the other major part of the social organization, which Marx called the *superstructure.* The superstructure is built onto the core or base of forces and relations of production. Accordingly, norms, rules, and laws reflect this core organization. And deviance is created as a part of the superstructural arrangements. Marx would agree with Durkheim that deviance reflects the organization of society. But the organization is more than just one of many possible forms that have some survival value. It is also an arrangement that has built-in advantages and disadvantages, different amounts of power, and different interests, all of which depend on one's location within the organization.

Deviance and social control take on political qualities when viewed from Marx's point of view. These qualities are implied in the example that began this chapter and in the "campus gays" editorial. Both descriptions suggest differences in rights and privileges. Still, deviance is seen as an integral part of the social order. What is the organizational character of deviance according to Marx? Very much as Durkheim did, Marx implied that deviance may be functional. But his analyses suggest other conclusions as well.

Laws and other parts of the superstructure of society reflect production arrangements. Norm violations (again, real or perceived) stand in some relationship to ongoing structural arrangements and the existing equilibrium or balance. Some violations are selected to be treated as crime or deviance; which ones and how many depend on the type and level of integration. But here we need to consider Marx's conclusions. The organization of society is not simply a matter of an evolving arrangement of parts with different survival values. And the balance of the arrangement (however dynamic) is seen as more precarious. Social organization includes hierarchies of interests and power. An assessment of the functions or positive consequences of any arrangement must consider its "contribution to the survival of the society" and its consequences for the hierarchies of interests and power (see Stinchcombe, 1968:93–95). Furthermore, Marx did not assume that social arrangements tend to be self-maintaining through functional organization. Instead, he asserted that such arrangements contain the "seeds of their own destruction." The parts (material conditions, forces and relations of production, and superstructure) are related in ways that ensure continuous change.

Let's consider again the example of sexual norms and their violation. Real and imagined violations of sexual norms in our society support the arrangement of civil and religious monogamy that operates as one way of replacing societal members. If the arrangement is functional, then both the norms and the compliant behavior, on the one hand, and the norm violations, on the other, will be perpetuated, according to the logic of Durkheim's functionalist explanation. But the norms, their violation, and their enforcement have different consequences for people in different locations within the society. In addition, the continuing tensions may result in radical changes in the parts and in the society as a whole. The following account of a recent Supreme Court decision raises important questions:

> The Supreme Court's ruling Monday [June 30, 1986] that there is no constitutionally protected right to engage in private, homosexual conduct has implications far beyond the bedroom.
>
> On a practical, legal level, the high court's decision upholding state laws banning sodomy could provide ammunition against homosexuals seeking custody of their children, fired from their jobs, or fighting discrimination in housing or other situations.
>
> "The most important effect of this case is not legal—it's social," said Thomas B. Stoddard, executive director of the Lambda Legal Defense and Education Fund, a gay-rights organization. "The most important judicial body in the United States has expressed a certain distaste for gay men and women and suggested that they be treated differently from other Americans. . . . This opinion will fuel bigotry, apart from its legal implications" [Marcus, 1986:A1, A8].

The Supreme Court decision is an example of an activity in the domain of the superstructure. It supports the sexual norms of civil and religious monogamy, which are, in turn, related to the relations and forces of production. The ruling indicates an unwillingness on the part of the majority of the justices to protect acts of oral and anal sex as matters of privacy rights. Contrary to popular opinion, the Constitution does not protect the conduct of adults in the privacy of their homes. The word *privacy* does not appear in the Constitution. Instead, some provisions for protecting privacy have been inferred by judges from the language on personal liberties in the Bill of Rights (Yoder, 1986).

The ruling in this case—Bowers v. Hardwick, 1986—has different consequences for heterosexuals and homosexuals. First, while it limits the number and variety of heterosexual sex acts covered by privacy rights, it virtually eliminates protection for the sexual activities of homosexuals. Second, and very closely related, the decision leaves intact the judicial idea of "rights of privacy" for heterosexual couples (married or unmarried), but leaves the impression that homosexual couples may have *no* privacy rights.

The differences in consequences may seem subtle and unimportant. After all, the decision supports the prohibition of certain acts no matter who performs them. Consider a parallel: It is equally unlawful for the wealthy and for the poor to take property that does not belong to them. In philosophy, the prohibitions apply equally to all, but the practical consequences are quite different. Those who have no property are not protected by property laws, and those laws do not appear to be in their best interests. Social control (the norms and their enforcement) supports certain arrangements and the interests represented in those arrangements. At the same time, these norms, rules, and laws may be contrary to other interests and may limit the power of those with different interests. The Supreme Court's decision clearly perpetuates disadvantages for adults with certain sexual preferences, interests, and practices.

THE MARXIAN DIALECTICAL VIEW The Marxian view, which can be called *dialectical*, differs from Durkheim's functionalist explanation in three ways: (1) Marx paid more attention to differences in interests and power within social arrangements, (2) he observed that social arrangements have different consequences for different people and groups (compare Gans, 1972), and (3) he asserted that social systems are, by nature, in continuous change. This third point concerns the relationships among the parts of society. Durkheim and the functionist view generally saw the parts as interdependent pieces of some evolving, adapting whole. Marx questioned and extended the idea of interdependent parts.

The functionalist approach assumes interdependence that creates a balance in social organization. For example, family patterns and related norms support patterns of production: Large families predominate in agricultural societies with high demands for relatively uneducated labor; small families predominate in advanced industrial societies that require a mobile labor force; and laws against homosexual activities support the practices of religious and civil monogamy. The Marxian view recognizes balanced interdependence as one possibility. At the same time, however, Marx asserted that there are tensions within the organization that do not resolve in some balanced equilibrium. In fact, one simple way of understanding dialectical relationships is that they involve things that are both complementary and contradictory (at least potentially).

According to Marx, all social arrangements involve tensions that may result in a radical change. Even revolution produces an arrangement that is tempo-rary—that is, it is vulnerable to new and different tensions. For example, the prevailing norms constrain different people and groups in different ways. Norms and laws concerning sodomy have different consequences for heterosexuals and homosexuals. The norms and laws limit the variety of heterosexual sexual expressions, but they prohibit almost all homosexual alternatives for sexual activity. Sodomy involves conduct that could undermine the societal require-ment for replacing members as it is currently done through monogamous mar-riage. As a result, the functionalist view sees the Supreme Court's decision as an instance of ongoing fine tuning of a social system's balance.

Note, however, that the resolution does not eliminate the tensions and, in fact, may increase tensions. Fallout from the decision may include increased political activity by gay-rights groups. Such actions could result in more direct assaults on existing norms, rules, and laws. One result could be a repeal of sodomy statutes, which would mean that the Supreme Court's decision was not a contribution to the functional maintenance of the social order (the status quo). Instead, the decision was a catalyst (tension) for change. But if the court decision is effective, sexual activity is limited to married heterosexuals and to the kinds of sexual activities that tend to produce new members of society. The result could be an increase in the population that the society could not support in its environment. In that case, the consequence is not a viable resolution for maintaining the existing order.

The functionalist model portrays social organization as evolving through adaptations. Parts are interchangeable as long as survival needs are met, and change is relatively slow (and, perhaps, moves in one direction, along some traceable line of adaptation). In contrast, Marx's dialectical model views parts and the whole as inextricably linked within arrangements that are continuously vulnerable to change. The parts may be interdependent, but there is no as-sumption that the resulting arrangements are viable resolutions or patterns that are adaptive within an environment.

In the following summary of the Marxian dialectical explanation of devi-ance, note the similarities and differences with the functionalist explanation.

Social control, the structural arrangement of norms and provisions for their enforcement, is part of society's superstructure.

The superstructure, including social control, is shaped by the forces and relations of production.

At the same time, the superstructure supports and constrains the organizational base of society (the forces and relations of production).

Norm violations, real or perceived, and social control are parts of a society's organization, which is vulnerable to change as tensions emerge and persist in a context of different interests and power.

Norm violations and social control have different consequences for different people and different parts of society depending on their position within the social order. They also have different consequences for existing arrangements that constitute the social order.

The Marxian dialectical view is largely consistent with Durkheim's functionalist model and, in a sense, encompasses the basic funtionalist logic. Accordingly, the two suggest some of the same questions in our efforts to understand deviance. The implied questions listed toward the end of the discussion of Durkheim's work are equally relevant here. The dialectical view suggests these additional questions as relevant to understanding deviance and social control:

Additional Questions

What interests does the existing organization serve and maintain?

How is power distributed in the organization?

How do deviance and social control relate to the distribution of power?

What are the consequences of deviance and social control for the society and its assorted parts?

Weber: Shared Understandings, Deviance, and Social Control

Norms, rules, and laws are central elements of social organization. Social control, as seen by Durkheim and Marx, is a part of a social system and is external to individuals. Most of the time, however, people are only vaguely aware of any social system or any organization of norms and laws. Instead, we connect with our community and society through shared meanings. The norms, rules, and laws often seem far removed from everyday experiences in which the reality of social control operates. For example, most Americans, including contemporary college students, do not have to wonder if homosexuality violates any norms or laws. They may ponder the matter in the abstract or if asked to in a class assignment, but they join the majority in viewing it as something generally undesirable. And many people would continue to disapprove of homosexuality even if there were no laws or formal injunctions against it. Our ideas about homosexuality have developed over a long time, and our understandings have deep roots. These understandings are of primary concern in the works of Max Weber.

Many people believe that the Bible specifically condemns homosexuals and homosexual acts. Some quote from scripture to explain and justify their negative attitudes toward homosexuality. Genesis 10:4–11 is cited frequently as the Christian teaching on the matter (from Greenia, 1984):

> Lot and the two angels had not gone to bed when the house was surrounded by the men of the town, the men of Sodom both young and old, all the people without exception. Calling to Lot they said, "Where are the men who came to you tonight? Send them out to us so we may know them." Lot came out to them at the door and having closed the door behind him said, "I beg you, my brothers, do no such wicked thing. Listen, I have two daughters who are virgins; let me bring them out to you and do to them as you please, only do nothing to these men for they have come under the shelter of my roof."

Greenia (1984:1) noted that this passage "has been interpreted to mean that the men of Sodom wanted to have sexual intercourse with the strangers and that God annihilated the city for that reason." He contended, however, that the verb *to know* is used 943 times in the Old Testament. It is used to mean sexual intercourse only 10 times and then refers only to heterosexual intercourse. Greenia (1984:1) reviewed the history of interpretation of the passage and concluded that "All modern scripture scholars now agree the Sodom story was meant as a condemnation of *inhospitality* [emphasis added]."

It probably does not matter for our purposes whether the passage really condemns homosexuality. What does matter is that people in Western societies have *understood* that the Bible condemns it. Whether this interpretation is correct has had no bearing on centuries of church teaching. And these Christian traditions have helped to shape Western and American views on homosexuality. Religious exhortation is a powerful social control and condemnation is a powerful sanction. People may or may not know of disputes over scriptural interpretation. If known, these disputes may or may not have any effect on feelings or understandings about homosexuality.

Weber struggled with the meaningfulness of human conduct (what he called *social action*) and the place of subjectivity in the order and change of social life. He observed that human experience is not bound by the directly apprehensible physical world of sensory stimuli. Human conduct is *not* just a matter of rational behavior based on facts and knowledge. Neither is it simply behavior that responds automatically to social constraints and determinants (see Ritzer,

1975, 1983:133). Weber proposed to understand social reality through the method of *verstehen*, the interpretive or subjective understanding of the meaning of *social action*.

To understand deviance and social order, in Weber's terms, means to examine the shared beliefs that are created and sustained as parts of social reality.[3] Social control (including religious exhortation and condemnation) has little consequence unless those involved share some understandings of good and bad, appropriate and inappropriate, admirable and embarrassing. By extension, a substantial part of the reality of deviance is found in its *subjective* character.

FORMS OF AUTHORITY AND SOCIAL CONTROL Weber's study of forms of authority and law contributes directly to our understanding of deviance and illustrates his method of understanding. Specifically, his work on authority helps to frame a fundamental issue of social order and the negotiation of deviance: Who has the right, power, or ability to create and apply definitions of deviance and impose consequent sanctions? Weber thought of authority as *legitimate domination*. He defined *domination* as the "probability that certain specific commands (or all commands) will be obeyed by a given group of persons" (Weber, 1968:212). Weber recognized that there are illegitimate forms of domination, but he focused his efforts on the "legitimate" forms, which he identified as rational, traditional, or charismatic.

Sodomy laws and judicial decisions (like the Supreme Court decision described earlier) are expressions of *rational authority*. The authority can be exercised through arrests, conviction, and punishment by state officials. Generally, however, widely shared understandings (*traditional authority*) shape the development of sexual orientations, preferences, and practices. These understandings (and this authority) are sufficient to limit the probability that people will engage in homosexuality. The understandings support norms, rules, and laws. People comply with these rules and laws because they "know" what is right and wrong, good and bad, moral and immoral. Obviously, some people engage in homosexual acts in spite of both laws and cultural understandings— but most do not, even if they are tempted or feel so inclined.

Sometimes cultural understandings grow out of, or are reinforced by, activities of people who are regarded as exemplary, heroic, or otherwise exceptional. These *charismatic* people provide a different kind of authority for social control (understandings, norms, rules, and laws). In a sense, Christ, the disciples, and various other contributors to the Bible were charismatic leaders. People can understand the scripture discussed earlier as a kind of lesson taught by example or parable and reflecting the authority of the ultimate Christian charismatic, Christ.

As we begin to ask more systematic questions about deviance, we need to be attentive to how certain things are selected to be treated as deviant while remarkably similar things are ignored or even treated as praiseworthy. Does the *type* of authority influence the selection of things as deviant? Is it possible that societies will select types of violation dependent upon the predominant form of authority (for example, rational versus traditional)? It seems likely that this is the case. For example, because we are a constitutional democracy, we may be more likely to exercise social control through law (*rational* authority). It is relatively difficult to prohibit beliefs through law. If social control were organized through ideology (for example, by *tradition*), such prohibitions might be more likely.

LAW AS A SOCIAL REALITY With that in mind, Weber's study of law, as a social reality, has obvious relevance to our study of deviance. Weber (1968:750–780) pointed to the rationalization of law in the West as an important part of the emerging social organization. He saw a historical movement away from authority based on tradition and shared, informal expectations and toward more complex, formal, bureaucratic organization. As a formal codifying of shared norms, the law may, in part, reflect the informal, shared beliefs of the people. But as with other social realities, law tends to take on a life of its own. Lawmakers (or others charged with creating and enforcing local or national rules) may or may not fully represent the "will" or shared beliefs of the collectivity.

Weber's study of law illustrates a point of view that I have integrated into the proposed approach. He urges attention to the subjectively meaningful character of social reality. At the same time, he has a clear appreciation for the ways in which social realities are external to people. Social life is arranged in various ways that influence conduct, beliefs, and outcomes. Shared understandings shape these arrangements, and, at the same time, the arrangements shape the shared understandings.

Consider an example from contemporary American family life. Norms and laws support a particular arrangement: the nuclear family (husband, wife, children); sex (primarily for procreation) between married heterosexual pairs. This arrangement is supported and reinforced by widely shared beliefs, some of which derive from the Bible and interpretations of it. American adolescents begin to get interested in the opposite sex as they approach puberty. They date, go steady, become engaged, and marry in predictable and routine ways—in spite of the apparent fragility of contemporary marital arrangements (for example, high divorce rates, widespread adultery, and spouse abuse). And they do all of this because they "know" that it is expected and good.

They know, also, that nonmarital sex is generally bad and that homosexuality is unfortunate at best, probably immoral, and illegal. Which comes first:

the organization of American society and the nuclear family, or the shared understandings about Biblical prescriptions and Western Christian traditions? Clearly, patterns of social life have more than a single dimension. There are objective, organizational, and external features and properties. And there are subjective, shared understandings.

Weber's collected works suggest that he was aware of this multidimensional character of social reality (compare Collins, 1985:84; Alexander, 1982; Kreps, 1986). He urged a method of research that emphasized the human, subjective qualities of social life. At the same time, his own work reveals a clear appreciation of social organization that stands apart from subjective matters. His work on authority and law (and, perhaps even more, his study of religion and capitalism) suggests a solid appreciation of the logic and operation of functional organization (Weber, 1968, 1958).

The research and theory Max Weber contributed introduce important questions to be answered in our effort to understand and explain deviance:

Implied Questions:

What are the types and sources of authority that create expectations, rules, or laws in the community or society?

How are violations handled and through what kinds of authority?

Do the types of authority influence the kinds of violations that are treated as deviant?

What shared understandings or subjective meanings define authority and deviance?

The key themes from the works of Durkheim, Marx, and Weber can be summarized:

Deviance is partly a matter of selection.

The selection reflects and supports the existing organization of a community or society.

Deviance and social control are related to the distribution of interests and power in a community or society.

Deviance and social control have different consequences for different segments of a community or society.

Deviance is partly a shared understanding, and it is related to other understandings that are characteristic of the community or society.

Authority is part of a community's organization. It influences the selection and treatment of deviance.

Putting It Together:
Toward a More Complete Understanding of Deviance

In Chapters 3 and 4 I will introduce a general theory of deviance. My convergence theory draws together the insights and approaches developed by Durkheim, Marx, and Weber. For now, let's consider the broad outlines of a synthesis. The works of these classical theorists demonstrate a keen appreciation of the complexity of the world that they sought to understand. (Alexander, 1982; Kreps, 1986)[4]

Deviance is elusive because it is multidimensional and a part of a multidimensional world. We try to understand and fail, often because we are trying to understand in only one dimension. We think of deviance as perversion, or illness, or evil, or harmfulness. In those efforts, we *reduce* deviance to something that it is not. We focus only on those who we believe are departing from the norm and overlook the ways in which our reactions shape (maybe even encourage) the things we treat as deviant. Or we focus on those who are creating and imposing definitions and we overlook the objective realities of norms, rules, laws, social control, and the social order. But because deviance is a *negotiated outcome*, we must give equal consideration to expectations and violations and to interpretations and outcomes.

I do not intend to excuse, justify, or apologize for any thing or anyone. Durkheim's observation is pertinent here:

> Although crime is a fact of normal sociology, it does not follow that we must not abhor it. Pain itself has nothing desirable about it; the individual dislikes it as society does crime, and yet it is a function of normal physiology. Not only is it [pain] necessarily derived from the very constitution of every living organism, but it plays a useful role in life, for which reason it cannot be replaced. It would, then, be a singular distortion of our thought to present it as an apology for crime. We would not even think of protesting against such an interpretation, did we not know to what strange accusations and misunderstandings one exposes oneself when one undertakes to study moral facts objectively and to speak of them in a different language from that of the layman. [Durkheim, 1966:72].

With no apology, we begin our analysis with the assertion that deviance is a normal part of society. It is a part of the organization of social life, and it performs useful functions within that organization. At the same time, we recognize that both the organization and deviance are partly matters of selection. There is nothing normal (that is, *natural* or *inevitable*) about any organization or any instance of deviance. As an example, through many series of selections, we have come to meet requirements for replacing societal members through a from of serial monogamy (one wife and one husband at a time, sometimes in rapid succession) and relative sexual exclusiveness. Operating from that normative order, certain things have a higher than average probability of being selected as deviant (for example, prostitution and homosexuality). The arrangement could have been different.

The selection of the social order and the selection of things treated as deviant reflect both the organization of our community and society and the shared understandings that give meaning to our social existence. The selection is not usually a matter of individaul intention or purposeful behavior. Rather, ways of acting develop, persist, and change over time, partly as they contribute or fail to contribute to the society's survival. At the same time, shared meanings develop around the patterned ways. These meanings support and sustain the existing organization while the organization confirms and perpetuates the meanings. And the meanings give rise to changing organization forms while changing patterns and organization sponsor new meanings.

The social order is always in process. It is always becoming. It is continually constructed and reconstructed. In a word, it is dialectical. Social control and deviance are parts of the ongoing social order. They support the social order and reflect existing interests and differences in power among groups and parts of society. Both Durkheim and Marx suggested that there are always forces operating to change the existing order, and there is organizational resistance to change. For Durkheim, the resistance came from the already existing organization (the "collective conscience"). Marx saw resistance from the existing order, from the hierarchy of interests and power within the society, and from the relationships among the parts and the overall organization—that is, the dialectical relationships. These interdependent parts are related to the whole. At the same time, the parts and the whole stand as potential sources of major change for each other. Marx's view can encompass the possiblity suggested by Durkheim, but the reverse is not true.

Meanwhile, shared understandings and subjective experiences reflect and support the existing social organization. These subjective meanings are sometimes formalized as rules and laws. When that happens, the meanings are given a certain kind of legitimacy. Weber's studies of authority provide clues for understanding how the objective social order and subjective experiences become intertwined; they both complement and contradict one another—or, again, they are dialectically related.

The central questions of the proposed functionalist, dialectical, social action approach, which is here called simply *dialectical*,[5] cut across the questions identified earlier in the chapter:

Implied Questions

How are social organization and deviance socially created and maintained?

What are the consequences of social control?

The key themes of the proposed theory are, likewise, synthetic:

Deviance is a social reality.

Deviance is an integral part of society.

Deviance and the social order are linked dialectically.

Explaining Deviance:
Basic Concepts, Classical Theories,
and Rates of Deviance

Deviance is normal. That sounds like a contradiction in logic, but it expresses the way deviance and social organization are related. Societies are created and change—usually slowly over a long time. We are seldom aware of the activities and processes that produce the persisting forms and patterns that we call society. We are equally oblivious to the creation and perpetuation of deviance. When and how did it become appropriate for men to shave their faces and women to shave their legs? When and how did it become bizarre for men to wear lipstick and women to smoke pipes?

Deviance as Part of Society

In what sense is deviance a part of society? There are some obvious examples: Crime supports an entire network of law enforcement and justice agencies and, thus, provides jobs for hundreds of thousands of people; mental illness is big business, driving an economy that includes income and profit from sources as diverse as institutional care (food, clothing, shelter, and recreation), psychiatry, and pharmaceutics; marijuana may be the most profitable crop in the United States. These examples suggest how deviance "supports" the conventional order—but they do not really tell the whole story.

We could observe, from a different angle, that deviance reinforces the rules and laws of a community or society. The rules are more certain when they are broken and when violators are identified and punished. We are reminded of our common standards. The line that separates "us" from "them" (the rule breakers) is highlighted, and our commitment to the conventional order is enhanced. (This is partly what Durkheim had in mind in his analyses of the functions of deviance; see Chapter 2.) Still, reinforcement of the status quo and increased community spirit (cohesion) are only part of what I mean by asserting that deviance is normal.

Deviance is a part of the nuts-and-bolts operation of society. It is a part of the *design* of collective living. Note, however, I do not mean that societies or any of their characteristics result from anyone's intention. That is a separate question. Consider an example:

The American system of public education is highly regarded around the world. Students learn to read and write, to solve mathematical problems, and to understand the physical and human world that surrounds them. They learn to apply themselves in order to achieve, they learn to compete, and they learn to see accomplishment partly in terms of material symbols of success (first, little letters on cards; later, little letters on jackets; and still later, little numbers on contracts and checks). So organized, the public schools contribute to the larger social order that is modern America. Graduates leave their schools and take their places in the "real" world prepared to pursue the "American dream" and to continue cultural traditions.

But there is another side to this story. Not everyone succeeds. Some do not learn to read or write or master the times tables. Some find achievement, as defined by our educational system, irrelevant or beyond their ability or patience. Some youngsters with interests (and maybe talent) in music can not afford to rent an instrument. Some who are fascinated by government and politics can not afford to make the class trip to Washington, D.C. But the system and its relevant beliefs are sustained: Those who are "most deserving" are most rewarded in this society organized by competition.

Our educational system, like our larger society, is designed in such a way that it produces both winners and losers, material wealth and poverty. This is not an indictment against the school system or the society. It simply describes how the organization works. No one needs to apologize for anything or to blame anyone. Those who value competition as a system believe that it results in the "greatest good for the greatest number"—and they may be right. The point remains: The system that produces valued results also produces things that are despised—failure, poverty, and crime.

The matter of crime may provide a more direct example. In our contemporary society, the criminal law is seen as the embodiment of collective values. We generally understand that the law makes explicit what is important and good and that it specifically prohibits what is bad and wrong. As such, the criminal law affirms the common good and the collective sentiments. Criminal laws prohibit certain actions and threaten violators with state-imposed punishments. In doing that, the people who violate laws are transformed into criminals. Criminal statutes and the agencies that enforce them make up a system dedicated to protecting the common good. The same system makes criminals out of those who violate the law. Are those people *less* likely to violate the law as a result? The answer is far from clear. It would be ironic to learn that the system that protects the public good and the collective order works in such a way as to produce and perpetuate a class of people (criminals) who are more likely to violate that good and order.

But why should people violate the norms, rules, or laws in the first place? If these expectations and standards really represent the collective sentiments or common good, should not everyone comply *naturally*? Recall the discussions from the previous chapter. Durkheim noted that not everyone will share equally in the collective sentiments and that the "collective conscience" must not be so powerful as to be inflexible (and thus resist adaptive change). Marx noted that the organization of society will always reflect and support some interests over others. Both arguments support the idea that norm and rule violations are normal and inevitable. Is it possible, then, that agencies and systems that enforce norms and rules (for example, a criminal justice system) partly control violations and partly perpetuate them?

I propose that deviance is an integral part of social organization, having defined deviance as a negotiated outcome that reflects society's organization. The potential for violation and social control are built into the structure of society. Under certain conditions, deviance is normal and functional. At the same time, deviance reflects the distribution of power and interests, contributes to the maintenance of the society, and is a source of change as well as the potential destruction of the society (according to Marx). Finally, deviance reflects the shared meanings that organize social life and give it coherence (according to Weber). I will detail my general approach through a consideration of key ideas. These ideas are summarized and focused in concepts, which are proposed as tools for understanding the social realities of deviance.

Explaining Deviance: The Concepts

The following concepts serve as building blocks to describe the emergence, persistence, and change of society and deviance. I take as given that social interaction and social structure are the fundamental elements of sociological description and explanation. *Interaction* is the process in which two or more people take each other into account and orient their conduct on the basis of their relationship. It is the source of all social realities. As we interact, we create, perpetuate, and change our social world(s) within the constraints and demands of the social and physical environment. (Recall the discussion of the nature of social organization in Chapter 2.)

Social structure refers to patterns of relationships among parts of some social entity (event, group, institution, society). The parts may be behaviors, beliefs, relationships, or other social realities. They may be related by hierarchy, symmetry, space, or time, among many possibilities. Structure refers also to patterns of relationships among positions, including, for example, hierarchies and divisions of labor. And it refers to patterns of belief that are more or less internally consistent, mutually supportive, and connected to other parts of respective social forms. Consider the following description of the structure of a predominant form of the American family. The major positions include husband, wife, mother, father, son, daughter, grandparent, aunt, uncle, and cousin. Major types of relationships include hierarchy (parent-child) and division of labor. Among the related beliefs and norms are those concerning the sanctity of marriage, the obligations of parenting, and the power of love. The following discussions cover the basic concepts for the proposed approach to deviance.

Social Action

Social action is patterned behavior that develops through interaction. Participants and members of the general society understand the behavior's meaning. Most human behavior is complex and reflects more than a random configuration of neuromuscular, skeletal motions. It is more accurately described as social action: people acting together in ways that are coherent—at least to those involved. Behaviors recur and are parts of ongoing human experiences, complete with expectations about what should be said and done.

Consider hooking as an example of social action. Usually, there are two main participants: a prostitute (or "hooker") and a customer (or "john" or "trick"). They engage in predictable interaction, which varies somewhat depending on the situation. Often, the hooker will approach a prospective customer and ask if he wants to "party." The knowledgeable (and interested) customer will then ask the price of services and the prostitute will describe a "menu." The words and actions are well known to and understood by most participants.

The concept of social action refers to instances of meaningful human conduct such as these. Social actions can be limited in time, space, and inclusiveness of participants (as hooking tends to be) or they can be very encompassing, involving nearly everyone in the society.

Social Niche

A social niche refers to a space in society that supplies a context for human social actions. It consists of roles, relationships, and rationales (Miller, 1978). It also provides an interpretive context within and through which people understand experiences (Bryant, 1982). As people enter social niches, they find that they are expected to act in certain ways and perform certain activities. These expectations are specific to positions within the setting and are called *roles* (see Biddle and Thomas, 1966). The social niche of a college classroom, for example, includes the easily identifiable roles of professor and student. Professors and students generally do not have to think about how to act in this setting. Their roles are well defined and understood. Roles are inherently relational. The expectations are always relative to others within a situation. The role of professor is defined largely in terms of the role of student, for example. Relationship, then, refers to the convergences between and among roles. Roles and relationships make up the social structure of social niches.

Rationales refer to the shared meanings within the niches. Professors engage in certain gestures that participants recognize as lecturing or teaching. Students go through motions of writing and staring that are understood as taking notes or learning (or so it seems!).

The concept of social niche refers to how people and groups are distributed into specialized living arrangements. We are not just Americans, but also Midwesterners or Southerners; urban or rural; young, middle aged, or old; and professionals, managers, laborers, or unemployed; and so on. We live within specialized contexts that I will refer to here as *niches*. Social niches can be described, in part, by observing and reporting the social actions that are characteristic of people who live and act in that context—their roles. An adequate description also requires an accounting of the physical and social geography of the setting (see Linton, 1936; Blumer, 1951; Stryker, 1980).

A pickup bar is an example of a social niche in American society. It is characterized most obviously by the social actions of drinking, partying, and hustling and the roles and relationships of bartender, customers, and "working girls." It is different from other kinds of bars and nightclubs in at least one way: It accommodates prostitutes who regularly ply their trade. This special feature is social and creates requirements for special physical properties. If the club is to survive, it must be designed so that some of the ongoing activities can be concealed from public view, for example.

Social actions persist and change. Social niches emerge, expand, contract, change, and disappear. In spite of this potential transience, a larger order emerges and reflects meaning and coherence in human social life. Social actions are woven together to form larger patterns of persisting practices. Social niches become interlocked or become parts of alliances or settlements that are tenuous or viable. This larger patterning or order is called *social organization.*

Social Organization

Sociologists often describe social organization in terms of the number of human relationships involved. There are dyads and triads (groups of two and three persons), small groups, large groups, classes, subcultures, and other configurations that are organized in various ways. Society is typically the most inclusive level of social organization of concern to sociologists. *Social organization* is the arrangement of persisting and changing patterns of social action and interrelated social niches.

Forms of organization are shaped partly by social and physical environmental requirements and partly by the operation of social processes such as interaction, competition, conflict, cooperation, imitation, invention, and social control—among many others. Social organization includes social control and, by implication, deviance.[1] More specifically, social control is that dimension of social organization that enforces expectations and laws through sanctions.

Groups, communities, societies, and other social entities are organized in diverse and dynamic ways. Their organization reflects the operation of environmental demands and social processes. And the organization has consequences for people who live and act within its context. Note that no form of organization is necessarily right or wrong—or better or worse than any other. My definition of organization disavows concepts such as disorganization because they suggest value judgments. Alternatively, differences in organization are recognized and considered important for understanding social realities (compare Sutherland and Cressey, 1978, especially the theory of differential organization, pages 83–97).

We often can see social organization most directly in the expectations that guide behavior in everyday experiences. These expectations take different forms. One important variable concerns formality. Some expectations are written and typically are enforced by some official agent or agency. Others are simply understood and no one in particular has the right or responsibility to enforce them. Laws and rules are examples of formal expectations. Norms and understandings illustrate informal expectations.

I have organized the following description through the use of the basic concepts (social action, social niche, and social organization).

. . . "[I]n 1979 Americans age 18 and over spent more than $32 billion so that each could drink, on the average, 34 gallons of beer; 2.7 gallons of distilled spirits; 2.6 gallons of still wine; and 1/6 gallon of bubbly wine" (Ray, 1983:145–146). Alcohol use and the control of alcohol have varied over the history of our society. Some drinking patterns came with the early settlers to the colonies. The first colonial American law pertaining to alcohol was passed in Maryland in 1642 and made drunkenness a punishable offense. Virginia passed a law in 1644 that prohibited ministers from drinking to excess. Other colonial laws prohibited being drunk in one's own home and drinking for more than half an hour at a time (Ray, 1983:148–149).

Drinking was pervasive through the colonial era and into the nineteenth century. Congress authorized giving soldiers and sailors rum, brandy, or whiskey from 1790 until the middle 1800s. In 1834, Congress enacted legislation that prohibited the sale of liquor to Indians. The temperance movement gained momentum during the 1820s, and by the turn of the century, a full-fledged abstinence and prohibition effort and been launched. The National Prohibition Party was formed in 1874, and in 1895 the American Anti-Saloon League was organized.

Between 1907 and 1919, 34 states enacted prohibition legislation, and over 100,000 licensed bars were closed. Liquor consumption increased by 16 percent. People drank more (*illegal*) distilled spirits, and they drank patent medicines that were not illegal—even though some contained 25 percent or more alcohol. Whisko, for example, was a "nonintoxicating stimulant" that was 55 proof; Kaufman's Sulfur Bitters was advertised as "containing no alcohol," but, in fact, it was 20 percent alcohol and had no sulfur. In January of 1919, the Eighteenth Amendment was ratified and Prohibition went into effect nationwide a year later. The Eighteenth Amendment was repealed by the Twenty-First Amendment, ending Prohibition in 1933 (Ray, 1983:149–151). In the early years of national prohibition, alcohol consumption went down. Toward the end, the rates were very similar to those of the years before Prohibition.

Alcohol use per capita has roughly doubled since the end of Prohibition. And drinking patterns are clearly established. A higher percentage of men than women drink and among those who drink, men drink more. Among male drinkers, young men are most likely to be heavy drinkers. Whites and blacks are about equally likely to drink, but blacks have a rate of alcoholism that is more than double that of whites. American Indians and Irish-Americans have very high rates of heavy drinking. Italian-Americans consume more alcohol per capita than their Irish-American counterparts, but they have a much lower rate of alcoholism. American Jews begin drinking at an early age, but few drink heavily and the rate of alcoholism is very low. The proportion of Catholics who drink is higher than that for Protestants, but conservative Protestants have a high rate of problem drinkers among those who drink. Similarly, more people of high socioeconomic status drink, but the lower socioeconomic status groups have much higher rates of alcoholism. Drinking is most prevalent in the Northeast and least prevalent in the South.

Drinking occurs in a variety of settings; heavy drinking often occurs in taverns. Kotarba (1984:153) reports research on a particular type of tavern: those found in predominantly or exclusively white lower-middle-class neighborhoods. Most of the customers are male, middle-aged, ethnic (Polish-, German-, and Irish-American), and hold low to medium status, high-paying jobs. Many of the regulars regard themselves as "heavy drinkers," defined as "one who visits the tavern almost daily and consumes a minimum of five drinks" (Kotarba, 1984:154).

The interiors of the taverns are decorated simply and are painted in dark colors. There are revolving beer signs, a pool table, a jukebox, and a long, wooden bar. Drinking and driving are virtually inseparable activities for the regulars. They stop at a bar on their way home from work (and many stop in the morning on their way to work), and they move from tavern to tavern pursuing different interests with groups that congregate at different bars. (Some are ethnically oriented, others are hangouts for people who work together, and still others are meeting places for softball and other recreational teams.)

We can see social organization in descriptions of historical variations and in the description of differences in contemporary beliefs and drinking patterns among groups and classes of people in our society. (See Bennett and Ames, 1985, for descriptions of various American patterns of drinking, including those of Italian-Americans, Polish-Americans, and Americans living in Appalachia.) The arrangement of social actions and social niches supported various drinking behaviors in the period immediately preceding Prohibition. Few laws controlled the production, distribution, and consumption of alcoholic drinks. Drinking was widespread and people earned livings by owning, operating, and working in the bars and taverns. Prohibition reflected and introduced major changes in social organization. New laws were created. Understandings about alcohol use changed, from mild general acceptance to public rejection (at least, official rejection) of drinking. The idea that alcohol is the root cause of much human suffering was increasingly accepted, and bars and taverns were closed.

Prohibition was later repealed. Since that time, and in spite of state and federal laws that set limits and prescribe and proscribe conduct, patterns and beliefs about drinking alcohol vary greatly by social class, gender, education, income, age, and ethnicity. Throughout, social processes such as competition (among groups for or against Prohibition) shaped the form and consequences of the emerging and changing organization. Indeed, some have suggested that Prohibition was partly a political effort to control the poor and immigrants (Thio, 1983:378; Gusfield, 1963).

An obvious example of a social niche is the neighborhood tavern, a physical setting with particular attributes. It is also a social setting defined in part by the characteristics of the participants and their behavior. Taverns share some things in common with other ethnically oriented settings. (There are some common social actions, such as ways of relating to friends and styles of dress and grooming.) Other social actions are unique. Social roles and relationships may be similar in form but quite different in content from one tavern to the next. And what is appropriate and characteristic in the tavern may be inappropriate in neighborhood homes or at family reunions.

The social actions that characterize one social niche do not fit in a different niche. In local churches, the most salient social actions typically will be identifiable as praying and worshiping. In the tavern, typical social actions revolve around drinking, socializing, and relaxing, even though what is relaxing in one tavern may not be in another.

A Definition of Deviance

The basic concepts of interaction, social structure, action, niche, and organization allow a more specific and explicit definition of deviance. Deviance involves both violation and social control. *Violation* is a social action (an act, event, meaning or characteristic) that departs from an expectation, norm, rule, or law. Violations may be real (that is, factually true and demonstrated by evidence) or only alleged (not true or true but not demonstrated by evidence). And the norms or laws may be shared and supported widely within the group or society, or they may reflect very narrow and circumscribed interests. Norms and rules also may be implicit and usually unspoken (informal) or explicit and written (formal). *Social control* is social action that imposes a penalty or sanction.[2] The penalty or sanction is related to some violation, but the violation may be real or only alleged. *Deviance*, then, is an outcome that links *violation* and *social control*.[3] Violation without social control is still violation, but it is not deviance. However, social control can combine with alleged violation (in the absence of actual violation) to create deviance. Finally, as noted in Chapter 1, deviance is both an objective and a subjective reality. It is created when real or suspected violations are joined with sanctions.

Violation, Social Control, and Deviance in Context

Violations and social control are not randomly distributed. Whether or not a rule violation or an accusation of violation becomes an instance of deviance depends on surrounding and related social actions, the characteristics of the social niche(s), and more general social arrangements (the social organization). In short, it depends on the core variables identified in the preceding discussion of concepts. Compare two groups described by Chambliss (1978). Do the variables identified through the concepts make a difference in how the behaviors of these groups are understood?

> **"The Saints"** included **"eight promising young men—children of good, stable, white upper-middle-class families, active in school affairs, good pre-college students. . . . The Saints were constantly occupied with truancy, drinking, wild driving, petty theft and vandalism"** (Chambliss, 1978:294). **The boys skipped school nearly every day during the period of observation. They did so by faking "legitimate" releases from school for extracurricular activities. Weekends were occupied with illegal drinking, drunk driving, and vandalism. Again, these activities occurred nearly every weekend during the period of observation. None of these boys was arrested.**
>
> **"The Roughnecks"** were six lower-class white boys who attended school regularly even though they saw it mostly as a burden. Their grades averaged around C. No one failed and no one had better than a C average. They engaged in fighting and drinking occasionally and petty theft frequently. They were constantly involved with the police. **"Over the period that the group was under observation, each member was arrested at least once. Several of the boys were arrested a number of times and spent at least one night in jail"** (1978:301).

The "Roughnecks" experienced these differences in police contacts and arrests "even though their rate of delinquency was about equal with that of the Saints" (1978:294).

The general community and societal organizations clearly favor the Saints. They are "good" students from "good" families. They are seen by the community as "normal" boys sowing their wild oats. The Roughnecks come from families and parts of town that are associated with trouble. They hang out in highly visible areas and act in ways that are considered improper. According to Chambliss (1978:299), "Townspeople would say, 'You can can see the gang members at the drugstore, night after night, leaning against the storefront (sometimes drunk) or slouching around inside buying cokes, reading magazines, and probably stealing old Mr. Wall blind'." The social niches are different. The Saints are involved in school and community activities. Their behavior violating norms and laws occurs in settings (niches) that are not part of their usual social settings. Their violating behavior is similar in content but much different in meaning. For the Saints, the behavior becomes the social action called "mischief." The Roughnecks' behavior is seen as trouble symptomatic of their badness and indicative of future problems.

That the deviance outcomes of these two groups are radically different is no surprise. The factors identified by the key concepts provide good clues for anticipating which norm violations will be joined with sanctions to produce the social reality of deviance. Recall that deviance has been defined as a probability-type *outcome* from the beginning.

Explaining Deviance: Theories

The classical theories of Marx, Durkheim, and Weber provide a foundation for a general theory of deviance. Note, however, that any explanation must answer at least two major and distinct sets of questions. One set of questions concerns the *occurrence, distribution,* and *rate* of deviance in a society. These are matters of the *epidemiology* of deviance: (1) whether or not instances of deviance will occur, (2) where instances of deviance will occur (if they do), (3) the rate of deviance generally, and (4) the rates of particular types of deviance.

A second set of questions concerns the *causes* (or *etiology*) of instances of deviance: Why did a person act in a certain way? What "causes" homosexuality? Why do men drink more than women do? These questions are relevant, but they must be approached carefully. When we start with these causal questions, we often get deceived into treating deviance as a kind of pathology, disease, or assumed, objective condition. Sometimes our failure to distinguish between epidemiological issues and causal questions results in confusion in logic and concepts. Most of the traditional sociological theories of deviance, for example, have been interpreted to suggest a link between social class and crime (deviance). The idea that people in the lower social classes are more criminal and deviant than those in the upper classes is consistent with common sense perceptions. And it had circulated for many years with little criticism as an implication of sociological theory until Tittle (1983:352) pointed out that "none [of the major deviance theories] actually provides a sufficient rationale for predicting such a relationship." (See also Tittle and Villemez, 1977, and Tittle, Villemez, and Smith, 1978, for a critical assessment of the empirical evidence for the assumed relationship.)

We can avoid some of the pitfalls of previous efforts by focusing clearly on the *sociological* reality of deviance. Sociologically, deviance is a negotiated outcome and a part of the social organization of human life. We must first try to understand deviance and social control within their context. Accordingly, we begin with the epidemiological theory and then proceed to consider the causal implications. Deviance and social control are to be understood as matters of probability. Explanations focus on the conditions under which the probability of deviance is increased and variables or factors that encourage or fail to constrain the occurrence of deviance.

Two separate but integrated theories will be presented. After I present the epidemiological theory in this chapter, I will review contemporary deviance theories. Chapter 4 presents the causal theory.

Before we continue, I will clarify a few points about convergence theory. It consists of two separate theories: One explains the epidemiology of deviance; the other explains the etiology of deviance. The epidemiological theory is presented in Postulate 1, Proposition $E1$, Proposition $E2$, and Postulate 2. The propositions of the epidemiological theory are marked with the letter E. Chapter 4 presents the causal theory in Postulate 1, Proposition $C1$, Proposition $C2$, and Postulate 2. The propositions of the causal theory are marked with the letter C. Note that the postulates are the same in the two theories. They are thus linked together to form a general theory of deviance. Arrows are used to describe relationships among the concepts of the theory. Arrows pointing up ($\uparrow$) indicate a pattern that is increasing; arrows pointing down ($\downarrow$) indicate a pattern that is decreasing. Subscripts $_1$ and $_2$ indicate different "system states," as described by Dubin (1978:144–151). The idea of system states is to describe some aspect of society and then treat the description comparatively. For example, the integration of society (abbreviated as I) might be described at system state 1 (I_1) and as changed at system state 2 (I_2). In this example, the system states seem to refer to different periods of time. Note, however, that time is only one possible source of difference between system states.

Explaining Rates and Patterns of Deviance and Social Control

Postulate 1: Social control is selective.

Some norm violations (real or alleged) are joined with sanctions; others are not. The things selected as deviant will tend to reflect the existing social organization. However, social control activities sometimes introduce changes in social organization. For example, efforts to control drinking led to the elimination of jobs and businesses as bars, taverns, liquor stores, and breweries were closed. The control efforts, then, resulted in state intrusion into private enterprise, an outcome that clearly is contrary to the prevailing social order. A more general example follows:

> Property laws reflect and support our existing capitalist social organization. Laws against theft, for example, protect those who have property from those who do not. Antitrust laws are also property laws, but they appear to *contradict* dominant features of our social and economic order. In a sense, they protect the have-nots from the haves by controlling monopolistic practices that might tend to be exploitive. In that way, they *restrict* the private accumulation of wealth.

Social control and social organization are related dialectically: they *complement* one another (they support and reinforce each other), and they *contradict* each other (their characteristics conflict and cause changes). See end note 1.)

Proposition E1: Integration and social control are dialectically related. As integration decreases, social control increases; as social control increases, integration increases.

$$I_1 \downarrow SC \uparrow I_2 \uparrow$$

The relationship between integration and social control parallels that between social organization and social control—that is, they are complementary and contradictory (dialectical). More specifically, integration is a dimension of social organization. Social control has been defined, but *integration* is a new term. The meaning and relevance of integration and social control can be seen through the works of the classical theorists. The following discussion draws from the works of Durkheim, Marx, and Weber to specify the meaning and measurement of integration. This analysis identifies three separate dimensions of integration: *solidarity, equilibrium,* and *commonality.* Note the overlap among

T A B L E   3 . 1

Measures of Integration: Durkheim, Marx, and Weber

	Characteristics of Social Order	General Theories' Measure of Integration
DURKHEIM	Order is based on nature and strength of relationships among the parts	*Solidarity* (Mechanical and Organic)
	Order is based on functional balance among system parts	*Equilibrium*
	Order is based on shared beliefs or collective representations	*Commonality*
MARX	Order is based on dynamic (dialectical) tensions among parts with different power and interests	*Equilibrium*
WEBER	Order is based on shared meanings	*Commonality*

the classical theorists in their ideas about social order and integration. Table 3.1 summarizes the meanings and measures of integration.

Dimensions of Integration

When Durkheim wrote about integration, he seemed to have in mind all three of the dimensions summarized in Table 3.1: solidarity, equilibrium, and commonality. *Solidarity* refers to the nature of the parts and the form of their relationships. He described two basic types of solidarity: mechanical and organic. *Mechanical* societies are composed of a few parts that are very similar. Parts refer to groups and other social structural arrangements. Solidarity results from the parts' similarity. *Organic* societies, in contrast, are composed of diverse parts (groups, social niches, patterns of conduct) that are interdependent. Each part performs some service or function for the other parts and the system as a whole. This interdependence is the basis of solidarity: the higher the level of mutual dependence, the higher the integration. Declining integration means something different for mechanical solidarity than it does for organic solidarity. Declining mechanical solidarity refers to differentiation: The number of parts increases and the parts become dissimilar. Declining organic solidarity means that the diverse but mutually dependent parts become less interdependent.

Equilibrium refers to the balance of the system, in this case a *social system*. Durkheim was much concerned with how societies were organized such that they did or did not survive within their environments. He saw the parts of society (for example, institutions) as intricately and functionally related, producing some equilibrium that has relative value for the survival of the system.[4] Declining integration refers to changes that somehow diminish the survival capabilities of the overall societal arrangement.

The third dimension or measure of integration is suggested by Durkheim's concept of "collective conscience." Also translated as "collective consciousness," this concept refers to widely shared beliefs that support and underpin customs, norms, and other aspects of social organization. Integration here refers to *commonality*, or the level of shared beliefs within a group or society.

Marx's conception of integration is very close to Durkheim's idea of *equilibrium*. Societies and other social systems are always in process, always undergoing change. The continuing dialectical relationships among the parts ensure change. Recall that for Marx, the "parts" are composed of forces and relations of production and the superstructure. Marxian theorists often describe the change process as resulting from interaction among "thesis," "antithesis," and "synthesis." I describe this process in terms of *complementary* and *contradictory* relationships. (See Chapter 2.) As integration decreases, conflicts and contradictions increase. These contradictions move the system toward some antithesis or some new synthesis. The distribution of power and interests influences the direction and result of change. For Marx, declining integration means movement away from the ideal state. Historically, the ideal state is the state of nature in which each person takes from the environment that which he or she needs for survival and nothing more. In Marx's view of the future, the ideal refers to a socialist state in which each contributes according to his or her ability and receives from the collective according to his or her need.

Weber's work on authority (1968; see also Chapter 2) suggests an understanding of integration that is similar to the *commonality* dimension described in Durkheim's research. Authority, the legitimate use of power, varies in part depending on the level and types of shared understandings in the community or society. When *informal* understandings are not widely shared, as the *commonality* dimension of integration decreases, formal means emerge to enforce at least some understandings. Laws are created, enforcement agencies develop, and rules replace informal understandings. A change from traditional authority to rational authority—for example, police departments take the place of civic and religious leaders in managing the conduct of citizens—illustrates this type of shift. The change would not mean necessarily that social control would increase. However, increase is likely because formal social control is less flexible than informal means. Violations of formal rules create more obligations for reaction and enforcement because such rules typically include provisions for enforcement.

Note that decreasing integration involves an increase in diversity and the disconnectedness of the parts, no matter which of the dimensions is examined.

(The parts of society are institutions such as family, economy, and polity, which in turn consist of social arrangements including norms, roles, relationships—or social niches.) For example, when *mechanical solidarity* decreases, the society becomes more complex, groups and classes of people live differently (there are more social niches), and there is less consensus of beliefs and expectations. As another example, declining integration may refer to threatened equilibrium, which involves the prospect of extinction of the society. This threat operates as a catalyst to produce potentially off-setting changes that may be adaptive and, thus, enhance the survival of the system.

There is an important exception to the argument that decreasing integration means increasing diversity. When integration refers to *organic solidarity*, social niches will be diverse and heterogeneous *and* interdependent. Accordingly, the niches will be different but connected by mutual dependencies. When integration is low or weak, niches will be diverse and disconnected. Conventional or official norms and values—*those that are most likely to be enforced*—will not be reflected strongly in the disparate niches. Decreased integration, then, means increased diversity and disconnectedness within and among the parts of society.

Proposition $E1$ concerns the relationship between integration and social control. The primary focus is on the *level* of integration. Classical theorists recognized the importance of integration and their work suggests a multidimensional understanding of it. Integration refers to the organization of society. I have specified three distinguishable dimensions of integration from the works of Durkheim, Marx, and Weber. The relationship between integration and social control is the same for all three dimensions. In each case, low levels of integration threaten the viability of the organization. For example, if solidarity breaks down, the system may not survive; when commonalities decrease, the maintenance of a meaningful community is threatened. When viability is threatened by some internal or environmental change, social control increases and may have the effect of resisting or managing the threat.[5]

The enforcement of norms and the punishment of real or alleged violations (that is, social control) reinforce the existing arrangements. In addition, other social control activities, such as policy decisions to implement or change enforcement activities, facilitate and enhance some interests and contradict or restrict others. In mechanical societies, integration (solidarity) means conformity—maintaining similarity. Deterrence is a key concern. Organic societies operate differently. These societies have more complicated arrangements, such as a division of labor with workers performing different tasks as parts of a complicated production. Social control cannot operate by simply enforcing conformity or uniformity because the organization (integration) requires differences. Instead, social control is oriented toward restoring the deviant part (pattern of conduct, group, niche) so that its function is performed. The commonality or shared understanding dimension of integration is maintained by social control that reinforces common beliefs. Commonality is symbolic in character. It consists of shared meanings that may take any of a variety of forms.

The Relationship Between Violation and Social Control

Proposition E2: Integration, violation, and social control are dialectically related. When integration decreases, violation and social control increase; when social control increases, integration increases.

$$I_1 \downarrow V \uparrow SC \uparrow I_2 \uparrow$$

The logic of Proposition $E2$ parallels that of Proposition $E1$. However, Proposition $E2$ has some important distinctions. First, note that there is no direct relationship between violation and social control—for example, increased violations do not lead, necessarily, to increased social control. Further, the relationship between integration and violation is inverse and moves in one direction: Violations increase as integration decreases. This relationship, like the one between integration and social control discussed earlier, holds true with all of the meanings and measures of integration. For example, when equilibrium declines, human behavior becomes more variable. Social structures, such as norms and laws, are less effective in constraining and limiting the range of behaviors and options. Similarly, as commonality decreases, more diverse meanings give rise to more variation in conduct.

Both propositions ($E1$ and $E2$) deny or play down the simple and "obvious" relationship between violation and social control. The common assumption is that social controls increase when (and because) violations increase, and violations decrease when social controls become pervasive and effective. Note this departure from the conventional wisdom for at least two reasons. First, empirical evidence *does not* support the "obvious." And second, the taken-for-granted understanding leads to questions that have not proved useful. These points are developed more fully in the following paragraphs.

Postulate 1 presented the argument that social control is selective. Most violations do not result in social control. For example, most people who drive over the speed limit, drink before the legal age, engage in prohibited games of chance, steal from department stores, or cheat on their income taxes do not get caught; they do not experience social control. Sometimes social control activities increase regardless of rates of violation. For example, the current massive drug education and enforcement programs (social control) were initiated during an era (mid-1980s) in which drug use was steadily decreasing. However, social control efforts often are stopped or reduced regardless of the rates of violation. This happens fairly often in the episodic and highly variable enforcement of prostitution statutes.

The widely shared (but highly questionable) idea that social control develops as a reaction to violation is part of the traditional image of deviance. It leads us to treat deviance as an objectively given reality rather than to question it as a negotiated outcome. We ask questions like these: Why do people violate rules? Why does the crime rate continue to increase even when we spend more money on enforcement? At the very least, these questions are premature. More importantly, they disregard the negotiated character of deviance.

Proposition $E2$ directs attention to a critically important theoretical matter. Recall that deviance is defined as the convergence or concomitance of violation and social control. Accordingly, the proposition (and equation) can be restated by substituting deviance (D) for violation and social control (V and SC): Integration (I) and deviance (D) are dialectically related ($I \downarrow D \uparrow I \uparrow$). This dialectical relationship is the core idea of my convergence theory.[6] It is *not* a new idea. It is anticipated in the works of Durkheim, Marx, and other contributors to functionalist sociology. One implication of the theory is especially important: Social control programs do not eliminate deviance. Indeed, deviance probably will not go away no matter what we do.

Postulate 2: Social control and violations are dialectically related. (Social control shapes and sustains deviance.)

The convergence theory begins and ends with the assertion that deviance is a matter of selection (Postulates 1 and 2). Negotiations determine whether or not something is deviant. My argument is that the selecting and negotiating operate to maintain, rather than to eliminate, the objects of control. Some kinds of things can be "selected" to the point of extinction—for example, killing off of certain species of birds and animals. But deviant selection does not necessarily reduce the stock of things selected—except, perhaps, through execution or expulsion. Prohibition did not eliminate drinking. The Harrison Act did not eliminate drugs or their use. Neither have criminal laws, wars on crime, and increased funding for police, courts, or corrections programs eliminated (or reduced?) rates of law violation. But all of these efforts, and probably all other social control efforts as well, have shaped and formed the objects of their concern. Illegal drug use is different from the drug use that preceded the legislation, just as drinking during Prohibition was different from drinking that preceded it. Hookers cannot approach customers directly to offer their services, and gay support groups often must meet under the cover of darkness.

Social control does not eliminate violations, but does it shape and sustain them? If violations persist in spite of social control, then they persist in some relation to it. Behavior that violates norms and laws, or that might be so interpreted, must be adapted to avoid continuous efforts to control, constrain, or eliminate. Through adaptations, violating conduct takes on certain characteristics. These features directly reflect the social control efforts. For example, prostitution statutes typically prohibit solicitation. It is against the law to offer sex for money. As a result, prostitutes cannot display signs advertising their services and prices, but they can advertise their availability by their dress, location, and demeanor. To avoid charges of soliciting, they must hint at what they have in mind and encourage the prospective customer to make the offer.

An extended example follows to make more concrete the proposed explanation and its implications.

Events surrounding the turn of the century (1880–1920) illustrate the assertions and relationships proposed by convergence theory. By 1880, the industrial revolution was well under way. American society was moving rapidly from an economy dominated by family farm agriculture to one in which factory production was central. Factories were becoming larger and more encompassing, and capital resources were increasingly concentrated in the hands of wealthy entrepreneurs. Industrial production required huge numbers of unskilled laborers. Millions of people entered this country during the period from 1900 to 1920. These immigrants and farm workers who were displaced by the mechanization of farming settled in growing cities of the Northeast and Midwest.

Compared to rural communities of earlier times, these cities brought together people with marked differences in life-styles, beliefs, interests, and habits. Observers of that time describe radical social change and increasing conflicts of interest. By any of the definitions, integration was decreasing. New demands challenged structural arrangements. (For example, technological innovations in farming undercut the value of large families.) Communities and the general society became more differentiated. Some of the differentiation contributed to increased interdependence. As one example, rural communities were replaced or consumed by growing metropolises, and fewer people grew, raised, or made the things they needed for survival. Common life experiences and shared understandings (commonalities) gave way to uneasy and tentative alliances and accommodations. Diverse ethnic groups living together in inner cities learned to tolerate, accommodate, or ignore their "strange" neighbors if they could not exclude them.

During this same period, there were important developments in law and public regulation. Compulsory education, child labor laws, and the juvenile court emerged as public and "rational" solutions to difficult "social problems" of the time. (Note that *rational* here, following Weber's lead, means *rule based*. The change involved, in part, a shift from traditional or informal social control to legal, formal means.) Labor laws severely restricted the use of children in industrial production and changed dramatically the status of young people in the economy and before the law. Legislation requiring school attendance made "criminals" of those who failed to go. At the same time, a new justice system emerged to "serve the needs" of this new class of citizens (that is, "children," as illegal laborers, truants, and delinquents); some have argued that the programs *controlled* rather than served children (compare Platt, 1969).

This description of life in turn-of-the-century America suggests three general conclusions: (1) change was dramatic and widespread, (2) the variety of social conduct increased sharply (foreigners introduced foreign ways), and (3) agencies and programs emerged and responded to some of the diverse behaviors and conditions of the era. Selectivity of social control can be seen in the developing programs that focused on care and control of children.

Social control programs were aimed at reinforcing and preserving traditional understandings and interests (commonality). Leaders of reform movements were openly critical of "foreign ways" and the threat of the "dangerous classes" (from the title of a book by C. L. Brace, *The Dangerous Classes of New York*, 1872). John P. Sloan, superintendent of the John Worthy School, observed:

> "From the crowded slum-life of a noisy, disorderly settlement, where seventy percent of the population is of foreign parentage, these boys should be sent to the open country, with regular methodical existence and a training and education that will develop and promote habits of industry" [Proceedings of the Illinois Conference of Charities, 1901, in Platt, 1969:66].

The interests that supported the reform-oriented social control efforts have been described more generally by Hofstadter (1955): "The Progressive mind . . . was pre-eminently a Protestant mind; and even though much of its strength was in the cities, it inherited the moral traditions of rural evangelical Protestantism."

The example suggests ways in which changes in social organization affect patterns and rates of violation and social control. In Chapter 4, attention is directed to contemporary deviance theories and matters of causation.

Explaining Deviance: Contemporary
Theories and Causes of Deviance

The epidemiological theory presented in Chapter 3 suggests certain causal questions:

1. Under what conditions will any individual engage in some conduct that has a relatively high probability of being identified as a violation?

2. Under what conditions will any instance of violation (real or alleged) have a relatively high probability of being sanctioned?

The theory asserts that deviance (the convergence of violation and social control) is related to social integration. As social integration decreases, the probability of violation and the probability of social control both increase. That is not a novel idea. A brief review of major sociological theories of deviance reveals the complementary themes that have developed and suggests their contribution to the proposed approach. It also provides additional foundation for a general causal theory.

Contemporary Deviance Theories
Functionalist Theories

In Chapter 2, we looked at *functionalism* as a general theoretical perspective through a consideration of the works of Durkheim and Marx. When it is applied to questions about deviance, this approach suggests that deviance is an integral part of society and performs useful functions in the organization and mainte- nance of the social system. Kingsley Davis (1937, 1948, and 1976) provided a contemporary and more specific functionalist explanation of deviance in his theory of prostitution. He argued that prostitution is supported by the social organization and in turn supports the conventional society:

> The demand for the prostitute's services arises out of the regulation of sex itself and the limited liability of the commercial relationship. If the cus- tomer has the money, he can obtain satisfaction with no further obliga- tions. . . . The division of labor by sex, derived from the female's greater association with reproduction and hence the family, makes women depen- dent to some extent on their sexual attractiveness and gives men more control of economic means. . . . Since the economic means are distributed unequally between classes but female attractiveness is not, some women of lower economic means can exploit their attractiveness for economic gain. For these reasons, demand and supply are broadly based and inextinguish- able [Davis, 1976:247].

Davis argued that prostitution supports the conventional order by providing a sexual outlet for men that does not disrupt conventional sexual and family relationships. At the same time, prostitution is a part of the social order because it reflects conventional arrangements such as the distribution of economic means and the "dependent" status of women. (Note that Davis's analysis appears to be time bound, given the increasing independence of contemporary American women.)

Functional theories of deviance have been concerned with social integra- tion in two major ways. First, as noted earlier, Durkheim proposed a relation- ship between integration and rates and types of deviance. Kai Erickson's (1966) study of Puritan settlers in seventeenth-century Massachusetts provides an excellent example of work related to this functionalist approach. Erickson's research described the consequences of religious persecution in defining and reinforcing the social and moral boundaries of the early Puritan colonies. This point of view is reflected directly in convergence theory.

Second, through the work of Talcott Parsons (see especially Parsons, 1951), functionalist theories considered the problematic relationship between integra- tion and deviance. If people in social systems are seen as voluntary actors, as Parsons and his students suggested, how can integration be maintained? How and why do people act in accordance with social arrangements rather than pursue selfish wants and goals?[1]

Parsons contended that the social order is maintained essentially through four social processes. People comply with and contribute to the ongoing order because (1) they are *socialized* to act and believe in certain ways, (2) they find *profit* in compliance with and connection to the ongoing arrangement, (3) they are *pursuaded* by ideological agencies such as education, and (4) they are *coerced* by normative and legal systems and various arrangements for imposing sanctions. Parsons's (1951:287–291, 428–479) analysis of the "sick role" and the ways in which the role limits the rights and opportunities of its incumbents provides a good example of how social control operates to *contain* deviance and maintain the social order. The proposed epidemiological theory does not deal with individual levels, patterns, or processes of integration. However, the processes identified by Parsons may be experiences that intervene between levels and types of social integration and individual conduct. This issue will be considered later in this chapter.

Anomie Theory

Anomie theory contends essentially that certain structural arrangements *promote* deviance or, more accurately, *violation* as a viable adaptation. In his review of Robert Merton's (1938, 1957) signal contributions to this theory, Goode (1984:25) asserted that the central thesis is that deviance results from a "*mal*integrated" [emphasis added] society. Anomie means normlessness, or a social condition in which the norms are not effectively organizing human behavior. It is not lack of integration but a form of integration that is not adaptive that is strongly related to deviance, according to this theory. Deviance is seen as symptomatic of this malintegration. Merton's analysis focused on structural arrangements in American society that define major goals and the normatively approved means for achieving those goals. More specifically, he examined the commonly shared belief in success and the ways in which our society is organized for the pursuit and attainment of these aspirations. Most Americans believe in the rightness of these goals, but access to the means for achieving them is not freely or equally available to all. The normatively approved means for pursuing the "American Dream" include education, hard work, inheritance, and professional sports.

But not everyone can get a good education or play professional basketball. What happens when the goals of success are held to be applicable to all but the means for achieving the goals are limited to some? Merton contended that this *structural conflict* produces a requirement for adaptation. He considered the possibilities for adapting by examining the logical possibilities given the combinations of accepting or rejecting the goals, the means, or both. If the goals and means are not wholly compatible, some people are caught in a structural bind (a condition of anomie). They could accept or reject one or the other, or reject both. This analysis produces a description of types of deviance that result from social "malintegration."

Richard Cloward (1959) and Cloward and Lloyd Ohlin (1960) expanded Merton's anomie thesis by suggesting a different kind of relationship between cultural goals and the means for achieving those goals. Specifically, these researchers noted that there are both legitimate and illegitimate means. Both are distributed unequally. Those who have limited access to conventional means (or no access at all) cannot turn to illegitimate means unless such opportunities are available. How many people know how to become a numbers runner or a pimp? Where do you go to apply for a job with the mafia? Although anyone can violate norms or laws, most people cannot do so with much chance of succeeding. Accordingly, the probability of violating conventional norms is not simply a matter of the extent to which the goals are accepted but legitimate means are blocked. There is at least the other problem of gaining access to illegitimate opportunities.

Convergence theory does not adopt the concept of malintegration. However, the idea that social arrangements encourage or promote violation and social control is completely consistent with the theory. The beginning and ending postulates point to the intimate relationship between conventional social arrangements and deviance. But anomie theory goes further. It suggests that people experience a kind of social condition that has been described variously as normlessness, powerlessness, and meaninglessness. Rates of deviance go up when anomie increases, and anomic people are more likely to commit acts of deviance. I will consider this point further later in this chapter.

Social Pathology Theories

Theories of *social pathology* seem naively judgmental, but they are similar in some ways to the seemingly more sophisticated versions of anomie theory and functionalist theory. Functionalists, anomie theorists, and pathologists all describe society as an organized system of parts that functions to maintain some balance. The pathology perspective in its simplest form contends that deviance and crime are reflections of fundamental disorders in society or in the individual or in both. Explanations proceed from a medical analogy in which societies resemble organisms, organized systems of parts that are susceptible to disease and malfunctioning. Individuals, likewise, are understood as complex biopsychosocial systems that can become sick or diseased. Ideas about sick or malfunctioning systems are not greatly different from anomie theory conceptions of malintegration.

However, the social pathology perspective is linked more inextricably to moral judgments than are the other theoretical efforts. (Compare Kavolis, 1977 who argued for an objective criterion of pathology, and Carl Rosenquist, 1940, and C. Wright Mills, 1943, who, respectively, described the "moral premises" and the "professional ideology" of social pathologists.) The approach was strongly influenced by various reform movements around the turn of the century. Social pathologists failed to develop an objective criterion of either normalcy or pathology. My proposed theory is related to the social pathology theory only to the extent that there are similarities between social pathology explanations and those proposed by functionalist and anomie theories.

Social Disorganization Theories

Many of the *social disorganization* theories are also limited by implicit middle-class values. (Merton's work on disorganization appears to be an exception. See Merton, 1976.) These theories developed principally from the work of sociologists at the University of Chicago. (Because of this, the approach is often referred to as the Chicago School of thought.) Sociologists who worked from and contributed to this perspective were much impressed by the seemingly negative qualities of city life: impersonality, diversity, rapid change, and mobility. Neighborhoods were characterized as "disorganized" based on descriptions of their characteristics, including the number of foreign-born residents, the level of poverty and unemployment, and the physical condition of streets, buildings, and houses.

Sociologists working from this point of view contributed remarkably detailed field studies that described the everyday world of deviant actors in their disorganized neighborhoods. See, for example, Anderson's (1923) study of the hobo, Zorbaugh's (1929) study of the slum, Thrasher's (1927) study of delinquent gangs, Shaw's (1930) study of a delinquent boy, and Cressey's (1932) study of the taxi-dance hall. At the same time, Chicago School sociologists used demographic methods to describe the distribution of deviance across neighborhoods and social and geographic areas. They documented concentrations of deviant patterns in areas with certain characteristics—that is, "disorganized" segments of communities. Their observations revealed that mental illness, crime, prostitution, and many other "social evils" were located disproportionately in the slum and low-income areas of urban communities. The central thesis that developed is that the breakdown of community and social control causes deviance. That thesis reflects what the researchers believed to be solid evidence describing the patterns, rates, and distribution of deviance. It is also a clear statement about the causes of deviance. As seemingly obvious as this thesis is, it is based on observations that may be misleading.

Researchers in the Chicago tradition were not much aware of the problems of using official or public agency data to describe patterns, rates, and distributions of deviant events. The possibility of bias in reporting of crimes, in decisions to arrest, and in the laws themselves did not occur to most researchers of the time (compare Kitsuse and Cicourel, 1963). There may be more crime in low-income neighborhoods as revealed in police records. Or the police may be more likely to arrest low-income people for the kinds of violations they commit. They may be less likely to arrest people who commit typically middle-class violations, such as tax fraud, employee theft, and embezzlement. Disorganization theorists were not entirely aware of their own rural, middle American biases. To them, the deteriorating and deteriorated inner cities were obviously disorganized and problematic. But recall (from Chapter 3) that what seem to be disorganized groups or neighborhoods may be described more precisely as organized differently (for example, organic solidarity versus mechanical solidarity). The central concerns of disorganization theories are included within the proposed conception of varying types and levels of integration.

Labeling Theories

Labeling theories represent a sharp change in the viewpoint of those interested in understanding deviance. Theorists working from this perspective do not see deviance as a matter of functional social organization, malintegration, or disorganization. Neither is there anything wrong with people or with organizational efforts to contain deviance. Instead, the problem is that groups, communities, and societies are organized in such a way that some people and some things get singled out for special and punitive treatment. The significance of this theoretical development for raising new questions and for turning upside down the old ones cannot be overemphasized.

In a sense, labeling theories take the first proposed postulate—social control is selective—to extremes. Not only is social control selective but it is also arbitrary. The only important difference between the deviant and the nondeviant is that the deviant was selected for punishment. Some versions of the theory suggest that both rules and violations of those rules are virtually irrelevant. The central (if not single) concern is with the reactions of others who treat some matters as deviant. Other varieties of this approach suggest that the selection is not so much arbitrary as it is a matter of accident. That is, things are selected because of contingencies that are irrelevant to the behaviors. Among the contingencies are the relative power and status of the actor (who may be accused of deviance) and the audience (those who may impose some sanction or other social control).

Labeling researchers contributed studies of marijuana use (Becker, 1953), check forging (Lemert, 1953, 1958), victimless crimes (Schur, 1965), and mental illness (Scheff, 1966), among many other deviance topics. Throughout these studies, the researchers attended to the ongoing interactions between actors who were the subjects of deviance labels and audiences who were actively creating and applying deviance definitions. Labeling theories share a concern about the consequences of deviant labels for those so defined. These researchers have advanced the claim that labeling of some earlier conduct or episode becomes a cause of subsequent deviant behavior. That assertion clearly is consonant with the second postulate of the proposed convergence theory: Social control and violations are dialectically related.

Conflict Theories

Conflict theories derive from the work of Karl Marx (as reviewed in Chapter 2). The dialectical explanation proposed here reflects many of these ideas as a consequence. Although several versions of this approach exist, conflict theorists typically are concerned with an issue that labeling theory raised but did not pursue: How and why are some things selected to be treated as matters of crime and deviance? The answer offered most often is that those with the greatest power are able to have their interests represented and enforced. Norms and laws do not necessarily reflect consensus in a group or society. And law enforcement does not necessarily protect the interests of the majority. Gusfield's (1963) work on the temperance movement, Chambliss's (1964) study of vagrancy laws, Turk's (1969) study of the legal order, and Quinney's (1974) critique of legal order are representative of the conflict point of view. My proposed theory does not provide a definitive answer to the central question raised from the conflict point of view. It does contend that the organization of society, in terms of both the level and type of integration, shapes and constrains violations and social control and thus deviance.

Social Control Theories

Social control theories directs attention to the matter of integration in a way different from other theoretical approaches. Various control theories focus on the extent of integration of individual actors. The central theme of these theories is that *people are constrained from violating norms, rules, and laws to the extent that they are integrated into the conventional social order.* Although there are important differences among them, theories proposed by Nye (1958), Hirschi (1969), and Reckless (1973) assert that people are not so much pushed to violate norms and laws as they are contained, controlled, or constrained from acting in those ways. The primary question is why don't more people violate more rules and laws? And the general answer is that various aspects of social organization and certain kinds of socialization experiences impose limits.

Travis Hirschi's (1969) assertion that people develop relationships that bind them to conventional values and ways of acting provides a useful summary of this approach. He described four ways in which people become "bonded" to society: (1) through attachment to others, (2) through a commitment to conformity, (3) through involvement in conventional activities, and (4) through beliefs in the validity of the rules and laws. My proposed epidemiological theory connects generally with the idea that integration is related to levels of violation. It does not deal with the origin or development of patterns of conduct.

Differential Organization and Association and Learning Theories

Edwin Sutherland's *differential organization and association theory* is the last major theoretical effort that I will review here. The basic postulate of his theory is that "crime is rooted in the social organization and is an expression of that social organization" (Sutherland and Cressey, 1955/1978:83). Sutherland was concerned primarily with the consequences of social complexity and diversity on crime rates. He argued against disorganization theories and suggested the concept of differential organization as an alternative. Nonetheless, he concluded that the complex and heterogeneous organization of modern American cities may tend to maximize rates of crime and deviance.

The theory of *differential association* builds from these ideas and focuses attention on social learning and cultural conflict. It has provided a point of departure for more elaborated and sophisticated learning theories, including most notably those suggested by Robert Burgess and Ronald Akers (1966; Akers, 1973). Sutherland asserted that crime is behavior and, like all other behavior, is learned through interaction within interpersonal relationships:

> When criminal behavior is learned, the learning includes (a) techniques of committing the crime, which are sometimes very complicated, sometimes very simple; (b) the specific direction of motives, drives, rationalizations, and attitudes.
>
> A person becomes delinquent because of an excess of definitions favorable to violation of law over definitions unfavorable to violation of law [Sutherland and Cressey, 1978:81].

The theory speaks of "motives, drives, and rationalizations," but in most of his writings Sutherland referred to definitions, especially *definitions favorable to law violation*. What Sutherland meant by *definitions* is unclear, but research reported by Sykes and Matza (1957) seems to provide some specification.[2] They describe "techniques of neutralization," which they assert operate to "free" individuals from the *controls* or *constraints* of social organization. They identify five such neutralizers: denial of responsibility, denial of injury, denial of the victim, condemnation of the condemners, and appeal to higher loyalties.

The first three of the definitions "excuse" violations because of contingent conditions: The person couldn't help himself, no one was hurt, or this person or group deserved what they got (they weren't really victims). The last two devalue the norms, rules, and laws by pointing to faults in those who represent the social order or by asserting some more compelling standard (for example, "I know it's wrong, but I have to do this for my friends").

Sutherland's theory of differential organization is reflected in the proposed epidemiological theory. "Complex" or "differential" organization, as he described it, is comparative and may reflect a change in the level or at least in the type of integration. The comparison or change may be from mechanical (homogeneous) to organic (complex, heterogeneous), or it may involve some other dimension of integration. The epidemiological theory does not deal with learning crime or deviance. As noted earlier, such matters are of concern as we turn to the origins or causes of conduct.

The Proposed Causal Theory

The causal theory must be consistent with the proposed epidemiological explanation. And if it is general in character, the theory also must reflect insights from contemporary theories—at least to the extent that those theories connect with the empirical world.[3] Recall the general assertion of the epidemiological theory: Social control and violations both increase as social integration decreases. What does that suggest about the causes of patterns of individual violation, social control, and deviance?

The level and type of integration in the society directly affects the composition and diversity of social niches and relationships among social niches. (Recall the discussion of integration and the diversity of social niches in Chapter 3.) When integration is high or strong, niches will be small in number and relatively homogeneous, or diverse but interdependent. When integration is low or weak, niches will be diverse and relatively disconnected from each other and, potentially, from the conventional order. The *conventional order* is defined as *those norms and laws that are most likely to be enforced.*

People grow, learn, and develop life-styles and habits of conduct within social niches. Social actions, patterned behavior that participants understand, are shaped and sustained within these niches. They are peculiar to the niche, depending on the nature of integration and differentiation within the society. Interpersonal and group relationships are formed within niches and are a specific source of social actions and the teaching and learning of social actions.

These ideas are very similar to those Sutherland offered in his theory of differential organization and association and to those Hirschi suggested in social control theory (see Sutherland and Cressey, 1978; Hirschi, 1969). One important difference is that the concept of social organization is expanded and elaborated by specifying the dimensions of integration. A second difference is that the relevance of social organization for learning within interpersonal relationships is made more explicit through the ideas of diversity and disconnectedness. Yet a third difference is my focus on social action. Sutherland and Hirschi (and most other theorists to date) refer globally to "behavior" and do not distinguish between individually unique or peculiar activities, on the one hand, and socially patterned action, on the other. A final and most important difference is this: My proposed theory is intended to apply to more than the learning or enacting of violating behavior, which was the primary concern for Sutherland, Hirschi, and others. Given the proposed understanding of deviance, both the development of "violating" conduct and the inclination to treat differences of deviance must be explained. The connections among integration, diversity, violation, and social control are specified in the following theory.

Postulate 1: Social control is selective.

As noted earlier, the first and the last postulates are the same in both the epidemiological and the etiological theories. Let's begin by recognizing the selectivity of social control and deviance: Some violations are treated as deviance (they are connected to sanctions) and sometimes sanctions are imposed without violation—as a result of false allegation, for example. Because this is true, we must explain something that is more than and different from the development of violating behavior. The matter of concern is deviance: the convergence of violation and social control.

Proposition C1: Integration (I), attachment (A), violation (V), and social control (SC) are dialectically related. As integration decreases, attachment decreases; violation and social control increase. As social control increases, integration increases.[4]

$$I_1 \downarrow \quad A \downarrow \quad V \uparrow \quad SC \uparrow \quad I_2 \uparrow$$

All but one of the proposition's terms are familiar and have been defined. The concept of *attachment* (A) is new; it derives most directly from the work on social control or bonding theory. The central theme of social control theory is that people conform to prevailing standards (the conventional order) because of their bond with the social order. (Recall that the conventional order is understood simply as those norms and rules that are most widely shared or that are most likely to be enforced.) Generally, people are attached to the conventional order through their relationships with representatives of that order, including parents, teachers, and friends.[5] Relationships are not equal in their influence on people and social actions. Some are critically important because they come early in the development of individual conduct. Others are important because they are frequent or long lasting and occupy a large portion of the individual's experience. And still others have little effect because they are superficial, short lived, or infrequent. (See Sutherland and Cressey, 1978).

As described in Chapter 3, decreased integration means increased diversity, so social niches are less connected to the general social order. (Recall the exception: Organic solidarity involves diversity regardless of integration. Decreased integration here means increased disconnectedness resulting from lack of interdependence.) As a result, there is a decrease in the proportion of interpersonal relationships that reflect and support prevailing conventional arrangements. Interactions within diverse or disconnected niches create opportunities for behaviors that depart from conventional standards. This is true because there are fewer constraining relationships in terms of the conventional order. Opportunities for violating conduct increase. (Recall that I have defined *violation* as an act, event, meaning, or characteristic that departs from an expectation, norm, rule, or law.)

Note that Proposition $C1$ includes within it the terms and relationships of Proposition $E1$ ($I_1 \downarrow SC \uparrow I_2 \uparrow$). The point here may be obvious: Decreased integration is accompanied by increased social control, regardless of whether or not attachments decrease or violations increase. Accordingly, the causal proposition does not assert that deviance increases just because violations increase. The relationship between integration (I) and social control (SC) remains as previously described. And deviance (D) is still understood as the convergence of violation (V) and social control (SC): $D = V \cdot SC$. *The theory does not reduce to assertions about the causes of violation.* To simplify proposition $C1$, we can substitute terms as I did with Proposition $E2$: $V \cdot SC = D$. The restated proposition then reads:

$$I_1 \downarrow \quad A \downarrow \quad D \uparrow \quad I_2 \uparrow$$

This substitution is carried forward in Proposition $C2$.

> **Proposition $C2$:** Integration (I), learning violations (LV), and deviance (D) are dialectically related. As integration and attachment decrease, learning violations and deviance increase; as deviance increases, integration increases.

$$I_1 \downarrow \quad A \downarrow \quad LV \uparrow \quad D \uparrow \quad I_2 \uparrow$$

Again, there is one new term in the proposition, *learning violations* (LV), which points to the work of Sutherland and other learning theorists who have followed his lead. Drawn from the differential association theory, learning violations means learning both the specific techniques of performance and the meanings or definitions that support or encourage social actions that violate norms and rules. Some social actions involve very complex techniques (playing football; shoplifting), while others are very simple (wearing Levi's button-fly blue jeans; carrying a concealed weapon). Likewise, some definitions are very complex and subtle (religious faith requires obedience to civil authority; you can use heroin and not get hooked). Others are very simple (smoking is bad for your health; school is the pits).

The process of learning can be described and specified further through the work of contemporary learning theorists. Akers (1973, 1985), for example, provided a model that introduces principles of reinforcement and behavior theory into the framework Sutherland suggested. The result is a theory of differential reinforcement that purports to explain the development of deviant behavior. My proposed theory specifies this explanation by pointing out that learning is a part of a process that includes integration and attachment. And, most importantly, my causal theory does not reduce the explanation of deviance to causes of violation. The relationship between integration (I) and social control (SC) remains an integral part of the explanation.

Postulate 2: Social control and violation (not deviance) are dialectically related. (Social control shapes and sustains deviance.)

The causal theory, like the proposed theory of epidemiology, ends with the assertion that social control and violation contradict and complement one another. Social control is an effort to manage or eliminate certain types of conditions or actions (violations). However, social control does not eliminate violation. Instead, it creates deviance by transforming violation into something more than and different from violation.

Social bonding theory and differential association theory are reflected most clearly in the proposed causal explanation. Both are consistent with the proposed epidemiological theory. Others have suggested linking the ideas of bonding and association for a more complete explanation of deviance. Marcos, Bahr, and Johnson (1986:144), for example, proposed an "integrated bonding/association model of drug use" (compare Conger, 1976; Matsueda, 1982). Their model explained an impressive proportion of variation in drug use patterns involving four categories of drugs (cigarettes, alcohol, marijuana, and amphetamines and depressants).

Convergence Theory and Contemporary Deviance Theories

Table 4.1 summarizes the relationships among the proposed theories and contemporary sociological explanations. Generally, the epidemiological and causal explanations specify the terms of the previous theories. The table identifies points of overlap, but note that the connections are almost always *partial*. The overlapping cannot be more than partial because convergence theory develops

T A B L E 4 . 1

The Convergence of the Proposed Theories and Previous Theories of Deviance

	Conflict Theory	Functional Theory	Anomie Theory	Differential Organization Theory	Social Disorganization Theory	Labeling Theory	Social Pathology Theory	Differential Association Theory	Social Control Theory
POSTULATE 1: Social control is selective	×	×							
POSTULATE 2: Social control shapes/sustains violations	×	×	×	×					
PROPOSITION E1: $I\downarrow SC\uparrow I\uparrow$	×	×							
PROPOSITION E2: $I\downarrow V \cdot SC\uparrow I\uparrow$	×		×	×	×	×	×		
PROPOSITION C1: $I\downarrow A\downarrow D\uparrow I\uparrow$	×		×	×	×		×	×	×
PROPOSITION C2: $I\downarrow LV\uparrow D\uparrow I\uparrow$								×	

from and focuses on a conception of deviance that is fundamentally different from that underlying the earlier theories. For example, the various conflict theories define deviance basically as violation. Social control typically is considered the exercise of power in the pursuit of interests. And the theories usually do not make explicit that social control is selective or that social control tends to sustain violations. Nonetheless, the ideas are congruent and sometimes implicit in the writings of conflict theorists (compare Quinney, 1969; Chambliss and Seidman, 1971). Functionalist theories tend to treat deviance as violation and social control as a system response. Accordingly, there is seldom direct attention to the selectivity of deviance, but some functionalist explanations suggest strongly that the character and shape of deviance reflect the general organization of society (compare Dentler and Erickson, 1959; Erickson, 1966).

A Final Note on the Proposed General Theory

The epidemiological and causal theories proposed here identify the kinds of conditions and processes that increase the probability of deviance—generally, or of some particular type. When the concern is with individual conduct, the proposed explanation asserts that some kinds of arrangements and experiences will increase the likelihood of some deviant expression. We don't usually think about causation in that way in our everyday lives. Instead, we think about causes producing effects. The common sense notion of causality is deterministic more than probabilistic. Often, for example, we talk about some person engaging in some act "because he was mentally ill." In that instance, we are asserting that "illness" is the cause, both disposing the person to act some way and, in the specific event, making him act that way.

Many social scientists believe that human behavior is not really caused in exactly that sense. I will consider this issue more fully in Chapter 5. For now, consider the implications of probability explanations as compared to the usual way of thinking about causes. The theory asserts basically that identifiable variables will increase the likelihood that some person will act in some way that violates expectations *and* that certain conditions and processes will increase the likelihood of social control.

If we stacked up all the factors that increase the probabilities of violation and of social control in some situation, it could still happen that neither one actually occurs. Some missing element, perhaps as simple as opportunity, might operate to determine the actual course of events. If we want an explanation of the causes of deviance and social control in the usual, common sense meaning of explanation, we must be able to explain the transformation of *probabilities* into *actualities*.

Some attention has been given to this issue, but little progress has been made toward accounting for actual performances as opposed to dispositions to act or probabilities of acting in some fashion (see Gibbons, 1982:242–244, and his discussion of precipitating factors). Here, I recognize and accept the limitations of probability explanations.

Finally, the entire discussion of explanations of deviance and social control can benefit from a consideration of the research and theory in deterrence. What kinds of threats or punishments prevent people from acting in certain ways? Previous work on deterrence, especially that of the past 15 years, is rich in conceptual suggestions and empirical data. (See the following for a useful sampling of the relevant studies: Silberman, 1976; Grasmick and Milligan, 1976; Erickson, Gibbs, and Jensen, 1977; Anderson, Chiricos, and Waldo, 1977; Meier and Johnson, 1977; Jensen, Gibbs, and Erickson, 1978; Tittle, 1980; and Grasmick and Bryjak, 1980.) I will consider contributions from this area in subsequent chapters when I raise policy issues.

CHAPTER 5

Researching Deviance

How can we evaluate explanations of deviance? In Chapter 4, I reviewed previous theories and proposed alternative explanations. How are we to choose among these possibilities? The answer, in a word, is *research*. Theories can be tested and modified through research that produces the necessary information. Can we do research on the things that are negotiated as deviant? Laud Humphreys undertook a study in the late 1960s that suggests that research is possible even on very private conduct. Whether such research *should* be done is a different question. Consider Humphreys's (1975:24–25) description of the "research problem" as he confronted it:

> Like any deviant group, homosexuals have developed defenses against outsiders: secrecy about their true identity, symbolic gestures and the use of the eyes for communication, unwillingness to expose the whereabouts of their meeting places, extraordinary caution with strangers, and admission to certain places only in the company of a recognized person. . . . I had to enter the subculture as would any newcomer and to make contact with respondents under the guise of being another gay guy.

Such entry is not difficult to accomplish. Almost any taxi driver can tell a customer where to find a gay bar. The real problem is not one of making contact with the subculture but of making the contact "stick." Acceptance does not come easy, and it is extremely difficult to move beyond superficial contact in public places to acceptance by the group and invitations to private and semiprivate parties.

During the first months, I made the rounds of ten gay bars then operating in the metropolitan area, attended private gatherings and the annual ball, covered the scene where male prostitutes operate out of a coffee house, observed pick-up operations in the parks and streets, and had dozens of informal interviews with participants in the gay society. I also visited the locales where "instant sex" was to be had: the local bathhouse, certain movie theaters, and the tearooms.

From the beginning, my decision was to continue the practice of the field study in passing as deviant. Although this raises questions of scientific ethics, there are good reasons for following this method of participant observation.

Humphreys's study focused on brief, anonymous homosexual encounters between men in public bathrooms (known as "tearooms"). He observed directly hundreds of acts of fellatio by serving as a "watchqueen," a participant role that occurs naturally in this setting and protects those involved in the sexual encounter from arrest and harassment. The watchqueen is a lookout and his participation in sexual behavior is optional. Whatever its strengths or weaknesses, Humphreys's study suggests that research *can* be done on deviant expressions—even when they involve very private behavior.

Observing Deviance

Information about deviance is problematic, as was noted in Chapter 1. In considering the "heroin problem," we saw that even the simplest descriptions may be subject to distortion, misrepresentation, and bias. Imagine the problem of collecting information on topics that are even more controversial, issues that raise legal problems and put people in danger—for example, how is heroin bought and sold? How do people start using heroin? How are heroin habits supported financially? Who are the chief distributors?

Consider first the issue of finding or recognizing information. In sociology and the other sciences, information usually means *systematic observation*. Observations are not equal in their value and usefulness for scientific purposes. They must be evaluated in terms of their directness, accurateness, precision, completeness, and certainty. Table 5.1 notes criteria for evaluating information.

T A B L E   5 . 1

Criteria for Evaluating Information for Testing Explanations

DIRECTNESS:	Observation of objects or events is firsthand and without obstruction
ACCURATENESS:	Observation minimizes distortions from vantage point (physical or philosophical)
PRECISION:	Observation allows careful description of large and small details and distinctions
COMPLETENESS:	Observation encompasses the entire range of events or objects
CERTAINTY:	Observation is supported by other and separate experience

Observers, as well as observations, must be evaluated. Some observers are trained, careful, and able to distinguish the relevant properties of what they observe. Others are uncertain, careless, have impaired vision (or problems with hearing, touch, taste, or smell), and are poorly trained (or untrained) to observe. Typically, observers are evaluated by comparing their findings with those produced by other observers or other observation strategies.

Returning to the heroin example, we find that researchers have been able to gather information on matters that many people would think are beyond observation. Consider the study done by Hanson and his colleagues (1985) on the everyday realities of inner-city heroin users. These researchers used middle-aged black men who were former addicts as interviewers to collect information on current users who were not and had not been hospitalized for drug treatment. They described in great detail the daily routine, the hustling to support the heroin habit, and the personal experiences of inner-city users. Through interviews, the researchers described drug users' language, self-concepts, and opinions about treatment programs. Over 100 heroin users were interviewed for approximately two and one-half to three hours each. The resulting data can be evaluated using the criteria described earlier. The following accounts from the interviews illustrate the detailed information from this study.

"I got up as usual, you know I'm an early riser; it was between seven-thirty and eight, and well, I had to shave. I usually shave every day or every other day. . . . I put my radio on. I get news seven to eight; I try to keep up with current events of the day, 'cause, you know, that helps me spend my day. I don't usually eat breakfast. My biggest thing is coffee, and I have a cup of coffee and try to rationalize out things. You know, sort of decide what kind of pants I'm gonna put on with these shoes, so I won't mess my outfit up. It ain't up to par nohow, but I try to dress the best I can under the circumstances" [Hanson and others, 1985:33].

"Me and my partner, we need dope. We hadn't did too much hustlin' . . . so we went out and . . . try to raise this store. The guy got a pistol from somewhere and he just started firin' . . . he came so close to my head, I heard bells a week later. . . . It shouldn't've happened that way . . . just started shootin' . . . close range. . . . Got to be a better way" [1985:37].

"If I ain't got it, you've got it. You usually share your drugs to make ends meet. It takes the pressure off you from having to hustle. If you don't have nothing you can call up somebody you usually share with. 'What you got man?' You know, I take what they got. They're moral like that. If I share, if they got something, they gonna let me have some" [1985:54].

The information is rich in detail and provides an indirect but vivid description of the life of inner-city black heroin users. The picture it provides is different from that usually portrayed in movies and newspaper stories and differs from "common sense."

Researchers also have been able to collect information on the activities of social control and personnel agencies. This research often is historical and focuses on documentary information. (For example, it may trace the emergence and development of control activities and organizations.) Systematic research on the social control of drugs and drug use began only fairly recently because most attention had been given to the drug user as the problem. Still, consider some of the information provided by deviance researchers.

David Musto (1973) reported on the activities of the Narcotics Division of the Treasury Department following the passage of the Harrison Act of 1914. It required those who dispensed narcotics, including physicians and dentists, to register with the Treasury Department's Bureau of Internal Revenue. He described the activities of division agents who created and enforced regulations related (presumably) to the Harrison Act. He concluded that the Harrison Act was transformed from a tax law into the foundation for enforcement with criminal penalties and consequences. Donald Dixon (1968) provided related information on the agency and described its emergence as an organization with a mission: to stamp out drug use. Charles Reasons (1974) summarized some of the relevant findings:

By focusing upon judicial decisions, rather than Congressional action, the Narcotics Division circumvented the strong lobbies of physicians and pharmacists and was able to create a whole new class of criminals [that is,] the addicts. . . . Those invested with enforcing the law and the dominant moral order would prove to be very capable of maintaining such an approach.

Erdwin Pfuhl (1986) reported on the problems that social control agencies have measuring the extent of deviance and assessing its consequences. He noted that claims were made in the late 1960s and early 1970s that drug addicts committed about half of all property crimes in New York City. It was estimated that addicts were responsible for stealing property valued at $2 to $5 billion per year. The assessment (the "economic cost of addict crime") was made using the following numbers and calculation: amount of money necessary to support addiction ($30 per day average) × number of days in the year (365) × number of addicts (100,000) × the "depreciation factor" for fencing stolen property (4; stolen property usually yields about 25 percent of the market value of the merchandise). Singer (1971) challenged this assessment by noting, among other things, that the total value of all property lost annually in thefts from homes and persons and from all shoplifting incidents in New York City was only about $330 million for the period considered. Other researchers have noted and documented gross exaggerations of agents and agencies of social control in their efforts to describe the extent of the problem. Epstein (1977), for example, concluded that President Nixon's estimate of $18 billion per year as the cost of addict crime is more than 25 times greater than the value of all property stolen and unrecovered in the United States per year during that time.

The people, activities, and events that make up the realities of deviance can be observed and can be understood using the tools of science. Understanding deviance as a dialectical reality, as proposed and discussed in previous chapters, requires careful attention to different kinds of things. We cannot simply watch some people who have been identified as deviant and expect to understand their deviance by locating their similarities. Instead, we have to observe the processes through which instances of deviance are created. We have to observe the convergence of real or alleged violations and imposed sanctions. Finally, doing research is not enough. We must also evaluate the methods, strategies, and results of the research.

Evaluating Research

The relationship between explanations and information is more complex than has been suggested to this point. For one thing, explanations, such as the theories proposed in this book, emerge at some point in the midst of existing theories and ongoing research. Published research reports typically include a section called "review of literature" or "previous studies" to set the current work in the context of related efforts. One result is that theory and research are in continuous interaction. As noted by Merton (1949a, 1949b), among others, collecting information and developing and testing explanations are interrelated in many and complex ways.

T A B L E 5 . 2

Criteria for Planning and Evaluating Scientific Research

VALIDITY:	A measure of the appropriateness of the observations for representing the ideas of a theory
RELIABILITY:	A measure of the consistency of the observations (for example, among different observers, over some period of time)
CONTROL:	A measure of the extent to which the observations can isolate the relevant factors and their consequences
GENERALIZABILITY:	A measure of the extent to which the observations are representative of the collection of things referred to by the theory

As a systematic method for developing valid explanations, science involves a fundamental tension between ideas and realities that can be apprehended by human senses. Science is not just accumulated facts or simply a conglomeration of theories. The scientific method uses agreed upon rules, such as those of logic and probability. This method also uses criteria for planning research activities and for evaluating the information that is collected. Table 5.2 summarizes these criteria.

Validity

Ideas are abstract. Sometimes they capture and summarize experiences. But often they highlight some aspects of reality while minimizing or even disregarding other experiences. And sometimes ideas do not involve much experience at all. They may be matters of imagination or invention. The point is that ideas are often difficult to represent in research—and that is the issue of validity. Consider the following example.

We want to study violations of drug laws. We begin by defining the dependent variable as the uses of any substance controlled by federal or state law. We decide to observe instances of illegal drug use by examining police records in five major metropolitan areas, looking at arrests made by narcotics officers for a specific six-month period. Is the definition of illegal drug use valid? Maybe. But it probably will not stand up to careful inspection and specification. For example, do we intend to include prescription medications and their use? What constitutes control by law? The definition is clearly problematic. The proposed measures (or observations) are also likely to present problems as well.

For example, the police will not know of many instances of illegal drug use. Accordingly, many instances will not result in arrest.

A valid study of this topic requires that we recognize the constructed nature of the deviance of illegal drug use. Agencies of social control in our society probably will *not* treat underage drinking as illegal drug use, for example. Some people who use marijuana regularly—college students on campus, for example—are not likely to be arrested. And there have been episodes of use of prescription medications contrary to medical advice or prescription that were never treated as deviant drug use (for example, the use of Valium by middle-class women).

Many ideas are more abstract than deviant drug use is. Consider the problem of researching child abuse. In our everyday language, we use the term *abuse* as if its meaning were perfectly clear. But what constitutes abuse: Any form of corporal punishment? Verbal assaults on a child's worth? Harsh criticism? Threats of physical harm? Americans widely believe that child abuse has increased in our contemporary society. Could it be that the standards (shared definitions) have changed? Is it possible that we are now treating as abuse things that were once regarded as normal child-rearing practices? Child abuse almost certainly has increased in the past few centuries, because the modern idea of childhood is relatively new. Before a concept of childhood existed, child abuse would have had a different meaning or very little meaning at all.

The *validity* of the research depends on the researcher's success in defining the concepts (ideas) so that the relevant observations can be made. Some researchers have suggested that the criterion of validity is fleeting (see Dubin, 1978:200–203). They have argued that validity is really nothing more than the consensus among some group of researchers that some empirical indicator measures the concept of concern. However, even at that, the issues remain important.

Reliability

The criterion of reliability concerns the consistency of observations. The problem is to observe in such a way that the information can be checked and, if checked, will be confirmed. Observations by solitary researchers at some single point in time do not inspire much confidence. Their information may or may not satisfy the criteria summarized in Table 5.1. There is no basis for comparison and only relatively subjective evaluations can be made.

Confidence is increased somewhat if the researcher reports the methods of observing. The observations could be repeated to determine the level of consistency. Better still, observations by two or more people can be compared. Or observations may have been repeated in other ways that allow different comparisons.

Recall the interview study of heroin users discussed earlier in this chapter (Hanson and others, 1985). How can we evaluate the reliability of research of this type? Data collected by interviewers can be checked in several ways. Each subject could be interviewed twice, with some time lapse between interviews. Or each subject could be interviewed twice and by different interviewers. Then we could compare the information collected from the two interviews. In the first case, we are checking the reliability of the subject's memory or perhaps his honesty. In the second check, we are looking for unreliability that may be introduced by something the interviewer is doing or not doing.

Adequate and useful research requires more than valid and reliable observations. The collection of information also must allow the researcher to make certain connections or at least to rule out certain kinds of conclusions. The criteria of control and generalizability refer to matters of research design. Each is concerned with managing the effects of extraneous factors on the ideas being tested.

Control

Botanists long ago discovered a way to make careful and controlled observations while conducting experiments. Working with plants in laboratories, they observed growth under conditions that allowed them to hold constant all factors except the one they wanted to study. The classical experimental design, which allows that kind of control, has three essential parts: independent and dependent variables, experimental and control groups, and pretests and posttests.

1. Independent and dependent variables: Variables are observable instances of the ideas we are researching. *Dependent* variables are the things we are trying to explain. *Independent* variables are things that we think cause, influence, or otherwise are related to what we are trying to explain. Decreased integration, for example, might be an independent variable that causes increases in levels of social control (the dependent variable).

2. Experimental and control groups: "Groups" refer to people, objects, behaviors, or other things being observed to develop or test explanations. Experimental and control groups are matched to be as similar as possible, with one important difference. Experimental groups have been or will be exposed to the independent variable. Control groups have not been and will not be so exposed.

3. Pretests and posttests: The groups (control and experimental) are compared at the beginning of the research. This *pretest* measures or observes some aspect of the dependent variable that is the research subject. The groups are (ideally) identical at this point. The experimental group is then exposed to the independent variable. *Posttest* observations

compare the groups again. If the groups were similar in the pretests and are different in the posttest, the difference is attributed to the independent variable.

Sociological researchers rarely have the luxury of collecting data using the classical experimental design because of practical and ethical problems. (For an interesting collection of examples of experimental research in the field of deviance, see Steffensmeier and Terry, 1975.) Few of the things of interest to us can be manipulated in the ways that laboratory scientists can manipulate their subjects. For example, we cannot select some group of newborn infants and subject them to physical abuse in order to compare their development with that of other (control) babies. And we cannot ask some identified group (or audience) to react in certain ways (impose sanctions, for example) so that we can compare the results to a control event in which things were allowed to happen by chance.

Sociologists often find that they must select groups based on their existing characteristics—for example, drug users are treated as the experimental group and are compared to nonusers for control. More generally, sociologists and other social scientists often must be content to approximate the design in an effort to control extraneous factors (see Campbell, 1957). It may not be possible to identify a control group for comparison, or a pretest measure for the experimental group may be impossible, for example.

Vaughan Stapleton and Lee Teitelbaum (1972) conducted a "modified" experiment to test the effects of using lawyers on the outcome of cases heard in American juvenile courts. At the time of the study, juveniles were not automatically represented by lawyers in juvenile court proceedings. Notice how control over extraneous variables was approximated:

> Youths charged with delinquency were randomly assigned to experimental and control groups. The experimental group was offered specially trained law counsel whose caseloads were held to a maximum of six new assignments per week, far below that of the ordinary legal aid attorney. The control group, drawn from the same population as the experimental group, was left to the regular legal services available in the project cities. The impact of representation was measured through the use of "case reports" which were prepared by the project attorneys and contained a day-to-day summary of each case handled [Stapleton and Teitelbaum, 1972:50].

The research was designed to test the hypothesis that the use of legal counsel affects the way in which juvenile cases are handled and the final disposition of the cases. Variables that might affect case handling and disposition (other than the experimental variable of legal counsel use) were "controlled" by randomizing the assignment of youths to experimental and control groups. For example, since the youths were assigned to experimental and control groups randomly, the seriousness of offenses for the youths in each group should have been similar through the operation of chance assignment. On the other hand, the two groups should have been categorically different with respect to the experimental variable: all members of the experimental group should have used legal counsel (and, ideally, the specially trained project legal counsel) and none of the experimental group should have used legal counsel. Obviously, however, the *researchers could not deny the control group juveniles the right to use lawyers*. One result was that the groups were not as different as the experimental design requires. In one city, for example, 82 percent of the experimental group had lawyers, most of whom were project lawyers, but more than 38 percent of the control group also had lawyers [1972:52; emphasis added].

The study was done in two cities and the results were mixed. The researchers found clear support for the conclusion that using an attorney made a difference in one of the cities, but no support for that conclusion in the data from the other city. Stapleton and Teitelbaum provide some useful interpretations for the mixed findings. Note that the results may have been no clearer if the experimental design had been implemented fully.

Generalizability

Even if other criteria are met, research will be valuable for testing or developing explanations only to the extent that the observations are representative of the total reality referred to by the idea or concept. We cannot observe all drug users, all drug addicts, or all of most things. For that reason, we must carefully select the instances that we do observe so that we can estimate the likelihood that our findings are characteristic of the whole.

Sampling strategies guide researchers in selecting groups, events, or instances for representativeness. The strategies can be described in terms of one fundamental distinction: probability versus nonprobability. Probability samples are selected in such a way that we can mathematically estimate the likelihood that the observations are characteristic. The most general procedure for drawing a probability sample is to use some device that allows random selection, so that each member of the population has an equal chance of being selected. We could number the events, people, or incidents and use a table of random numbers to select the sample.

As was true with experimental design, probability sampling is an idea that often can only be approximated in social scientific research. Often the relevant population cannot be specified, and even if it could, it would not be possible to number population members or select them by some random process. How can we identify the population of illegal drug users or drug addicts? We can make rough estimates of the total numbers (based on police or treatment program information, for example) but we cannot pool them, identify their characteristics, and then systematically select some representative group. Probability sampling, like the experimental design, serves as a model for researchers. We can evaluate the strength and importance of a study in part by examining its sampling procedure and selected observations.

In summary, we develop and test theories of deviance and social control by collecting relevant information through observations. The quality of the observations can be evaluated using the criteria described in Table 5.1. And we can evaluate the method of collecting the observations using the criteria of adequacy of scientific research (see Table 5.2). A research project is described in some detail below. An evaluation of the study and the resultant data follows the description.

Homicide and Heterogeneity:
An Example

Hansmann and Quigley (1982) conducted research on murder in nearly 60 countries. Their study provides an indirect test of the theories proposed and discussed in Chapters 3 and 4. In simplified (and reduced) form, the theories assert that as integration (I) decreases, diversity of social niches increases; as diversity increases, attachment (A) to the conventional order decreases; both result in increased rates of social control (SC) and violation (V), or deviance ($D = SC \cdot V$).

Hansmann and Quigley presented their research as a test of a general hypothesis about the effect of population heterogeneity on criminality, in this case homicide. Their measure of heterogeneity was similar to those that might represent the effects of decreased integration, diversity, and attachment.

VALIDITY The central ideas of the theory are voiced in three observations: population heterogeneity (independent variable), homicide rates (dependent variable), and the relationship between them.

The researchers defined *heterogeneity* in terms of differences in income, language, ethnicity, and religion among groups within each country. Income heterogeneity was measured (observed) using the Gini coefficient. If all incomes are equal in a group (in this case, nation), the Gini coefficient is zero. As income differences increase, the coefficient approaches a value of one. Language, ethnic, and religious heterogeneity were measured using a coefficient that calculates both the number of different languages, ethnic groups, and religions in a nation and the proportion of people who speak or belong to each.

Hansmann and Quigley (1982:210) defined *homicide* as "all deaths purposely inflicted by other persons and by the state, except for deaths related to acts of warfare." They determined homicide rates from official crime statistics, but they do not say specifically how these were obtained.

A *positive relationship* is observed by examining statistical patterns of association, especially through the use of *regression analysis*, a statistical procedure that allows researchers to identify systematic mathematical relationships among observations represented by numbers such as Gini indexes of 0 to 1 and coefficients of diversity.

Are the observations valid representations of the ideas (concepts)? The researchers did not provide any formal measures of validity. They proposed definitions that seem plausible, and they described the kinds of information that they regarded as relevant. Simply put, they proposed observations that have "face validity"—that is, they seem reasonable. There may be validity problems. For example, the researchers recognized that what constitutes homicide may vary from society to society. They proposed a very broad definition to try to deal with that problem. But does the intentional taking of a life by the state, what we call an execution or capital punishment, qualify as homicide or criminal homicide? There are many opinions about capital punishment, but few people in our society consider execution as homicide or criminal homicide.

RELIABILITY The researchers did not report any tests for the reliability of their data. We could, however, test their information for consistency. The detailed descriptions of their methods of data collection would allow others to repeat the study and compare the resulting observations. Checking for reliability is easy because the researchers used existing data that are generally available in a standard form.

The researchers' treatment of the concept of homicide illustrates the problem of reliability and its relation to the issue of validity. The concept is defined very broadly so that it will be easy to identify instances that count from one society to the next. However, one result is that some of the things that were counted do not resemble what we think of as criminal homicide. In this case, the researchers have compromised validity of the measure slightly for an increase in reliability. This strategy could be taken to the extreme. A selected measure could maximize reliability but virtually lose validity. For example, the researchers might have counted all instances of death as homicide. That way, there would be no difficulty in deciding what to count, and the counting would be highly consistent. Obviously, however, that is *not* what we consider homicide.

CONTROL The dependent variable—that is, the thing to be explained—is variation in homicide rates. The proposed explanation (the independent variable) is the level of heterogeneity within the society. Given the nature of the study, the researchers could not practically or ethically use control and experimental groups or pretests and posttests. They did manage to introduce control through comparison and statistical matching.

We . . . obtained measures of several other social, economic, and demographic factors, primarily *to serve as controls* on the tests of the heterogeneity hypothesis. . . . These variables include population density, a
measure of urbanization (the percentage of people living in cities larger
than 100,000), gross national product per capita, and the percentage of
the population between 15 and 25 years of age [Hansmann and Quigley,
1982:213; emphasis added].

The researchers had reason to believe (from previous research and theories
on homicide) that such factors as population density and urbanization might
affect the homicide rate regardless of the level of heterogeneity. They wanted to
separate the effects of heterogeneity from the effects of other factors. Information
on these "extraneous" variables allowed them to compare homicide rates while
holding constant the differences among the countries on the "irrelevant" factors.

GENERALIZABILITY Data were collected to describe 58 countries, and data
from 40 were analyzed. Is that sufficiently representative of the nations of the
world to allow generalization of the findings? Maybe. But the sample was not
selected using any procedure that would allow calculation of the probability of
representativeness. Rather, the countries were selected in part because the
necessary data were available. The resulting sample is best described as a
"convenience sample" (convenient, that is, for the researchers). Still, though
40 is not representative in any known way, it suggests that the results have
merit.

FINDINGS Hansmann and Quigley concluded that their data "lend support to
the theory that the interaction within a society of heterogeneous cultural groups
tends to increase the rate of homicide" (1982:206). In very general terms, they
found that murder rates are highest in those countries that have the most diverse
populations. These findings lend indirect support to the dialectical theories of
deviance I have proposed.

   Their study illustrates how social scientists adapt research procedures in
an effort to approach the ideal standards of scientific research. Clearly, we
cannot have total confidence in the findings or conclusions from this research.
Note, however, that this is a good piece of work, and it is far superior to
speculative common sense, which is almost totally incautious by comparison.
Moreover, other scientific disciplines, including the hard sciences of physics,
chemistry, and biology, often must approximate design standards in similar
ways. In short, scientific conclusions and explanations are always "for the time
being" rather than final. Explanation is always *becoming*. The interaction
between theory and research continues.

Note that this study is not a *test* of the proposed theories. The two efforts are related, but they are not tied together in such a way that the homicide research can be treated as a source of the theory or as a test of its explanatory power. Before it can be tested directly, the theory and its central ideas need to be further specified. In addition, the research that tests it will need to reflect more completely and precisely the assertions of the theory. We can use previous research to assess informally the extent of empirical support for these or any other theories. And that will be a major strategy in the chapters that follow. Types of deviant behavior, such as prostitution, will be described and explained using the central concepts and the proposed theories. I will review empirical research on the topics and use it to assess the level of empirical support for the explanations.

Ethics and Deviance Research

A review of the tables of contents of professional journals, textbooks, proceedings of professional meetings, and other professional writings of sociologists would surprise many people. Research has been done and is being done on topics that many regard as inaccessible. And we have seen that such research can be done in a way that will produce reliable, valid, and generalizable results. The ethical question remains: Should such research be done? If the answer is yes, what are the responsibilities of the researchers?

Laud Humphreys's research on homosexuality in public places and the controversies that resulted are instructive. In response to the question of whether the research should be done, Humphreys (1975:168) said, "Let the clergy worry about keeping their cassocks clean; the scientist has too great a responsibility for such compulsions!" And to the question of the researcher's responsibilities, Humphreys answered, "I believe that preventing harm to his respondents should be the *primary* interest of the scientist" (1975:169). These seem like reasonable and straightforward answers and solutions. As usual, however, things are not so simple.

Consider issues raised by Humphreys's detractors. Nicholas von Hoffman (1975:181), writing in the *Washington Post*, wrote of Humphreys's study: "Incontestably such information is useful to parents, teen-agers . . . to policemen, legislators and many others, but it was done by invading some people's privacy. . . . No information is valuable enough to obtain by nipping away at personal liberty, and this is true no matter who's doing the gnawing, John Mitchell and the conservatives over at the Justice Department or Laud Humphreys and the liberals over at the Sociology Department."

Donald P. Warwick, a fellow social scientist, took a different approach. He found Humphreys's logic flawed: "There are three ethical objections. . . .

First, the researcher took advantage of a relatively powerless group of men to pursue his study. . . . Second, through his research tactics Humphreys reinforces an image already prevalent in some circles that social scientists are sly tricksters who are not to be trusted. . . . The third and strongest objection is that the use of deception, misrepresentation, and manipulation in social research encourages the same tendencies in other parts of society" (Warwick, 1975:211).

The American Sociological Association's *Code of Ethics* (revised in 1980 and subscribed to by most professional sociologists in the United States) asserts that "A first principle of ethics holds that people are always to be considered ends and not means, so that whether they are being studied or taught, their integrity, dignity, and autonomy must be maintained" (in Bailey, 1982:511). The code further maintains that "research subjects are entitled to rights of privacy and dignity of treatment" and that "research must not expose subjects to substantial risk or personal harm." Finally, the code indicates that "confidential information provided by research participants must be treated as such by sociologists, even when this information enjoys no legal protection or privilege" (1982:514).

A critical issue in deviance research concerns the sociologist's responsibility to protect research subjects who are engaged in behavior that is potentially embarrassing, discrediting, or illegal. That issue was raised in a case in which a graduate student researcher was subpoenaed to testify and to turn over his field notes in a grand jury investigation of a restaurant fire. In a hearing to quash the subpoena, Chief Judge Jack B. Weinstein ruled that "compelling production of a researcher's notes may inhibit prospective and actual sources of information, thereby, obstructing the flow of information to the researcher, and through him or her, the public. . . . Affording social scientists protected freedom is essential if we are to understand how our own and other societies operate" (American Sociological Association, 1984:11). This ruling provides limited protection. It does not grant confidential immunity equivalent to that of the physician–patient or lawyer–client relationship. As a consequence, the practical problem of protecting research subjects remains difficult.

James Inciardi (1986:120), reporting on research on drug users, described a different strategy for protecting research subjects:

> In research of this type [interviewing active drug users about their drug-using and criminal behavior] the Drug Enforcement Administration and the National Institute on Drug Abuse provide investigators with a grant of confidentiality. The grant is a signed document that guarantees that the investigator cannot be forced to divulge the identity of his or her informants to any law-enforcement authority, court, or grand jury. All informants were made aware of the grant and were given copies if they requested it. . . .

To eliminate any hesitation by informants, questions about their criminal activities were asked in a way that would be deemed no more than "hearsay" in a court of law. In other words, the dates and places of specific crimes were not asked. . . . Questions about any rapes or homicides committed were simply not asked, although a number of informants volunteered such information.

Law enforcement and court officials might or might not respect this "grant of confidentiality." Whether or not information about criminal activities should be protected is a difficult judgment. There are no easy answers. Ethical questions are always, in the end, questions of values. Scientists are likely to believe that knowledge and understanding are so important that other values can be compromised in the name of science. Others may place the value of privacy above all others, as von Hoffman appears to do. Still others worry most about abuse of power and exploitation, concerns expressed clearly in Warwick's criticism of Humphreys's research. When it is all said and done, what is ethical, like what is deviant, is a matter of negotiation.

Explaining and Counting Deviants

In Chapter 4 I raised some of the problems of explaining deviance (see especially the "A Final Note" section). Specifically, I noted that the idea of "causation" needs to be understood differently from our typical common sense. At least two major problems need consideration: (1) Few things have single causes, and (2) deviance is a negotiated outcome.

Many Causes and Partial Answers

People who are unfamiliar with the discipline and practice of sociology often find sociological explanations bothersome. They seem either incredibly simple (and sometimes simpleminded) or incomprehensibly complex because of the number of qualifiers. Part of the problem is that sociology deals with topics that often only *seem* familiar. As a result, "simple" explanations seem wrong because we can find important exceptions with little effort. And qualified explanations seem pretentious because the "real truth" is "obvious." Matters are made even worse because empirical tests of explanations often find that the proposed causes explain only a small portion of the variation in the object of study. In other words, the independent variable has little effect on the dependent variable.

Unless the world can be simplified in some way, sociologists and consumers of sociological knowledge will need to accept that our efforts typically produce *partial* explanations. That limit presents few problems for scientists most of the time because they understand science as a continuing and cumulative process. There are times, however, when sociologists and other scientists engage in prolonged debates as if there were only one explanation or one valid point of view. (See Hirschi and Selvin, 1966, for an excellent discussion of the problems of thinking about and establishing causal relationships.)

Determinism and Outcomes

From the point of view of the proposed approach, deviance is a probabilistic reality. The issue of causation is complex; causes are found partly in the activity of social control agents and agencies. People violate norms, but the norms are created by people with different amounts of power. If we take seriously the assertion that deviance is a negotiated outcome, we have to ask several causal questions:

1. Why did someone act in some way that violated a norm or law?

2. Why did someone accuse another of violating a norm or law (whether or not it is true)?

3. Why was social control applied in this instance?

4. What was the result of the interactions between the accused and the accuser?

Note that *none* of these questions really concerns the causation of deviance as we usually consider it. The relevant causal question is *what caused the interaction that resulted in creating an instance of deviance?* Simple, straightforward deterministic explanations do not fit very well for understanding deviance in this way.

Most human social experiences and events are complex. Single-cause explanations and deterministic theories have not survived empirical tests. If we are to move toward adequate and verified explanations, we will have to take things as they present themselves rather than try to bend reality to fit our poor efforts to understand. Goode (1984:10–11) posed the problem somewhat differently and suggested as a "modest resolution" what he called a "soft reactive" approach. His approach recognizes the relevance of norms and norm violation, but it does not assume that all violations are treated as deviance.

The dialectical approach that I propose is not markedly different, but it encourages researchers to recognize the *dynamic, interactive* and *social* qualities of deviance and social control. From this point of view, understanding deviance requires that we observe the creation and perpetuation of deviance through interaction. It also requires that we connect instances of created

TABLE 5.3

Counting Deviance: Public Perceptions of U.S. Crime Trends, 1982

Question: "Just as your best guess, would you say that the crime rate in this country is going up, going down, or what?"

	Going Up	About the Same	Going Down	No Opinion/ Refuse to Answer
SEX				
Male	80%	12%	7%	1%
Female	87	8	4	1
RACE, ETHNICITY				
White	82	11	6	1
Black	91	5	4	1
Hispanic	86	7	7	0
EDUCATION				
College	80	12	6	2
High school	85	9	5	—
Grade school	86	7	6	1

Source: Adapted from Edmond F. McGarrell and Timothy J. Flanagan (1985:168). Table constructed by *Sourcebook* staff from data provided by ABC News Poll telephone surveys of 2,464 persons 18 years and older during December 7–18, 1982.

deviance with larger social contexts. Whether or not something becomes deviant and what things are deviant are not arbitrary or matters of chance. The ongoing processes of violation and social control reflect and shape our social realities.

Research that is relevant to the theory, whether oriented to further development of the explanation or toward testing, will need to reflect this view of causation. We can see some of the issues suggested here in the collection and use of official information about deviants—for example, the number and characteristics of people in a mental health system, the number and types of crimes committed in some jurisdiction during some time, or estimates of the proportion of people who have had some homosexual experience or who have ever tried some drug.

Tables 5.3, 5.4, and 5.5 provide an illustration of deviance counting. Table 5.3 describes public perceptions of the recent trend in crime. Note the level of agreement. Males, females, whites, blacks, Hispanics, and those across educational levels believed that crime in the United States is increasing. The opinion poll provided other information (not reproduced here) that revealed

TABLE 5.4

*Counting Deviance: Index Crimes, U.S. Offenses Known to Police
(Estimated) 1980–1983*

	1980	1981	1982	1983
MURDER AND NONNEGLIGENT MANSLAUGHTER	23,040	22,520	21,010	19,310
FORCIBLE RAPE	82,090	81,540	77,760	78,920
ROBBERY	548,810	574,130	536,890	500,220
AGGRAVATED ASSAULT	654,960	643,720	650,040	639,530
BURGLARY	3,759,200	3,739,800	3,415,500	3,120,800
LARCENY-THEFT	7,112,700	7,154,500	7,107,700	6,707,000
MOTOR VEHICLE THEFT	1,114,700	1,074,000	1,048,300	1,004,400

Note: Arson is also an index crime, but is not included in these data.
Source: Adapted from Edmond F. McGarrell and Timothy J. Flanagan (1985:380).

similar levels of agreement across age levels, occupational differences, income differences, and other characteristics. The consensus is especially striking when we consider the data in Tables 5.4 and 5.5. These data strongly suggest that the "crime trend" is hard to describe and highly variable. The numbers of index crimes known to the police (Table 5.4) went up and down over four years. The general pattern, however, was toward fewer incidents. Murder, burglary, and car theft were consistently lower each year. And forcible rape, robbery, aggravated assault, and larceny-theft were mostly down.

A comparison with Table 5.5 raises even more questions. First, the patterns are mixed. For example, while the number of murders and nonnegligent manslaughters known to police were decreasing, the number of arrests for those crimes was increasing. Second, there is a remarkable difference in the numbers. In part, that is not surprising because Table 5.4 reports crimes known to police, while Table 5.5 reports arrests for those crimes. Still, consider how different crime looks depending on how it is counted. The point can be extended if we imagine that we have information describing the perpetrators of the offenses for both tables. Those arrested are not necessarily representative of those who committed the offenses.

TABLE 5.5

Counting Deviance: Index Crimes, U.S. Arrests, 1980–1983

	1980	1981	1982	1983
MURDER AND NONNEGLIGENT MANSLAUGHTER	16,229	17,544	18,511	18,064
FORCIBLE RAPE	28,805	29,268	28,322	30,183
ROBBERY	128,724	134,998	138,118	134,018
AGGRAVATED ASSAULT	222,865	228,215	258,899	261,421
BURGLARY	444,453	449,461	436,271	415,651
LARCENY-THEFT	778,172	832,060	1,416,705	1,169,066
MOTOR VEHICLE THEFT	117,011	109,026	108,736	105,514

Note: Arson is also an index crime, but is not included in these data.

Source: Data for 1982 and 1983 adapted from Edmond F. McGarrell and Timothy J. Flanagan (1985: 474–475). Data for 1980 and 1981 adapted from Edward J. Brown, Timothy J. Flanagan, and Maureen McLeod (1984:430).

Note that information from groups and organizations that produce and disseminate official data and statistics about deviants and deviance must be treated with extreme care. Most of these organizations are agencies of social control. The data that they collect and produce often tell us more about what the agencies are doing than they do about incidents of deviance. Singer (1971), Kitsuse and Cicourel (1973), Sutherland and Cressey (1978), and Aday (1979) have offered useful discussions of interpreting so-called official data.

Perhaps even more important, the illustration suggests how the reality of deviance is created and sustained. (It is probably more accurate to talk about the *realities* of deviance.) Does it matter that certain objective indicators (measures) of crime reveal that the crime rate is not going up consistently? Probably not. People are likely to make personal and political decisions on the basis of the widely shared (mis)perception that "crime is increasing at a steady and alarming rate." They may agitate for more police, tougher enforcement, more punishment, and more prisons. Deviance, then, is created and sustained not just in isolated incidents of interaction but also as broadly shared ideas about the way things are in our world.

Looking Ahead

Four of the chapters of Part II provide analyses of particular deviant practices. I explain each type of deviance using my conceptual framework and proposed theory to organize the relevant research information on the topic. These reviews will consider the full range of previous research, not just those studies that seem to support the proposed explanation. (Selective searching for supportive evidence introduces bias rather than objective testing.) *The reviews do not count as tests of the theory.* They are, instead, informal assessments as described earlier in this chapter. Moreover, note that this review process is not what we mean typically when we speak of sociological research. Rather, the tasks of explaining and testing explanations are active processes that require careful thought and systematic observation of the world out there.

PART TWO

Deviance: Social Organization, Niches, and Actions

CHAPTER 6

Heterosexual Deviance

Cheryl Costa tells "her" story:

> The first time I was caught playing with my mother's cosmetics was when I was six years old. Actually, I wasn't really caught in the act. My mother noticed some sort of red residue around my lip area and got very concerned that I was coming down with some dreaded childhood illness. After close inspection she realized that I had traces of lipstick on. This threw my dear mom into a tizzy. She called my dad into the room and gave me the third degree. WHY? I was honest with them and told them that I liked girls' things and wanted to play dress-up like my girl playmates. This was about 1959—the "Right Stuff" years. Steve Canyon, and the original seven astronauts were the image of the day.
>
> Mom pointed out that I had expressed desire to be a jet pilot when I grew up. With this she also pointed out that girls don't

do such things and boys don't wear lipstick. Like other transgendered persons, the softer persona never went away. I continued to experiment with mom's makeup and old clothes in the attic, all in secret of course. I went in the Air Force to make a "man" of myself. I was 105 lbs., 5'8" with a mild beard and rosy cheeks . . . a wimp! The USAF decided that I should climb telephone poles in South Vietnam. After getting shot off a pole I woke up to find myself in traction and unable to view my genitals. A pole climber's worst fear is that of running a pole (losing footing and sliding down a pole crotch first). In telephone school there were several gruesome stories about climbers that neutered themselves in such mishaps. Most guys would have been frightened to death. Part of me was saying "Oh, no," while another part was saying "Wonderful" [Costa, n.d.].

Transvestite? Transsexual? It is not mentioned in the quoted material, but "Cheryl" is married to a woman. Is she (or he) bisexual, heterosexual, or homosexual? What constitutes "normal" sexuality? Are some kinds of human sexual expressions inherently bad, sick, or deviant? Many people who approach these questions from a biological point of view assert that there are *normal* and *abnormal* sexual activities, preferences, and inclinations. Some have asserted that heterosexuality is normal and homosexuality is abnormal (Bieber, 1962; Socarides, 1975). One argument holds that "structure dictates function"—that is, men and women are anatomically complementary and various organs have distinctive and exclusive purposes (see, for example, Socarides's assertion, 1975:121, that the anus is a "purely excretory organ"). Others have developed evolutionary arguments that offer criteria of "normalcy." Gallup (1986:20), for example, asserted that males and females must pursue distinctive and conflicting strategies of sexual conduct:

> There is a basic and irreconcilable conflict between males and females in terms of their respective roles in evolution. When it comes to inclusive fitness, the best interests of females serve to constrain those of males, and vice versa. . . . there may very well be a biological rather than merely a cultural basis for the sexual double standard.

According to evolutionary theorists, members of species are "motivated" to maximize their representation in future generations. They "want" to pass on their genes. "Inclusive fitness" refers to the success of any individual in transmitting those genetic characteristics. Women and men must pursue different strategies to accomplish genetic goals: Men have abundant supplies of "seeds" to sow, but little control over the opportunity for "planting." Women, on the other hand, have a limited supply of eggs that can be fertilized and primary responsibility for the care and raising of infants (at least in the earliest periods before birth and prior to weaning). Therefore, the "natural" order dictates that men will want to maximize sexual frequency and variety while women will want to control and constrain both. Their optimal sexual strategies are in conflict.

By this logic, a number of sexual expressions would be "naturally wrong": homosexuality, female "promiscuity," prostitution, and practices that involve contact other than between the penis and the vagina, for example. Indeed, virtually any sexual activity that is not directly linked to the procreation of the species or that competes with "optimal" sexual strategies could be seen as deviant or pathological. Note the similarity of this point of view to traditional Roman Catholic and other Christian teachings on sexuality and birth control.

The question of sexual deviance or normalcy can be approached in another way. Viewed cross culturally, the variety of sexual practices is impressive. Moreover, there is considerable variety even within a single culture at a single time if we consider what people actually do instead of what they believe is ideal. The Kinsey reports (1948, 1953) surprised many Americans with their description of respondents' sexual practices. Many of these activities were and are prohibited by criminal law. Human beings are capable of a wide variety of behaviors that can be interpreted as sexual. And *interpretation* is a key issue. Consider all of the kinds of things that have sexual meanings or implications in our contemporary culture: lips touching, closing one eye, the back seats of cars, the raised middle finger, an unbuttoned top button on a shirt or blouse, tongue-moistened lips, a red handkerchief casually displayed in the left (or right, depending on location) rear pocket. These are only a few of the things that have no discernible connection with anything biologically sexual that nonetheless involve sex in some meaningful sense.

Again, the idea of *meaningful* is critical. As far as we know, humans are different from (most?) other animals because we can and do treat sex as something relatively independent of reproduction and procreation. Recall Max Weber's insistence that human behavior is meaningful and that it must be understood in terms of the *subjective* character of experience. As soon as we acknowledge that human conduct, including sex, involves meanings and social definitions, the idea of using biological and evolutionary criteria to determine normalcy and deviance becomes suspect. If human beings routinely engage in sexual acts that are unrelated to procreation, genetic and evolutionary variables and consequences are only marginally relevant for explanations of sex practices.

An alternative criterion of normalcy could refer to the survival of the race, nation, society, community, or other social unit. Those sex acts that support or contribute to the unit's persistence would be normal. Practices that conflict with these or that are unrelated to the perpetuation of the group could be identified as deviant or abnormal. As with the view from biology, this approach does not take into account the fundamentally *social* and *definitional* dimensions of human sexuality. Research in other cultures and over periods of human history reveals that sex and sexuality are matters of taste—more or less shared social definitions. For example, many people around the world are amused by the fascination of the American male with the size and shape of the female mammary gland. Similarly, Americans might be surprised by the interest of some African men in the length of the labia minora.

Data from cross-cultural research overwhelmingly support the conclusion that human sexuality is shaped largely by social learning (see Ford and Beach, 1951, and Gregerson, 1982). We learn when, how, where, and by what to be sexually excited. We even learn the proper frequency of sexual arousal and satisfaction. The people from Inis Beag (described in Chapter 1) provide an excellent example of this social learning—especially when their behavior is compared to that of the people of Mangaia (see Marshall, 1971). Recall that people in Inis Beag find sex and nudity embarrassing and appear determined to keep both to the bare, obligatory minimum. Mangaians, in contrast, literally seem to work at maximizing sexual activity, frequency, satisfaction, and skill. Married couples in Mangaia engage in sexual intercourse on the average of three times a night, seven nights a week.

A Sociological Conception of Sexuality and Deviance

Sociologically, human sexuality is learned and shaped by social experience. "From a sociological viewpoint, sexual activity is ordered and patterned by norms, including laws, and these norms are reinforced by social control: rewards for conformity to and punishments for deviation from them" (DeLamater and MacCorquodale, 1979:3; see also Gagnon and Simon, 1973). Sexual deviance is relative to the prevailing social patterns or organization. It is a *negotiated outcome*. We can describe and explain different types of deviant heterosexual practices by drawing from the core concepts and the proposed theories described in Chapters 3 and 4. (You may want to review the concepts and theories presented in those chapters.) The descriptions and explanations that follow begin at the broadest level with issues of social organization.

Prostitution

Prostitution is an example of a sexual activity that often is treated as deviant in our society. It is related to ongoing, conventional social arrangements (*social organization*, including family and gender structures, for example). Prostitution consists of events, acts, and actors that are variably legal, legitimate, and conventional or illegal or deviant. It involves developed and identifiable *social niches*, such as "the life," the generalized subculture of prostitutes, pimps, after-hours bars, and bars with topless dancers, for example. It also involves interactions that shape and reflect both special and more general social relationships, such as those between "hookers" and "tricks" and men and women. We can describe prostitution in terms of patterned and recurrent *social actions*. The descriptions and explanations that follow are drawn from relevant social research. Although diverse styles of prostitution exist, this analysis focuses on the prostitution of women.

> Newport News (VA), 11/3/85—Thirteen men were arrested late Friday night and early Saturday and charged with aiding and abetting prostitution in an undercover operation that involved two female police officers disguised as prostitutes.
>
> The arrests were part of an ongoing operation to keep prostitutes and their customers off guard, Lt. L. J. Goldstrohm said.
>
> Police decided to carry out the operation Friday because the *USS Dwight D. Eisenhower* is at Newport News Shipyard for an overhaul.
>
> The two female officers posed as prostitutes on Washington Avenue downtown. Goldstrohm said the two accepted car rides from men who approached them and rode to a nearby hotel. Once inside the hotel, the men were arrested [Police Arrest 13 in Prostitution Crackdown, 1985:C3].

This story ended with a listing of the names, ages, and addresses of the men arrested. (Incidentally, it is not apparent in the list that any of the arrested were sailors or assigned to the ship that was mentioned.)

Rasmussen (1984:208) reported the following discussion between a customer (L) and a woman (M) who worked in a massage parlor:

> L: Do you give extras (an insider term for sex)?
> M: What do you mean by extras?
> L: Like give head or things like that?
> M: Are you soliciting me?
> L: Well, yes.
> M: Yeah, I do, but it's really expensive now.
> L: How about $20?
> M: Yes.

The presence of prostitution is a crime against all people. It legitimates people treating others as objects to be bought and sold without respect to human dignity; it supports an illegal market place (police payoffs, pimps, drug pushers, etc.) which results in crime and violence; it enforces one-sided monogamy and it perpetuates racist and sexist attitudes, dehumanizing women and Third World people [Women Endorsing Decriminalization, 1973:160].

I spoke to a women's studies class here and they didn't approve of me at all because my job furthers men's ego, or whatever, and I kept trying to explain to them, "Listen, I can do more good for women in my job if I can show just one man how to get his old lady off and relieve her sexual frustration, don't you think that that's a valid position?" [An interview with "Shirley," a masseuse, reported by Lowney, Winslow, and Winslow, 1981:76].

The Difficulty of Defining Prostitution

What is prostitution? Is it police officers soliciting men for sex and then arresting them when they respond? Is it men soliciting women for sex—whether or not the women agree? Is it an affront to human dignity, an instance of dehumanizing racism and sexism? Or is it a service performed by some women for the general betterment of all women? Prostitution is often called the oldest profession. It probably is not. (The berry-picker and hunter undoubtedly preceded anything we could identify as prostitution.) But something recognizable as prostitution has existed in many societies for centuries. The need for an adequate definition is underscored by recent developments such as male escorts, male prostitutes, sex therapists, and masseuses who provide various services that have some sexual relevance.

Whatever the criteria may be, many people clearly have different and competing meanings about what prostitution really is. The examples just quoted point to some of the interactions and negotiations that shape the social reality of prostitution. The first task for analysis is to describe the thing of concern as *generically* as possible. (See the list of tasks for analysis in Chapter 1.) What do we want to examine under the heading of prostitution?

Gale Miller (1978:123) has provided a useful starting point. He summarized some of the cross-cultural and historical variations, and concluded that the "organization and meaning [of prostitution] varies from society to society based on the social niche occupied by prostitutes as well as the values that surround both the prostitute's role and sexuality in general." In similar fashion, John Gagnon (1977:277) asserted that "our contemporary versions of the prostitution of women emerge from the current economic and political status of women, combined with the sexual scripts that allow for and demand their existence as well as our cultural stereotypes about the prostitute as a sexual heroine or erotic object."

Is it really so hard to say what we mean to study here? Isn't prostitution simply the exchange of sex for money (or vice versa)? If it is, do we include the activities of concubines and slaves? Both of these involve a lack of "voluntariness" that may or may not be characteristic of prostitution. Many people who accept the "sex for pay" definition assume that the transaction is voluntary. By now you should not be surprised to find that deviance (in this case, prostitution) is more complex than is usually assumed. Benjamin and Masters (1964) claim that five elements define prostitution:

1. The seller of sexual services is free from coercion.
2. The prostitute receives direct payment from the customer.
3. The prostitute engages in sex with different customers.
4. The prostitute–customer relationship is temporary.
5. The prostitute–customer relationship is impersonal.

Miller (1978:125–126) argued convincingly that prostitution is not defined categorically by these characteristics. Instead, it tends to vary along these dimensions. Most prostitutes are not coerced, but some are. Most prostitute-customer relationships are temporary or impersonal, but some are not. There does not seem to be a really satisfying generic definition. In general, prostitution is "sex for pay," but *what it is specifically and precisely is determined by negotiations among those involved in various ways.*

Description: The Organization, Niches, and Social Actions of Prostitution

The neon calling cards of marquees begin to flicker out, giving the streets the appearance of semidarkness. The street habitués congregate in front of a steel-gated darkened movie house, silently conversing with passersby in the sign language of the street hustler. Squad cars prowl silently like hunting dogs sniffing the air for their prey, and then periodically the call of the wild streets pierces the night and the screeching banshees alert every denizen of the street that the hounds are in pursuit. Then just as quickly as they screamed their presence, it is quiet again. The crowded streets are beginning to thin now, people who sought their pleasure in movies, theater, and dining are bustling home. And those who are on the streets for business suddenly appear, as if on cue for their nightly debut, along with those who have no place to go and nothing to do but watch the unrehearsed choreography of this shadowy netherworld, another kind of street theater, where people play their roles, buying and selling the illicit "sins" of the city: a banned play of staged criminality where all participants know their part and act it out—police and prostitutes, junkies and narcs, muggers and the anticrime squads, fences and bargain-hunters. It is a symbiotic drama in a Stygian ["hellish"] world where everybody lives off one another's vices and vulnerabilities [Carmen and Moody, 1985:1–2].

SOCIAL ORGANIZATION Prostitution, at least as practiced in the streets, is organized and a part of an ongoing social niche. This niche, in turn, is a part of the larger social world of neighborhoods, communities, states, and nations. The analysis of the organizational character of prostitution begins at the broadest level: society. Recall (from Chapter 4) Kingsley Davis's (1937) *functional* explanation of prostitution (summarized and elaborated slightly here):

> The regulation of sexual activity is necessary to ensure the replacement of societal members.

> Regulation creates a demand for sexual services and outlets (that is, for those who want or need sex outside of the activities of procreation).

> Prostitution protects the existing organization by providing an outlet that does not undermine those arrangements.

This functionalist description probably does not capture fully the relationship between prostitution and society. Note, for example, that the "regulation of sexual activity" referred to as the origin of the demand for prostitution *includes prohibitions against* prostitution. Virtually all states prohibit prostitution and have for centuries. Most provide criminal penalties for violations. Definitions, laws, and penalties vary widely, but efforts to condemn and constrain have been persistent.

Beginning in the 1920s, a group of prominent lawyers, judges, and professors have been formulating recommendations for more consistent and rational law. As members of the American Law Institute, they have drafted documents that attempt to guide the reform of American criminal codes. Their recommendations are presented in drafts of the Model Penal Code and have had enormous influence on contemporary criminal statutes (see annual reports of the American Law Institute, 1954 to 1961; 1985). The model recommends the following provision for prostitution: "[A] person who engages or offers or agrees to engage in sexual activity for hire . . . commits a petty misdemeanor" (American Law Institute, 1959:sec. 207.12). It provides further that sexual activity includes carnal knowledge, vaginal intercourse, sodomy, fellatio, cunnilingus, masturbation, voyeurism, and male prostitution.

There is an interesting paradox: Prostitution has been prohibited for centuries by beliefs, morals, and criminal law, yet it has persisted with little change or decline. What are the sexual standards of our society? Have they changed? How are they related to prostitution? There is a common belief that we experienced a "sexual revolution" some time during the 1960s and 1970s and that contemporary Americans are much more "permissive" than before. Most of us are aware of our Puritan heritage (during the eighteenth century) and the Victorian era of the nineteenth and twentieth century. But few people know of research that suggests that one-third of the women marrying in puritan New England were pregnant (see Reiss, 1980:90; Calhoun, 1945:133). Nor are they aware that many women during this time slept with their fiancés—that is, they "bundled." This courtship custom, popular during winter, was not supposed to involve intimate contact.

Research by Ira Reiss (1973, 1986) and others has suggested that changes in sexual behavior have not been categorical but matters of degree. And the changes have been more complex than we usually recognize. Drawing from data collected by Alfred Kinsey and his associates (1948), Reiss (1980:168–174) summarized some of the changes by examining rates of premarital sex among women who were born before 1900 and in the decades up to 1930. The proportion of those who reported "none" in response to the question of premarital coitus was lowest for those born before 1900 (73.4 percent—not 100 percent). For those born in the next decade, the proportion was 48.7 percent. The proportion reporting virginity at marriage remained essentially the same for the next two decades (43.9 percent for the 1910–1919 decade; 48.8 percent for the 1920–1929 decade).

Terman's (1938) study provides some information for comparing the sexual activities of men. Approximately 51 percent of the men born before 1890 reported no premarital coitus; of the men born in the next two decades, 41.9 percent and 32.6 percent, respectively, reported virginity at marriage. If the data are accurate, we can see some problems. For example, 49 percent of the men born before 1890 were having sex with 27 percent of the women—or someone else.

Reiss (1980:177) has argued that there are several standards for evaluating premarital sex in our contemporary society. These may reflect more general social standards with respect to sexual activity in the United States. The standards are described as follows:

Abstinence: Premarital intercourse is considered wrong for both men and women, regardless of circumstances.

Double standard: Premarital intercourse is more acceptable for men than for women.

Permissiveness with affection: Premarital intercourse is considered right for both men and women when a stable relationship with love or strong affection is present.

Permissiveness with or without affection: Premarital intercourse is considered right for both men and women if they are so inclined, regardless of the amount or stability of affection present [Reiss, 1980:177].

The institutions of family and religion are the primary sources of norms and rules that govern sexual expression. Our Judeo-Christian heritage includes an orientation toward sex that emphasizes utility (as contrasted with recreation, for example) and procreation. Accordingly, sexual activities that have nothing to do with reproduction tend to be disvalued, discouraged, or prohibited. Marriage is the central structural arrangement for conventional and legitimate sexual expression in our society. We use the marriage relationship as the point of reference in characterizing a variety of sexual activities: pre*marital* sex, extra*marital* sex, and *marital* sex, for example.

The organizational context of prostitution suggests that changes in family and religious arrangements will be at least related to (if not causes of) changes in the activities of prostitutes and their clients. For example, as rates of premarital sex increase, incidents of prostitution (and other commercial sex) might decline, and religious teachings on matters of sex and morality probably are related to the nature and volume of prostitution. Of course, the relationships are not necessarily simple or obvious. For one thing, those who patronize prostitutes may not be the same people who are involved in premarital or extramarital sex. And changes in religious teachings or pronouncements may have different effects on people in different social niches.

Unfortunately, it is not possible today to describe the *epidemiology* of prostitution or to trace epidemiological changes over the history of our society. (Recall the discussion of epidemiology from Chapter 3.) We do not know the present rates in the United States. An estimate of 350,000 women who make some or all of their living as prostitutes is sometimes given. Akers (1985:205) estimated that there are 1,000,000 prostitutes who entertain approximately 300,000 clients each night. Official crime data estimate 125,600 arrests for prostitution and commercialized vice in 1983 (McGarrell and Flanagan, 1985). Arrest information, however, provides only a poor estimate of the number of incidents or participants. We cannot say with any real confidence what the direction of change has been in terms of the numbers of prostitutes or customers. We can examine indirectly some of the epidemiological patterns and causal relationships.

Hunt (1975:143–144) claimed that prostitution has been decreasing throughout the past several decades. Drawing in part from data collected in the Playboy Foundation survey, he offerred the following:

> A century ago, and even a generation ago, a considerable number of young males went to prostitutes for their sexual initiation, and some males— especially those in the lower social and educational levels—resorted to them often and reularly prior to marriage. . . . Our data show that . . . there have been distinct decreases in the past generation in the percentage of American males who are sexually initiated by prostitutes, in the percentage who ever have premarital intercourse with prostitutes and in the average frequency with which they have such experiences.
>
> This is a continuation of a long-term trend that has coincided with— and in large part been the result of—the long-range emancipation of women

and the decay of the double standard, for as dating partners have become sexual partners, prostitutes have become unnecessary and undesirable.

This research and that reported by Kinsey suggest some support for the functional explanation of prostitution. Both studies suggest that lower-class males (for example, those with low levels of education) want more sex and more variety than their traditional marriage relationships provide. Compared to their more highly educated counterparts, they engage in sex with their wives less frequently, limit foreplay, finish quickly, and engage only in traditional sex practices (such as vaginal intercourse in the so-called missionary position). The studies also suggest that lower-class men have been more likely to use prostitutes than their better educated counterparts. Other research suggests that men visit prostitutes in part because of their desire for more sex and greater variety (see Winick and Kinsie, 1971, and James, 1977). And Diana (1985:81) reported that fellatio is the service most frequently requested from prostitutes.

At the same time, Hunt suggested that some of the social class differences have diminished with general increases in education and sophistication—that is, more people at all educational levels are exposed to explicit discussions and portrayals of sexual activities. Both studies showed that husbands from all educational levels reported wanting a higher frequency of sexual activity than they have currently. Kinsey's study provided an interesting twist: Marital intercourse provided a *smaller* proportion of the total sexual experience in the later phases of the marriage for college-educated men than it did for those with less education. Does that mean that older, highly educated married men are more frequent users of prostitutes? Maybe. Or it may mean that higher status males are more likely to engage in extramarital affairs or use masturbation as an alternative outlet. (Higher-status males are more likely than their lower-class counterparts to use masturbation as an alternative prior to marriage; see Hunt, 1975:145.)

Prostitution supports existing conventional arrangements in complex and changing ways. The structural patterns almost certainly are more complex than was suggested by Davis's (1937) early functional explanation. There is an interesting combination of supporting and conflicting relationships between prostitution and parts of the legitimate order. Prostitutes have long provided a source for sexual initiation for young men and an outlet for sexual variety and quantity for others (especially married men). Prostitution continues to be a source of uninvolved sex for men who travel and others who treat sex as a physiological need. It does not challenge directly conventional marital or family relationships (Diana, 1985:xviii). At the same time, it is against the law in most places, and it is the object of continuing negative evaluation.

During this century, criminal law and its enforcement have been the primary control strategies used in our society. Prostitution was more or less tolerated in frontier towns of the 1800s, and little is known about its practice or control before that. By 1910, some systematic control efforts were developing in the form of educational and political lobby organizations. The American Society of Sanitary Moral Prophylaxis, the American Federation of Sex Hygiene, and the YMCA actively pursued policies to oppress and eventually eliminate prostitutes and their trade. Brothels that had operated openly were closed and red light districts of concentrated prostitution were reduced substantially (Anderson, 1974; McCaghy, 1985:362). The following groups, organizations, and collectivities have sought to control prostitution or reform prostitutes: the clergy, vice commissions, nativists, antinativists, news media, the police, civil liberties groups, and women's and feminist groups (Hagan, 1985:84–85).

Recently, prostitutes themselves have gotten into the fray, introducing their own ideologies into the control efforts. Groups such as COYOTE (Call Off Your Old Tired Ethics), PONY (Prostitutes of New York), and ASP (Association of Seattle Prostitutes) have emerged as unions and advocacy groups (Roby, 1969, 1972; Women Endorsing Decriminalization, 1973; Sheehy, 1973). Such groups often highlight the exploitive nature of control efforts and point to the hyprocrisy of laws prohibiting services that conventional citizens seek and buy. Themes such as "Whores have saved more marriages than marriage counselors ever will" often are sponsored and promoted by these organizations in response to condemnation by reform and prohibitionist groups.

Some of the professional associations and unions and some social scientists have recently recognized political and economic aspects of prostitution. Representatives from COYOTE, for example, have alleged that prostitutes are harassed and persecuted by the same people (or the same kind of people) who are their clients (middle-aged, middle-income men). Others, including some sociologists, have observed that prostitution in the United States is a direct reflection of the white, Anglo-Saxon, male-dominated, capitalist economy. From this point of view, prostitutes have found it necessary to separate themselves from their own sexuality to survive in an economy shaped by a distribution of wealth and resources that favors some to the considerable disadvantage of others.

The practices of prostitution probably are shaped by the particular structure and organization of the society. Hierarchical arrangements of age, race, social class, education, and gender are important features of social organization and social control that undoubtedly influence the emergence, persistence, and change of deviance and other social realities. For example, minorities, including blacks and immigrants, typically have contributed disproportionately to the ranks of prostitution. And women have recently become the purchasers, rather than just the providers, of sexual services. Perhaps American women have finally achieved sufficient control over their personal lives and finances to move to the other side of the professional-client relationship.

An uneasy alliance has developed between some prostitute groups and some feminist groups. While feminists tend to see prostitution as a continuing form of exploitation of women, they have recognized prostitutes' claims of freedom to do as they choose with their own bodies. And they join these women in their opposition to laws that penalize the women but not their male customers. In some ways, the paradoxical relationship between hookers and feminists reflects the broader paradox and dialectic of prostitution and the general society. This "love-hate" quality is reflected, in turn, in the more specific organization of prostitution in the diverse niches that constitute the everyday worlds of prostitutes and their customers.

> They come in all sizes and colors
> Black, Spanish, White, and others
> Tall, short, fat, skinny, and even out of shape
> Yes, yes, gentlemen, all to satisfy your taste
> On sale at a corner near you
> Anywhere in New York you choose
> Whether it's uptown, downtown, or midtown
> We're getting down everywhere in this town
> Thiefs, freaks, flatbacks, and sleaze
> Choose as you please, from any of these
> Ladies of the night.—Me (Anonymous)

SOCIAL NICHES This poem (in Carmen and Moody, 1985:1) points to variety and geographical dispersion in the practice of prostitution. Observers are agreed that the term *prostitute* refers to an impressive variety of styles and roles. Different niches include different roles, relationships, and rationales. In his description of organizational contexts and variations, Diana (1985:3–42) suggested the following categories of prostitution: street, brothel, truck stop, hotel-motel, roadside lounge, resident home, message parlor, call girl, and "other." Jennifer James (1977) pointed to yet other types: bar girls, studio models and escorts, stag party workers, convention prostitutes, Nevada house prostitutes, illegal house and apartment prostitutes, and circuit travelers. Gale Miller (1978:127–128) provided a more analytic description and identified four types, which are based on the exclusiveness of the customers served and the organizational affiliation of the women: nonexclusive, independent; exclusive, independent; nonexclusive, organizationally affiliated; and, exclusive, organizationally affiliated.

All prostitutes participate in some measure in the broad social and cultural patterns and meanings that define and shape prostitution in contemporary America. At the same time, the different types exist within different *social niches*—relatively specialized social and physical settings. Within these settings, different people encounter one another in different roles and in different relationships. Different patterns of *social action* emerge, persist, and change, and prostitution as a social reality is *negotiated*. What counts as prostitution in one niche might not be recognizable as prostitution in another. Employees of "escort agencies," for example, may make finer distinctions between on-the-job sex and prostitution than do streetwalkers.

The diverse types of prostitution and the various social niches reflect distinctions, social patterns, and broader social arrangements of the conventional culture. Highly paid professionals and executives seldom travel the streets and sidewalks worked by hookers, and most semi-skilled workers could not afford to support—or even visit—top-dollar call girls, for example. The brothels of western, frontier, and gold rush towns gave way to more discreet (or at least more hidden) forms such as "social clubs" and barrooms with "hostesses."

However, all of the niches include certain types of roles occupied by participants who carry out their duties. For example, there are service-providers, who may be hookers, bar girls, call girls, or escorts. And there are customers, who may be tricks, johns, customers, clients, or dates. There are also managers or supervisors in the forms of pimps, madams, bartenders, or booking agents. In addition, there are steerers who include cabdrivers, bellmen, bartenders, and convention directors. Profiteers provide services to the service providers, for example as managers of hotels and motels, as operators of massage parlors, as corrupt law enforcement officials who provide "protection," and as physicians who provide medical checkups. Publicists make money and advance careers through their descriptions and explanations of prostitution. These include journalists, politicians, and sociologists (among other researchers). Finally, there are agents of conventional society, or controllers (Becker, 1963:147, called them "moral entrepreneurs"), including police officers, judges, social workers, clinical psychologists, politicians, members of the clergy, morally indignant citizens, and teachers, for example. (See Miller, 1978:138–157, for a discussion of related roles. The concepts of steerers, profiteers, and publicists are borrowed directly from Miller.)

The activities of prostitution and the social niches in which they occur vary from one local setting to another. Both activities and niches change over time. And different kinds of prostitution occur within different social niches. Negotiations within each niche give prostitution its particular form at any moment. We can understand prostitution by examining the ongoing and changing interactions within the various social niches. The details will be different if we look at prostitution in Virginia or in a rural Kansas community. Prostitution today undoubtedly is different from that during the 1800s and the opening of the west. And the activities that characterize massage parlor hooking are different from those found in hotels and motels. Consider the following description of truck-stop prostitution (drawn in part from Diana, 1985:18–21; additional data from my files):

Physical and Social Setting: A complex of buildings located near an exit from a major federal highway. There is a service station, a restaurant, and a small building with rooms that can be rented by "professional drivers"—ostensibly, and often, for sleeping. The business is known as a truck stop and provides services primarily for truck drivers. Others stop on occasion, but few family travelers stop for anything other than gas. The restaurant looks like a greasy spoon and the entire complex has a seedy, transient quality. The quality and form of interactions such as buying gasoline, ordering and serving meals vary depending upon the participants' roles—especially, whether the customer is an "insider" or an "outsider."

Roles: There are "regulars" (drivers who stop with some frequency) and other "insiders" (drivers who know about and have stopped at other truck stops that provide prostitution). "Outsiders" are those who are unaware of the range of activities and who are not a part of the ongoing social world of the trucker. More specifically, there are drivers, mechanics, gas jockeys, waitresses, cashiers, desk clerks, and dates. The dates sometimes work as waitresses and provide sex for a price after normal working hours. At other times, the dates may be cocktail waitresses or customers at the bar. The steerers include the cashier and, most likely, the desk clerk who handles room registration and scheduling and payment for showers. Waitresses and gas jockeys sometimes serve as steerers. "Family men" are people who come into the setting without knowing its true nature—and include unsuspecting women as well as men. These intruders are part of the cadre of social control agents and agencies. Local police and sheriffs, federal agents, alcoholic beverage control officers, health inspectors, and agents of various licensing bureaus enter the setting periodically and introduce the possibility of sanction and control.

Relationships: The customer and the prostitute often refer to each other, and are referred to by others, as "dates." A waitress might ask a trucker if he has a date. The trucker often responds by asking if the waitress dates. A regular might be told by the cashier that his "favorite girl" already has a date for the night, or that his girl's "dance card" is full. Truck-stop owners sometimes act as managers of all the services and get a percentage of the income from prostitution. At other times, the owner is not visibly a part of the operation. The women typically split their fees with the managers. Some provide "tips" to steerers.

Prospective customers are sized up by the manager, cashier, or the prostitute. Diana (1985:19) provided the following description: "Customers other than truckers would be scrutinized as they drove in. Employees, including the girls, first checked the license plate and the car. An out-of-state plate was considered safe. The car gave an initial clue about the probable type of man driving it. As he walked in, all observed his manner and dress, for in ways they could not explain, a cop had a distinctive manner, and since local cops were not apt to be a problem, one had to be even more careful. The 'feds' were smoother. Cops, generally, they found, were apt to be brusk and authoritative, to have rough hands and to swing them widely from the sides of the body. They were likely to ask questions, especially about some aspects of the business. . . . Feds were apt to be smoother, more self-assured."

Rationales: Women who work the truck stops are regarded as "good-time gals" and "honky-tonk queens." Truckers are seen as hard-working, hard-living, modern-day gypsies. Sex-role stereotyping—macho men and sweet and sassy ladies—are salient features of the setting. The following excerpts are from an interview Diana (1985:120–130) conducted with a woman who started her career as a truck-stop prostitute. They reflect some of the meanings that prostitutes share.

> "I was tired of working and not having money to pay for things you didn't expect—and then would fall behind. Life's a struggle. There's always somebody's hand in your pocket.
>
> "You hear stories all the time about how hard the life of a prostitute is, but it hasn't been that way for me. I don't mean it's always pleasant—every job has its ups and downs. . . . The worse thing that happens is when a guy comes in drunk, slobbers over you, and gets nasty if he doesn't make it.
>
> "The money's good. The work isn't hard. You meet a lot of interesting people and the place where I work is nice.
>
> "You just do what comes natural except now you're getting paid for it.
>
> "I like men. Oh, sure, you see some who are downright obnoxious and there are things I don't like about men

generally. They act like they're so superior, like they're doing you a favor by being there.

"I know it's hard to believe, but I like my work. I like to be with them. I like their company—they're interesting. They're all alike in some ways, but they're different too.

"It's a sociable thing and a sexual thing. It's nice to know men want you. That makes you feel good and if the guy is nice—even if he's not young and good looking—it's pleasant. I don't expect to get turned on and I don't decide I want to get turned on. If I like a customer, I relax. If he goes on long enough, I often do get turned on."

The woman was asked if she felt much guilt about her work. She responded: "Much guilt? I don't feel any. I know some of the girls worry and wonder if other people look at them and say 'She's a prostitute.' That doesn't bother me. How can they tell anyway? . . . I don't believe it's immoral either. Look, I'm doing what I want to do. It's my choice. I can stop anytime I want to. The customers are doing what they want to do. I have something they want and I give it to them for a price. It's a mutual thing, an agreement."

SOCIAL ACTION: THE PATTERNED BEHAVIOR OF PROSTITUTION There are arrangements and patterns that characterize contemporary American prostitution in spite of the diverse niches and styles. These patterns or common features allow an analytic description of the initiation, development, and change of the activities that make up the social realities of prostitution. At the same time, social relationships define and encompass prostitution—for example, relationships between prostitutes and customers, agencies of social control, and the broader society.

Much of the research literature suggests that prostitution can be seen as a kind of "con" game in which customers are swindled by false promises (see Greenwald, 1958; Bryan, 1965; Milner and Milner, 1972). Holzman and Pines (1982) questioned this characterization by pointing to observations that suggest that at least some clients are well aware of the nature of the situation and exchange (compare Stewart, 1972). At the same time, their research suggests that the clients participate in creating and maintaining the fiction of something more than a physical encounter. Accordingly, the activities and relationships can be described by drawing from descriptions of confidence artists (see, for example, Maurer, 1974; Roebuck and Hunter, 1970; and Tatro, 1974). Maurer (1974:6) described a lengthy series of events that are typical of a "big con." Prostitution probably has more in common with "short cons"—those that involve fairly simple strategies and brief periods of time. Accordingly, the steps of the confidence game are abbreviated in the following account:

"Putting the mark up": A prospect is identified.

"Playing the con" or "telling the tale": The prospect is approached and enticed by promises of fulfillment of sexual fantasies, a "come-on," and suggestive conversation and gestures.

"Giving him the breakdown": The prostitute or her agent provides information on the cost of services.

"Taking off the touch": The customer is "serviced," that is, he is brought to orgasm or some other point of closure.

"Blowing him off": The encounter is ended and the customer is moved out with dispatch.

This description is not meant to suggest an evaluation or condemnation of prostitutes. Customers probably get what they pay for: quick, uninvolved sex. Still the image of "something more" is central to the exchange. The specific content and style of these activities and relationships no doubt vary depending on the social niche in which the operator and her trick encounter each other. The characteristics of the conventional society and its agents and agencies of control strongly influence (constrain and shape) these encounters. Streetwalkers, for example, don't work professional conventions, and expensive and sophisticated call girls don't work waterfront bars. Broad shared understandings define "appropriate" connections and the social niches in which they are likely to occur.

Toward a General Theory of Prostitution as Deviance

As we noted in Chapters 3 and 4, the explanation of deviance requires attention to the dialectics of *violation* and *sanction* and to the related matters of epidemiology and causation. The following presentation proceeds through the outline of the convergence theory of deviance. Recall that the central variable in the epidemiological theory is *integration:* As *integration* decreases, both *violation* and *social control* increase.

Explaining Rates and Patterns of Prostitution

The general direction of change in American society has been toward increasing differentiation. The direction, rate, and substance of changes have been uneven. There has been a long-term trend toward *decreasing* integration, at least in terms of Durkheim's conception of solidarity. Prior to 1900, the society was organized in mechanically solid form, with simple division of labor and few differences among social positions. Today's society is more organic in form with more complex division of labor and high levels of specialization. Some of these differences among people and positions contribute to solidarity through interdependence. However, it appears that integration has declined with these changes. The theory suggests two hypotheses: (1) rates of violation of sexual norms have increased; and (2) rates of social control have increased.

Judeo-Christian beliefs provide the foundation of broadly shared understandings about sex, sexuality, and sex-role behavior. These beliefs also underpin structural arrangements of class, gender, race, and ethnicity. Historically, some social and sexual relationships have been condemned and, at times, treated as deviant prostitution in American society. At any moment, those activities and relationships that are selected reflect the nature and the level of integration of the community and society. (Recall the discussions in Chapter 3: The *nature* of integration refers to the type of solidarity, the distribution of interests and power within the social arrangements of concern, or the types of meanings that are the focus of commonalities. The *level* of integration refers to the *viability* of organization.) For example, prostitution in the United States traditionally has involved women who were the object of scorn and were susceptible to arrest and male customers who were neither scorned nor arrested. More recently, male heterosexual prostitution has emerged following the redefinition of cultural roles for women and changes in the participation of women in jobs and careers outside the family home.

Enforcement of the norms, rules, and laws that govern sexual activity varies with integration. Social control increases as integration decreases. For example, the major moral reform activities of groups such as the American Society of Sanitary and Moral Prophylaxis and the American Purity Alliance occurred at the turn of the century during a period of massive immigration. Efforts to control or eliminate prostitution in the United States have included major moral reform movements, religious instruction and admonition, the criminal law and its enforcement (including undercover efforts), and legal and administrative regulation (such as in the state of Nevada).

The practice of prostitution reflects these efforts as styles develop to avoid detection and to adapt the activities and relationships to the limits set by control activities. As a result, prostitution changes and persists. Massage parlor prostitution provides an example. Most localities found it easy to prohibit brothels and other establishments that could be identified easily as "houses of ill repute." The massage parlor, however, provides a cover that is not easy to debunk. What is to be prohibited: rubbing? Providing rubs while either the "masseuse" or the "client" is nude or partially nude?

At times of high levels of integration (for example, during popular wars), communities and societies are organized around highly salient shared understandings. The high level of commonality in these shared understandings, such as the "righteousness" of American values and traditions, constrain social action. Activities that depart from these values, including disapproved sexual activities such as prostitution, occur at some minimal rate. Note: The theory does not assert that violation is eliminated or that it disappears.

In general, increased differentiation in American society (including the move from mechanical to organic solidarity) has resulted in increasingly diverse social niches (including those in which prostitution is a "normal" or routine feature). Accordingly, there are more styles and varieties of prostitution. More specifically, diverse social niches provide contexts for the emergence of expectations that diverge from conventional understandings and laws (including those that concern sexual activities). Because of these changes, the frequency and rate of prostitution activities have increased since the middle of the nineteenth century. Some researchers (Hunt, 1975) have contended that prostitution has been declining since the beginning of the so-called sexual revolution. Others, more recently, have speculated on the effects of the "AIDS epidemic." And "consciousness-raising" effects of the women's movement may have reduced participation in prostitution. In spite of these speculations, the theory asserts that prostitution has increased as a result of decreases in integration. The issue can be resolved only through the collection of relevant empirical data.

Prostitution activities emerge and change partly in response to social control efforts of different types. Social control activities shape and sustain prostitution by sustaining the conditions that produce prostitution as a solution to a problem and by requiring adaptations that protect the activities from control efforts.

Explaining Causes of Prostitution

Recall that the central variables in the causal theory are *integration, attachment,* and *learning violations:* As *integration* decreases, *attachment* decreases, and *learning* of *violations* increases.

Women who grow up in social niches at the margins of conventional society have an increased probability of learning meanings and patterns of conduct that depart from or violate conventional expectations. Because they are less *attached* to the conventional order, they are more likely to engage in *violating* behaviors. Those who are raised in social niches that include recurring patterns of sexual deviance, including especially patterns of prostitution, are more likely to *learn* about the specific activities of prostitution and to learn and accept definitions that support the activities and neutralize conventional prohibitions.

The importance of economic and social incentives for prostitution are easily misunderstood and misrepresented. Contrary to popular opinion, most of the women who engage in prostitution did not choose prostitution to avoid starvation. Most were not kidnapped into "white slavery" (Bracey, 1979). And most were not too lazy to get a "decent" job. Both the severity of economic hardship and the prospects for making money are frequently misrepresented in popular accounts. One particularly articulate prostitute explained the relative rewards as follows:

> All prostitutes are in it for the money. With most uptown girls, the choice is not between starvation and life, but it is a choice between $5,000 and $25,000 or between $10,000 and $50,000. That's a pretty big choice, a pretty big difference [Millett, 1973:55].

Winick and Kinsie (1971:40) observed that the choice for many women is between low-status, low-income jobs such as waitressing and low-status but relatively high income through prostitution. Those who are drawn to prostitution may exaggerate the amount of money to be made. Even so, it is nonetheless true that prostitution provides more disposable income than many conventional jobs. Income tax and social security tax are not withheld and payment is in cash. One result is a feeling of relative wealth—the money is there and can be spent freely because it can be quickly replenished. Moreover, Diana (1985:45–46) found that two-thirds of his sample of prostitutes ($N = 487$) came from families with low or marginal incomes. Three-fourths of their fathers were skilled or semi-skilled workers, while most of their mothers were either unemployed or worked at semi-skilled jobs. Thus, the incomes seem high relatively.

There are other rewards as well. Women may be attracted to the opportunities to buy and wear fancy clothes and jewelry and to live the "fast life" of late nights, after-hours parties and all of the things that go with "the life" (Gray, 1973:411). There is at least one other reason why the income may seem greater than it is. For the most part, nothing is saved from the earnings. All of the styles of prostitution appear to operate within social niches that emphasize fun, fast living, and immediate gratification.

The following account captures much of the flavor of the economic and social incentives:

> "My husband walked out on me. We were both working but now I had to pay for everything and I'd just bought a new car. I had some charge accounts at stores, too. The payments were just too much. It seemed like every day I'd get a letter or phone call and if I didn't pay my bills they'd take me to court. One company did and they took it out of my pay.

"At lunch one day, one of the girls said 'Hey, why don't you go work at a massage parlor? I hear they make good money.' We laughed and talked about what it would be like. But in my own head, I knew I couldn't do it. After my court case I wasn't so sure. . . .

"Afterwards I kept wondering what it could be like if I did do it, just after work and on week-ends to make extra money. I tried to picture the kind of men who go in there and what I would have to do. I like sex, so it wasn't that. It was not knowing the men.

"About two weeks later I got a summons to go to court—I was two months behind on my car payments and a month on my rent. That did it. I said 'what the hell' and went to a place on Broad street. . . . I took the job for nights and Saturdays. After two weeks I quit my other job" [Diana, 1985:70–71].

The level of integration and the relative diversity of social niches in a community or society strongly influence opportunities to make a living and enjoy material rewards. Merton (1938; see also Chapter 4) was among the first to recognize the link between limited opportunities and conduct that may be treated as deviant. Most people in American society can pursue the goals of personal success and material comfort by traditionally acceptable means: education, hard work, savings and investments, for example. When the conventional avenues are not available or when usual opportunities are limited, some may turn to unconventional or illegitimate means. Prostitution—in any style—is, in part, an unconventional route to very traditional goals. In a sense, "the life" represents an innovative adaptation to structural strain in the larger society.

One of the most consistent findings in research on prostitutes is that a high proportion have had early sexual experiences. This conclusion stands even when data are collected to represent a wide range of the styles, practices, and backgrounds of participants. For example, Davis (1971) found that most of the women in her prison sample ($N = 30$) had sexual intercourse at an early age (average = 13.6 years). Over 95 percent of Diana's (1985:xii) sample had sexual intercourse around the age of 13. And his sample included nearly 500 women who represented a range of styles from streetwalkers ($N = 26$) to call girls ($N = 78$). Diana (1985) and James and Meyerding (1977) all found that a significant number of prostitutes have been victims of incest or other involuntary sexual acts. And Davis (1971) found that virtually all of her respondents had been regarded as different and troublemakers by their families and teachers. Most had been confined to some juvenile home or institution for truancy, incorrigibility, or sexual misbehavior.

Findings such as these tempt us to look for exotic explanations for prostitution. Early, promiscuous, or forced sexual activities might have a profound effect on sexual development. Some researchers have suggested that these women have experienced some kind of trauma and are thereby suffering from some psychological or personality disorder. The evidence does not seem to support such conclusions. In fact, those who have been interviewed or surveyed provide widely different interpretations of these events (Diana, 1985:65). There is no clear pattern to suggest trauma or conflict of sexual identity for prostitutes generally or for those who had early sexual experiences. And many who have had experiences (early sex or incest) are not and have not been involved in prostitution or other forms of sexual deviance. The following quoted passages are representative of interpretations provided by prostitutes who reported early or unconventional sexual experiences.

"You don't have words to say how it felt. I really didn't feel anything. But your own father doing that to you—I felt like dirt for years."

"It didn't hurt but it didn't feel good either. At that age (11) I wasn't sure exactly what was going on. I couldn't understand why the old man was so excited. I thought he was going to die."

"It was no big deal. I didn't exactly like it, but I didn't not like it either. After we did it for a while I'd come, but it still was no big deal."

"My boyfriend forced me. But it was exciting, too. I liked the sex but I didn't like his making me do it." [Diana, 1985:65].

Nanette Davis (1971:305) has provided an alternative explanation for the data on sexual experiences: "The adolescent girl who is labeled a sex offender for promiscuity . . . may initially experience a conflict about her identity. Intimate association with sophisticated deviants, however, may provide an incentive to learn the hustler role." In other words, some of these girls drift into association with others who are also marginal or stigmatized. For them, deviance becomes a part of their acceptance into different associations rather than the source of rejection from conventional groups.

Davis's description of drifting into other associations or groups provides one example of the participation in diverse social niches that is described in the convergence theory. It also suggests the effects of diminished attachment. Women may start within any of a number of different social niches that make up the larger society. Their drifting may take different forms depending on the character of their early experiences—including sexual experiences. Those who ultimately participate on some regular basis in activities called prostitution undergo a process of learning. This learning occurs as part of a process that has been referred to as an "apprenticeship" (compare Bryan, 1965; Heyl, 1979)—a somewhat more directed drifting.

For most, the training involves listening and talking to more experienced women (Bryan, 1965). For others, the process may be more explicit and systematic. Heyl's (1979) description of "the madam as teacher" suggested that the training can be very explicit. "Novices" are taught how to "manage" clients, both verbally and physically, and they are taught certain values or shared meanings (that is, they learn to violate). The meanings can neutralize the conventional definitions that condemn prostitution (Sykes and Matza, 1957). Consider the following examples:

> "It's a good deal for the guy and it's a good deal for me. People lie to each other and use each other all over the country, everyday. At least what I do is honest and it doesn't harm anyone" [Winick and Kinsie, 1971:50].

> "I could say that a prostitute has held more marriages together as a part of their profession than any divorce counselor" [Bryan, 1966:443].

> "I make love to men other women only dream of" [Diana, 1985:93].

> "Where else can I make this kind of money? And so easy?" [Diana, 1985:93].

> "I put in eight hours a day. I work about two, and most of that is taking my clothes off and putting 'em back on" [Diana, 1985:76].

> "I dug the attention from men, the easy money. You can't beat the hours. The actual sex part took about thirty seconds" [Lowney, Winslow, and Winslow, 1981:140].

Policy Implications: Social Control and Deterrence Theories

Convergence theory includes the assertion that prostitution is shaped and sustained by social control. That suggests that efforts to control, limit, or eliminate it are not likely to be effective. The theory says nothing about whether prostitution or any other form of deviance *should* be controlled. Clearly, though, social control is an essential part of the reality of deviance. In its most elementary form, social control is a sanction, and sanctions come in a variety of forms. Likewise, sanctions can reflect different purposes or ends: Punishment, rehabilitation, retribution, and deterrence are examples. The following discussion of policy implications focuses on deterrence in an effort to further specify the role of social control in the construction of deviance.

Systematic empirical research on deterrence has been accumulating for more than 20 years, and the resulting literature is impressive in size and scope. In spite of these fairly sophisticated efforts, our understanding of deterrence is surprisingly modest. It is not clear what kinds of sanctions are effective for preventing which behaviors under what circumstances. Indeed, Charles Tittle's (1980) thorough review of the literature on deterrence ends with the very reserved conclusion that sanctions have *some* effects under *some* conditions. Matthew Silberman's (1976) effort provides some specification and suggests some progress toward a coherent theory of deterrence. However, his sample (174 undergraduates at a small private university) leaves some readers doubtful of the generalizability of his findings. Still, Silberman drew from his research and that of others to develop an explict theory of deterrence. The theory is informed by the research and is stated clearly in eight propositions.

In its general form, Silberman's theory provides a solid foundation for future and more focused research. For our purposes, several of the propositions are critically significant. They connect directly with the proposed theories of deviance and social control:

> Proposition I: The higher the degree of moral support for the legal regulation of an offense or offenses, the lower the probability that the offense will be committed. . . .

> Proposition III: The greater the degree of association with peers who have committed an offense or offenses, the greater the probability that the offense or offenses will be committed. . . .

> Proposition V: The greater the degree of moral support for the legal regulation of an offense or offenses, the smaller the degree of association with peers who have committed the offense or offenses [Silberman, 1976:457–458].

His remaining propositions deal with perceptions—of the certainty or severity of punishment, for example—and do not relate directly to issues of concern to the theory proposed here.

Silberman's propositions assert that violations will vary inversely with the level of moral support and the degree of association with peers who have committed an offense or offenses. In other words, "moral support" and "association with peers who have not committed an offense or offenses" *deter* people from violating norms, rules, and laws. Moral support probably can be understood as a part of social integration. It may refer to solidarity, commonality, or to another of the described dimensions. Or it may refer to some as yet unspecified aspect of integration. "Association with peers who have [not] committed an offense or offenses" resembles the concept of attachment as described in Chapter 4. Seen in those terms, the deterrence theory's propositions overlap substantially with those of the proposed convergence theory. We may view them as *inverse* statements of Propositions $E2$ and $C1$, except that the deterrence theory is not based on any explicit conception of deviance.

The combined theories suggest that "effective" social control of prostitution requires the following:

An overall increase in the level of social integration of the society

An increase in the integration experiences of those who have an unusually high probability of participating in "the life"

Increased moral support for the relevant norms, rules, and laws (increased attachment)

Decreased association among those who are "at risk" and those who are active participants in the subculture of prostitution (increased attachment)

This control strategy may seem grandiose and fantastic, but consider the following points: (1) Previous and current efforts to control prostitution through laws and their enforcement have not proved effective; (2) the proposals are consistent with the proposed theory and Silberman's deterrence theory; and (3) all of the proposed steps are within the capabilities of contemporary American communities. We will consider these "facts," in reverse order, in the following discussions.

It is easy to be overwhelmed by the apparent diversity of our contemporary society. We are 240 million people who pride ourselves on individuality and on the right to pursue life, liberty, and happiness as we choose. Moreover, competition and conflict among different interests have become increasingly salient as battle lines have been drawn among owners, managers, and labor, between white and black Americans, farmers and the federal government, women and men, smokers and nonsmokers,—and the list goes on. How, then, is it possible to increase integration generally or to increase the integrating experiences of those who are especially "at risk" of participating in prostitution?

We could begin by recognizing that considerable consensus or commonality exists in spite of our diversity. This consensus cuts across important divisions and differences in interests and life-styles. And it reflects at least some of the moral support that is central to social integration. Consensus is evident in part in the results of public opinion polls. For example, Americans share considerable agreement on the acceptability of abortion under certain conditions, the use of the death penalty, the registration of handguns, and the legalization of marijuana. Seventy-seven percent of those surveyed in a national probability sample reported that women who become pregnant as a result of rape should be allowed legal abortion—and that included agreement among 74 percent of the Catholics surveyed. This consensus has persisted over more than ten years, varying between a low of 75 percent and a high of 83 percent between 1972 and 1984 (see Flanagan and McGarrell, 1986:172).

Similarly, 72 percent of those surveyed (again as a part of a national probability sample) reported favoring the death penalty for those convicted of murder. This consensus has persisted for at least a decade, varying between a low of 60 percent and a high of 74 percent between 1973 and 1985 (Flanagan and McGarrell, 1986:176–178; surveys conducted by National Opinion Research Center and Gallup). And 85 percent of surveyed adult Americans favored registration of handguns as a way to reduce crime, according to a 1985 survey by Media General/Associated Press Poll, while 73 percent opposed the legalization of marijuana, according to a 1985 survey by Gallup. (Both surveys are reported in Flanagan and McGarrell, 1986:197,212.)

I selected these issues randomly to illustrate that consensus exists in our contemporary social lives. Consensus is not the same thing as integration, but it refers to at least one major dimension of it—commonality. Commitment to certain norms, rules, laws, and other social arrangements might be enhanced simply by increased awareness of the level of agreement among members of our communities. Perhaps the focus of consensus must be either broad or "generic" in order to minimize points of contention. Nonetheless, there is the possibility of increased integration through consensus. Applied to the issue of controlling prostitution, the relevant issue might be that of sexual behavior and its meaning. A campaign to promote some commonly acceptable theme that discourages sexual exploitation would be an example. The theme might take a form similar to the "Just Say No" campaign to discourage drug use. The widespread concern about the AIDS virus may provide a social context for a campaign to encourage not only "safe sex" but also "responsible sex." Ad Council messages on television might feature President and Mrs. Bush urging a kindler, gentler, and more caring attitude among friends and lovers. To be effective, the value-oriented campaign would need to discredit exploitive sex and encourage expressions of love and caring. Durkheim (1956) described two types of integration or "solidarity" (see Chapter 3). The first, mechanical solidarity, depends on the similarity of participants and diminishes with differentiation. The second, organic solidarity, develops from differentiation and increases as specialized and *interdependent* activities emerge. Integration could be enhanced by organizing to maximize the connections and dependencies among people, groups, and other parts of our collective lives. "Neighborhood Watch" programs, for example, have developed in recent years to combat crime (especially in suburbs) and illustrate the power of cooperative and voluntary efforts. Such programs rest on recognized interdependence and differences. If everyone in the neighborhood kept the same schedule (at home and away from home at the same times), these programs could not work.

Reorganization to enhance the integrating effects of interdependence might include increased opportunities for conventional and respectable careers for those who find traditional avenues difficult or impossible. Not everyone can or should go to college to seek her or his fortune in business, computers, or law. Service and craft occupations are critically necessary in our modern world and could be sources of rewarding and respected jobs and careers. Wider recognition of our dependence on those who care for our children ("baby-sitters"), who dispose of our waste ("garbage men"), who control pests and vermin ("bug sprayers"), and the myriad others who do what many regard as "menial" or "dirty" work might result in both higher pay and greater respect. It would, at the same time, increase opportunities for those who find themselves choosing between low-prestige/low-paying jobs and prostitution, which is low prestige also, but often seems to offer higher income.

We could increase integration through enhanced commitment to some set of norms, rules, and laws *and* through organization that recognizes and maximizes interdependencies. The examples provided here are no more than crude beginnings, but they suggest some of the theoretical implications in action. Some of the changes are fundamental. They would not be expensive necessarily, but they could involve changes that are costly from some points of view. At the same time, it is intriguing to think about the possibility of planning and implementing social change on the basis of some careful effort to understand.

Our current social control strategies and those of the past developed without much consideration of the nature of the problem or any careful planning for results. We passed laws, created law enforcement agencies, passed more laws, increased the size of police departments, spent more money on equipment and tactics, and built more jails and prisons. What were the goals or purposes of these efforts? The answer is not clear. However, if we hoped to eliminate or substantially reduce prostitution, we have not been successful. Instead, our control efforts have *shaped* and *sustained* prostitution by creating the conditions under which the activities can continue *regardless of law enforcement efforts.* The only potentially effective means of enforcing the laws is through questionable (if not outright unethical) behavior on the part of police officers. Recall the examples at the beginning of the chapter. Police officers, posing either as prospective customers or as prostitutes themselves, *invite participation in prostitution in order to arrest those who accept the invitation.*

To be effective, social control efforts must neutralize some causal factor. Most of our efforts, now and in the past, have instead exacerbated the conditions that give rise to the problem. Or, they have compounded the effects of these conditions. Making prostitution illegal and criminal probably does not enhance integration overall. Durkheim's work (as discussed in Chapter 3) suggests that social control, regardless of its character, generally has the effect of increasing integration. However, it does not follow that all types of social control are equally integrating or that any act of social control has *only* or *optimal* integrating effects. In the case of prostitution, our law enforcement efforts may tend to further alienate those who are subject to control. If lack of integration, diversity, and diminished attachment are primary causes of deviance, then encouraging more of these conditions cannot be an effective strategy of social control.

The Need for Research

At least two kinds of research need to be pursued further toward specifying and beginning to test the proposed theory of the deviance and social control of prostitution. One type of study focuses on the relationships between the social conditions of integration and diversity of social niches, on the one hand, and the rates and distribution of prostitution, on the other. The theory should allow accurate epidemiological predictions. The second type of research focuses on the patterns of attachment and the learning experiences of those who participate in prostitution. The theory suggests several hypotheses that can be tested at least partially through a strategy of field research. The following discussion provides an illustration of the kinds of research that might be pursued. As you consider the proposals, you may want to review Chapter 5.

RESEARCHING RATES AND PATTERNS OF PROSTITUTION Communities of different size within a common geographical and cultural region could be sampled to ensure at least some variation in heterogeneity. By selecting a single geographical or cultural region (such as the rural Midwest or the urban Northeast) you could provide some control over *extraneous variation,* characteristics of social life in a particular context that are not really related to rates and practices of prostitution. Select six communities: two large (populations of more than 500,000 within the commonly recognized community area), two medium (populations of approximately 250,000), and two small (populations of approximately 50,000 and not more than 100,000). Although there may be no correspondence between size of population and levels of integration and diversity, start with variations in size in order to identify variations on the relevant factors.

Researchers would collect data in each community to describe the level of support for identified "moral" issues. The selected issues should be clearly related to sexual behavior and, more specifically, to the social realities of prostitution. By sampling the populations of each community, you would ensure representation across important differences of age, race, social class, education, occupation, religion, neighborhood, and related demographic variables. You could do the sampling through a random procedure or through some more purposive procedure that would ensure representativeness.

Those selected would become respondents to a survey questionnaire designed to collect information describing (1) personal commitment to identified norms, rules, and laws (integration through commonality or moral support for norms, rules, and laws) and (2) participation in activities typically regarded as prostitution. Recognizing the negotiated character of deviance in general and prostitution in particular, you would begin your study by asking respondents to identify those events (from a list you provide) that are acts or instances of prostitution. Respondents then would be asked to provide descriptions of their experiences in these activities using "self-report" questions. (See Arnold and Brungardt, 1983:404–419, for an excellent discussion and evaluation of self-report data.) The responses would provide a measure of the level of participation in prostitution as respondents define it.

To measure "integration through interdependence," you would ask respondents to evaluate the level of community support and appreciation for their occupation or vocation or for their unemployed status (for example, retired, welfare, homemaker). You would next ask them to evaluate and rate the importance, value, and appropriate level of salary or other reward for a series of occupations and related statuses.

The collected data would be analyzed to identify patterns of association between levels of integration and levels of prostitution.

RESEARCHING CAUSES OF PROSTITUTION Several of the important studies reporting on experiences of samples of prostitutes have included field observations and interviews of working prostitutes. These studies have provided descriptions and insights, but few have been designed to test theoretically derived hypotheses. Moreover, most of the studies have focused on streetwalkers and other styles that tend to be both lower on the hierarchical scale and more accessible to researchers (and, for that matter, to agents of social control).

I will describe a study that continues the tradition of ethnographic or field research, but departs from that style of research in being guided by an explicit theory. Samples of those identified by themselves and others as prostitutes would be selected to represent the analytic types of prostitution Gale Miller (1978:127–128) proposed: nonexclusive, independent; exclusive, independent; nonexclusive, organizationally affiliated; and exclusive, organizationally affiliated. This sample should include at least 100 women with each "type" represented equally. Researchers would select a second sample of women who are not involved in prostitution, but who are similar in demographic characteristics to the first group for comparison.

Both samples of women would be interviewed at length to gather the relevant information. For those identified as prostitutes, researchers would collect data following the example provided by the "Heroin Lifestyle Study" (Hanson and others, 1985). In that study, former heroin users who were intimately familiar with the local drug scene were used to identify respondents and, subsequently, as interviewers. In my proposed study, women with experience in the different types of prostitution would be used to select relevant samples of prostitutes.

They also would contribute to the formation of questions and interview schedules, especially in translating the relevant questions into a form that communicates with the intended audiences. Finally, these women would be trained as interviewers and would conduct the interviews under the supervision of trained field researchers. The conventional sample of women would be interviewed by women with similar characteristics also trained in appropriate interviewing techniques.

Then researchers would ask respondents from the two samples to describe people and relationships from their adolescence and up to the present. They would be asked to recall events and experiences that shaped their lives. And they would be asked about people they have known who are or were involved in prostitution. The women would be asked to describe conventional, unconventional, and anticonventional friends, acquaintances, and experiences. They also would be asked to rank the relationships and experiences in terms of their importance or intensity, their duration, and their frequency.

The collected data would be analyzed to reveal patterns of association within and across the samples. The sample of conventional women would be compared to that of the prostitutes in terms of types of relationships and types of experiences. And the subsamples of prostitutes would be compared to identify important differences and similarities.

The proposed studies, described briefly here, provide examples of the kinds of research implied by the description and explanation of prostitution and my convergence theory of deviance and social control. Neither study would provide a real test of theories. Instead, both would build on existing research. If the data tended to support the theories, the studies would provide further empirical grounding.

Mental Illness

Mr. Turner (a fictitious name) has been a patient at the State Hospital for the past eight months. He has been in this mental hospital and others like it episodically for more than 20 years. He is diagnosed as "schizophrenic—chronic, undifferentiated." He has come to our attention because he wants to discontinue use of his prescribed antipsychotic medication. As members of the Patients' Rights Committee, we have been asked to hear Mr. Turner's complaints and to rule on his right to refuse medication and to participate in treatment decisions.

A review of the patient records reveals that Mr. Turner first came to the attention of authorities because he refused to go to work, he did not bathe or attend to personal hygiene, and he stayed in bed for long periods. His aunt and sisters described him as withdrawn when they were interviewed by case workers at State Hospital. It is not clear from the records how Mr. Turner was referred to the hospital at the time of his first admission. The records also indicate that the patient is a black male, 55 years old, has suffered from pneumonia, and is a college graduate who had worked as a teacher and personnel manager before his admission to the hospital. During the year of his first admission, Turner had surgery to remove thyroid gland tissue and was despondent over the death of his mother.

Taken together, descriptions of Mr. Turner's admissions and releases from the hospital during the past 10 years suggest a pattern. When he is not in the hospital, he lives with his aunt. He has usually been referred to the hospital by this aunt, who complains that Turner is not attending to personal hygiene, seems to be saving and hiding his waste (urine and feces), and refuses to take his medication. He is admitted, antipsychotic medication is prescribed and administered (sometimes with some measure of force), and his attention to personal hygiene improves. He is then described as more lucid by hospital staff, and he is released when the medication regimen is restored. After some weeks or months, Mr. Turner stops taking the medication. Some time later (varying between weeks and as much as a year), Turner's aunt contacts hospital officials with the concerns described above, and the cycle begins again.

During the course of the hearing, the committee learned that Mr. Turner has never received counseling or behavioral therapy and that no one on the staff is aware of Mr. Turner's thyroidectomy, his career experiences, or his level of education. The head of the treatment team, who is also the attending physician, expressed his resentment that the Patient's Rights Committee is interfering and that anyone should question his treatment decision. He is absolutely certain that treatment with antipsychotic medication is the only viable strategy. The committee also learned that Mr. Turner dislikes the medication because he believes that it causes slurred speech, blurred vision, and impotence. He believes that it interferes with his reading and sexual activity, both of which are extremely important to him. Turner also is concerned because he has read that the medication causes tardive dyskinesia, a condition in which the side effects of the medication (including muscle spasms, sucking and smacking movements of the lips and tongue, and tics of the eyes and lips) become permanent and irreversible. It is generally known, and was confirmed by psychiatrists who appeared before the committee, that the medication has the side effects that concern the patient (American College of Neuropsychopharmacology-Food and Drug Administration Task Force, 1973).

The committee concluded that Mr. Turner has a right to participate in making treatment decisions and that he is within his rights to request alternative treatment—that is, without medication. The committee noted that Mr. Turner is willing to cooperate in counseling and various behavioral programs. The director of the hospital accepted the recommendations, and medication was discontinued briefly. The committee chairman learned four weeks later that the head of the treatment team had decided to reimpose medication because he believed that Mr. Turner's behavior had degenerated to the point that he represented a danger to himself and others.

This case description is fictional, but is based on a compilation of incidents, people, and cases known to me through professional and volunteer work in public mental hospitals in 2 states over a period of 12 years.

A Sociological Conception of Mental Illness

What is wrong with Mr. Turner? Is it mental illness, physical illness, or a problem of living? The diagnosis sounds medical and, in fact, there is some evidence that schizophrenia is a biochemical disorder. There is also good reason to question the reliability and validity of psychiatric diagnoses (compare Ash, 1949; Kendall and others, 1971; Krohn and Akers, 1977; Rushing, 1978). Mr. Turner suffered from some disorder of the thyroid and had surgery the year he was first admitted to the mental hospital. The disturbed behavior of concern in that year may have been related to the thyroid disorder or the thyroid surgery, and, in that sense, the problem is physical illness. Or perhaps the death of his mother, the thyroid disorder, and other experiences created stress to which Mr. Turner simply could not adjust.

Few issues have generated as much controversy and persistent ambiguity as "mental illness"and "mental disorder." The controversy may be the result of the diversity of things included in these categories. (In the following discussions, I will use the terms *mental illness* and *disorder* as they are used in our everyday language. Given the approach described here, the terms should appear in quotes each time ("mental illness") to emphasize the *problematic* and *negotiated* nature of the social reality. To avoid belaboring the point, quotation marks will be discontinued at this point.) The terms are applied to behaviors, events, and characteristics that are sharply different in origin and form. Some may be accurately described as mental illness: diseases or pathological conditions of the brain or those that have some observable effect on mental processes. "Organic brain syndromes" such as syphilis of the central nervous system or intracranial infection would be examples. The medical model, which treats behaviors and conditions as either *medical in fact* or as being *very much like physical medical problems* may be appropriate for understanding these problems. Within sociology, Walter Gove (1970, 1972, 1982) has been the major defender of this model.

Some problems called mental illness may be included because they have some organic or biological link and resemble physical illnesses or medical problems—for example, depression and schizophrenia. Research suggests some genetic vulnerability for schizophrenia (Kallman, 1953; Rosenthal, 1970; Kohn, 1973). And there is evidence of a biochemical or genetic basis for psychotic depression (Rosenthal, 1970; Gershan, Targum, and Kessler, 1977). For these, the medical model may be appropriate. A social stress approach that emphasizes environmental experiences might fit. Kohn (1973:74) illustrated a stress model:

> The thrust of the argument is that the conditions of life experienced by people of lower social class position tend to impair their ability to deal resourcefully with the problematic and the stressful. Such impairment would be unfortunate for all who suffer it, but would not in itself result in schizophrenia. In conjunction with a genetic vulnerability to schizophrenia and the experience of great stress, however, such impairment could well be disabling.

Some of the events and behaviors that frequently are labeled mental illness probably do not belong in the category at all. For socially disapproved behavior, such as delinquency, violent crime, and transvestism, there is no convincing evidence that these activities have any origin in illnesses of the mind, in pathological conditions of the brain, or in any identifiable mental process. A societal reaction approach that emphasizes the *selection* of certain behaviors and events for special attention might be most useful for understanding these (compare Lemert, 1951; Goffman, 1961; Rushing, 1979a). I will describe the issues of societal reaction, or labeling, more fully later in this chapter.

Three related but distinct points of view contribute to a sociological conception that encompasses most of the behavior that is identified as mental illness. The first approach recognizes the diversity of things called mental illness and directs attention to the selection of behaviors, events, and people. Thomas Scheff (1966) observes that various things called mental illness have very little in common. Fundamentally, they share the trait of being *violations* of expectations. In addition, they violate expectations that are not clearly specified. In contrast, some expectations are clearly defined, and their violations are readily identified and named. Violating the norm of sexual intercourse with someone of the opposite sex is homosexuality; snorting cocaine is drug abuse; belching in public is bad manners. According to Scheff, we could identify all of these clearly specified expectations and set them aside. There would remain vague and ambiguous expectations—a residue of rules of living: understandings about the appropriate length for staring into space, about the proper way to imagine or fantasize, or about the acceptable level of physical activity. Violations of these expectations are not readily specified or easily named and, at least in our culture, get lumped into the large *residual* category of mental illness. *Residual rule violations* (as Scheff called them) arise from diverse sources. Most of these violations are not defined as symptoms of mental disease. When residual rule violations are selected and treated as symptoms of mental illness, the effect is to shape and stabilize the undesirable behaviors into forms that are regarded as "typical" of "mental illness."

The second approach questions medical and psychiatric ideas about mental illness and proposes that the behaviors and events are more accurately described as "problems of living." Thomas Szasz, psychiatrist, is a leading proponent of this point of view. He has called mental illness a "myth" and contended that much of our current thinking is based on an analogy that is both faulty and out of control. He has gone further: "According to the view I have endeavored to develop and clarify . . . there is, and can be, no such thing as mental illness or psychiatric treatment; the interventions now designated as 'psychiatric treatment' must be clearly identified as voluntary or involuntary: voluntary interventions are things a person does for himself in an effort to change, whereas involuntary interventions are things done against his will; psychiatry is not a medical, but a moral and political, enterprise" (Szasz, 1974:xii).

The third point of view suggests that mental illness is troublesome behavior that may (or may not) be related to some physiological problem. More specifically, the behavior may be "inappropriate" given the situation or stimuli, "deficient" in terms of usual or ordinary skills, or "delusional," that is, out of touch with observable or shared understandings. Akers (1985:330–331) described the nature of such behaviors. Symptoms are understood as "conditioned responses to the environment. . . . The process may start and end simply as behavioral idiosyncrasies either not very distinguishable from other individual differences or not sufficiently different to be defined as serious deviance. . . . Whether a person takes on such a role [that is, a 'stabilized deviant role'] is determined more by the nature of interpersonal relationships and the changing environment than on the unfolding imperatives of an underlying dynamic illness."

Taken together, the approaches imply an understanding of mental illness as a *negotiated outcome*. Scheff's concept of residual rule violation points to selective identification of the relevant events and people. Moreover, the selected events and behaviors are shaped and become stable through the activities of people who react in certain ways—for example, by introducing social control.

For Szasz, the term itself is a cultural invention rather than an accurate description of an empirical reality. The alternative he prefers emphasizes the *problematic* nature of the social reality. Things are "problems of living" or they are not depending on what the actor and those around him do about it. Acquaintances, friends, and relatives may do nothing. Or they may encourage voluntary efforts to deal with the problem. Akers and others who have pursued behavioral explanations have recognized the problematic nature of mental illness diagnoses and imply negotiation through their attention to interpersonal relationships and the changing environment as sources of "outcomes" (in this case, whether or not the person takes on a "mental illness role").

Mental Illness as a Negotiated Outcome

John P. is 31 years old, black, divorced, and childless; he lives at home with his mother. He has worked as a semi-skilled laborer in a large corporation in his home town since his graduation from high school. For approximately six years, John has experienced difficulty with sleeping and has had attacks of dizziness, weakness, and blurred vision. For the past six months, John has awakened frequently at night unable to breathe and expressing fears about death. Three months ago, his mother told him to "straighten up" or she'd have him put away at the State Hospital. John currently is hospitalized in the admissions/short-term care unit of the State Hospital. The clinical social worker who was on duty at the time of John's admission diagnosed his problem as "anxiety neurosis." The medical director of the unit, a psychiatrist, has recommended a change of diagnosis to "schizophrenia—undifferentiated."

Meryl J. is 38 years old. She is white, single, has never been married, and lives alone in a small condominium. A laboratory technician who has worked in hospitals in several states, she is currently a senior staff member of a Veterans Administration Hospital in a large city. Meryl has had difficulty sleeping for several years. She has told family members and friends that she worries about disease and death. She eats very selectively, avoiding meat ("because it causes cancer"), sugar ("because it promotes dental decay"), and eggs ("because cholesterol causes heart disease"). She is uncomfortable when she visits in other homes because she believes that others are not careful about dirt and germs. She washes her hands frequently, sometimes as many as 12 times in an hour when she is away from her home. She cleans her apartment fully and disinfects her sink, stove, refrigerator, cooking utensils, silverware, and dishes every day. Meryl sees a private psychiatrist once a week. Her problem has been diagnosed as "obsessive-compulsive neurosis."

Diana T, 35 years old, is white, married, and mother of three children. She works at home as a babysitter and homemaker. Diana believes that she has an abnormal metabolism that causes her to be overweight, chronically weak and tired, and unusually susceptible to injury and illness. During the 12 years of her marriage, Diana has sought medical treatment in one form or another more than once a month. During pregnancy, she has sought treatment at least once each month for problems unrelated to childbearing, in addition to regular obstetrical examinations. She routinely limits her activities because of illnesses and weakness. At least three physicians have advised Diana and her husband that she is healthy and that there is no evidence of metabolic problems or any other chronic medical condition.

The "cases" reported here are composites from my files. They reflect factual events, but the identities of the subjects are fictional. These three cases involve behaviors and events that are understood within the field of mental health as symptoms of neuroses, relatively mild disorders that involve anxiety (inappropriate fear). Experts estimate that as many as 25 percent of the general population have neuroses (Kolb, 1973; Gallagher, 1980). John P. has been diagnosed as having anxiety neurosis, but there is disagreement; he is in a state mental hospital. Meryl J. is undergoing treatment with a private psychiatrist; her diagnosis is obsessive compulsive. And Diana T's fears cause her to limit her activities and to organize her life around alleged disorders. However, she has not been identified officially or effectively as mentally ill.

How can we account for the different ways in which these *potential* instances of mental illness are defined and handled? When instances of residual rule breaking are identified, how are decisions made about treatment or other forms of management or social control? These brief case histories suggest *selection* in the identification and treatment of mental illness. They illustrate the *problematic* character of mental illness and the selectivity of social control as described in my proposed theory.

What is the rate of symptoms of mental illness (that is, problems of living or residual rule violations)? Estimates are difficult to make and even harder to evaluate. Beginning in the 1930s and continuing to the present time, researchers have sought to determine the prevalence of mental illness symptoms in two major ways: (1) by counting the number of people who are receiving services and extrapolating or (2) by surveying samples from the general population, identifying symptomatic characteristics, and generalizing (Faris and Dunham, 1939; Hollingshead and Redlich, 1958; Jaco, 1960; Dunham, 1965; Srole and others; 1962; Levy and Rowitz, 1973). The estimates have ranged from a low of about 5 percent to a high of approximately 25 percent of Americans. There is some agreement around an estimate of 15 percent (Dohrenwend and others, 1980; Reiger, Goldberg, and Taube, 1978).

What proportion of those with "symptoms" are treated for mental illness? The President's Commission on Mental Health (1978) estimated about 3 percent of the population—or approximately 20 percent of those who exhibit symptoms. It might be argued from a clinical point of view that the problem is that 80 percent of these mentally ill are not receiving treatment. From a sociological point of view, however, the critical concerns are the *selection* and *differential treatment* of those with similar patterns of behavior. I will use the concepts of social organization, social niche, and social action (as introduced in Chapter 3) to raise and consider these issues. Following that, I will present a general sociological theory (convergence theory) of mental illness.

Social Organization: Demographics and Mental Illness

There is an order to social life that creates a sense of coherence for most people in a community and society. The sorting of events, behaviors, and symptoms typically does not appear random or nonsensical. We do not find it entirely strange, for example, that low-income, minority people usually are treated at public mental hospitals while upper-income, professional people are more likely to be treated by private psychiatrists. Many would assume that the difference results simply from relative resources. But what if the cost of psychiatry *is not* the only or the central issue?

A number of researchers have observed that there are no objective or universally applicable standards for admission to mental hospitals (Goffman, 1961; Mishler and Waxler, 1963; Rushing, 1971; Gove and Howell, 1974). The overrepresentation of the poor and minorities in public mental hospitals may result from differences based on social class in response to troublesome or unusual behavior. For example, lower-class people and families appear to be more tolerant of diverse behavior and residual rule violation among family members, friends, and acquaintances than are middle-class people. Once the tolerance level is exceeded, however, they tend to react more punitively than their middle-class counterparts. They may call the police or turn to other outside agencies for help in controlling or removing the source of the trouble. Middle-class people are more inclined to intervene early when they perceive a problem. At the same time, their reaction appears to be more therapeutic than punitive. Family members and friends are inclined to see the problem as medical or medically related and to seek medical or other professional therapy for the troubled person (compare Hollingshead and Redlich, 1958; Freeman and Simmons, 1961; Horwitz, 1977; Kulka, Veroff, and Douvan, 1979). The selection of the mentally ill may be explained partly by these social-class differences.

Once people are identified as mentally ill, they receive different forms of treatment. Higher-income patients usually receive some kind of psychotherapy, while lower-income patients are more often treated with some sort of physio-logically-based procedure (medication, electroconvulsive therapy) or are simply held in custody (compare Gallagher, 1980:268; Schwab and others, 1968; Myers and Schaffer, 1954). Lower-class people also are more likely to be misdiagnosed (Karno, 1966), although we recognize that the whole issue of diagnosis is problematic.

Explanations of class-based differences in reaction and treatment have included the following factors: the capabilities and amenability of lower-class people to psychoanalytic and other verbal therapies, the biases of treatment agents and agencies, and differences in the resources of prospective clients. Hollingshead and Redlich (1958) note that lower-class people are less likely to attribute personal problems to mental disorder. Mayer and Schamess (1969) and Rowden and associates (1970) have contended that patients from the lower classes do not understand the psychotherapeutic process and lack "insight-verbal ability." McMahon (1964) pointed to biased therapists as the explanation for differential treatment by social class (compare Gallagher, 1980:251). And Marx and Spray (1972) found evidence that psychiatrists prefer college-educated patients and those from their own religious background.

Scheff (1966) has long maintained that the selection and treatment of those with symptoms of mental illness depend primarily on social characteristics rather than on objective evaluations of behaviors or mental conditions. Krohn and Akers (1977) reviewed research on the effects of nonpsychiatric variables on identification and treatment decisions. They found that all 18 studies of involuntarily committed patients supported the conclusion that social charac-teristics significantly affect admissions and discharge decisions. Rushing (1978) reported support for a "status resources hypothesis," which asserts that individuals with higher social status are more likely to be admitted *voluntarily*, while those with lower status are more likely to be admitted *involuntarily*. However, extremely disruptive people are likely to be dealt with coercively regardless of their status.

In general, definitions of mental illness are resisted and avoided when possible (Phillips, 1963; Linsky, 1970; Rushing, 1971). There is evidence that public attitudes have softened and become more tolerant toward mental illness (Lemkau and Crocetti, 1962; Dohrenwend, 1966; Clausen and Huffine, 1975; Cockerham, 1979). However, it seems likely that negative stereotypes about mental illness encourage efforts to resist labels and diagnoses (compare

Nunnally, 1961; Scheff, 1966; American Psychiatric Association, 1978). Research suggests that families often will contribute to efforts to resist designation of mental illness (Yarrow and others, 1955; Sampson, Messenger, and Towne, 1962) and that people with certain characteristics are decidedly more likely than others to seek psychiatric help (Greenley and Mechanic, 1976). Women, Jews, people with little or no religious affiliation, those who live in urban and suburban areas, and those with more income and education are most likely to seek help voluntarily for mental disorders. Men are less likely than women are to seek treatment, and Horwitz (1977:175) notes that "the men who enter psychiatric treatment are often in a weak position of power which allows others to coerce them into entering treatment."

There are clear patterns of association between rates and types of mental illness and assorted social variables, such as class, race, and gender. The associations undoubtedly reflect differences in the ways in which instances are identified and treated. They also may reflect how the structure of society constrains and shapes the development of conduct.

SOCIAL CLASS: OCCUPATION, EDUCATION, AND INCOME The organization of American society includes differences among people and life-styles that can be described as hierarchically arranged categories. These categories, or classes, are relatively homogeneous groupings that reflect differences in education, jobs, income, housing, leisure activities, and other matters of daily living. Studies of rates and patterns of mental illness have measured social class in different ways. Some researchers have chosen one of three popular indicators to identify and describe differences: occupation, education, or income. Others have combined two or three of these indicators. Still others have used composites that include these and other variables such as religion and ethnicity.

Researchers consistently have found an inverse relationship between occupational prestige and rates of mental illness (Blauner, 1964; Gallagher, 1980). The nature of the relationship is not clear. Some have suggested that greater stress is found in jobs that are at the bottom of the prestige scale (Kornhauser, 1965; Liem and Liem, 1978). Others have examined the effects of occupational mobility (or, more generally, social mobility) on mental health, but research findings have been inconsistent (compare Blau, 1956, and Clausen and Kohn, 1959). Karen Horney (1937) argued that personality disorders *cause* striving for mobility rather than the reverse, and Ellis's (1952) research provides some support for the assertion. Still other researchers have pointed to "status inconsistency" as the key to the relationship between occupations and mental illness (see Dunham, Phillips, and Scinivason, 1966; Hollingshead, Ellis, and Kirby, 1954; Eitzen and Bair, 1972).

Complex relationships probably exist between occupational variables and mental illness. And the key factors may have more to do with "vulnerability" and "selection" than anything else. Jobs may vary in terms of power, resources, and other characteristics that do or do not help to protect or insulate individuals from assorted deviance definitions—including mental illness. College professors, for example, are somewhat insulated from imputations of mental illness by cultural stereotypes that suggest that they are, by nature, "eccentric." They are further insulated by the relatively high level of independence that goes with their role.

Some research also suggests an inverse relationship between level of education and rates of mental illness (compare Meile, Johnson, and St. Peter, 1976; Gallagher, 1980:247–248). Hollingshead and Redlich's (1953, 1958) research on social class provides additional support for the relationship. They included education in their composite measure of social class, and they found a link between social class and both *prevalence* and *type* of mental illness.

Few studies have focused on income and mental illness. Instead, researchers have examined various clusters of resources as they relate to treatment decisions. As already noted, there is good evidence that these resources (such as family and marital status in addition to education and occupation) are related closely to intervention and treatment decisions to admit, to commit, or to release.

MARITAL STATUS, GENDER, AND ETHNICITY Patterns of association between marital status and mental illness are striking and complex. Researchers have consistently found higher rates of mental illness among single men than among married men. In addition, among those who are diagnosed as mentally ill, married men have a better prognosis of recovery (Gove, 1972; Pearlin and Johnson, 1977). And married men who are institutionalized stay for shorter periods than their single counterparts do (Gallagher, 1980). In contrast, married women do not have lower rates of mental illness than single women do (Gove, 1972; Cockerham, 1981:216–218). Explanations for the differences have included the following: (1) Women are more likely to be mentally disordered than are men, and marriage does not change that; (2) marriage is more difficult for women than it is for men; (3) marriage is a "status resource" for men that helps to protect them from mental illness definitions. Women do not benefit in the same way because, traditionally, their marriage status has not signified any special competence (such as working outside of the home); (4) being mentally ill reduces men's chances of finding a marital partner; mentally ill women are less easily identified because of the traditional passive role of women in courtship (see Gallagher, 1980:204–209; Cockerham, 1981:215–218; Rushing, 1979b; Meile, Johnson, and St. Peter, 1976).

There are interesting patterns of association between mental illness and gender, beyond those that have to do with marital status. Women and men are equally likely to manifest psychotic symptoms in general and those of schizophrenia in particular. Women are more likely to be diagnosed as having affective and anxiety disorders. And organic brain syndromes caused by aging are slightly more common for women. Men have higher rates of personality disorders and substance-induced and substance-abuse disorders (see Dohrenwend and Dohrenwend, 1974, 1976; Dohrenwend, 1975; Cockerham, 1981).

Prior to 1965, women were more likely than men were to be hospitalized in state and county institutions. Since that time, men have surpassed women as a proportion of institutionalized populations (National Institute of Mental Health, 1978; Cockerham, 1981). Rates of institutionalization may be explained by differences in types of disorders (for example, depression may be treated medically without in-patient care), by gender characteristics (women are culturally more compliant and thus less threatening), or by the orientation of screening and other social control agencies (see Gove and Tudor, 1973; Doherty, 1978; Phillips and Segal, 1969).

Cockerham (1981:218–219) has contended that there is no evidence to suggest significant differences between whites and blacks in rates of mental illness. Where differences are found, they are most likely the result of social class rather than race (Warheit, Holzer, and Avery, 1975). However, there are some interesting patterns of symptoms by ethnicity within the United States. For example, Dohrenwend (1966) found higher rates of reported symptoms among Puerto Ricans than among Jews. Jaco (1960) found significant differences in rates of psychoses among Mexican-Americans and Anglo-Americans living in Texas. Rates of psychosis were 50 percent lower for Mexican-Americans than for Anglo-Americans. And Japanese-Americans are known to have very low rates of mental illness (Kitano, 1962).

In sum, organizational and structural variables influence the selection and treatment of incidents of mental illness, problems of living, or residual rule violations. For example, people in different social classes react differently in part based on the social class, education, and occupation of the person of concern. Social structural variables also seem to influence the development of particular patterns of behavior—in this case, patterns that have an unusually high probability of being treated as problems or symptoms of mental illness. For example, men are more likely to engage in unaccepted patterns of substance use (drugs), and women are more likely to engage in disapproved forms of emotional expression (depression).

Social Niches and Mental Illness

Identification, selection, and treatment of certain behaviors and people as mentally ill occur within particular settings. If the behaviors in question share the quality of being residual rule violations, as suggested by Scheff (1966), negotiations among those in certain roles and relationships are likely to be critical. Research suggests that certain social niches are central to the process of identifying and treating mental illness: the family, work, mental health and social service agencies, and the police. We can describe these niches in the abstract, such as the *system* of mental health with the pertinent roles across different levels (national, state, local). That kind of description also would include the patterned relationships among clinicians, clients, administrators, and others, as well as the shared understandings about mental illness, medical practices, and related activities. Niches also can be described in more local or discrete form. For example, the description might focus on a particular family or a specific pattern of family relationships such as "equalitarian" or "patriarchal." In the analyses that follow, the relevance of social niche variables for identifying and selecting instances of mental illness are illustrated through a description of family patterns and the organization of mental health services.

FAMILIES AND THE SELECTION OF MENTAL ILLNESS Yarrow and her associates (1955) studied women whose husbands eventually were identified as mentally ill. They noted that the wives initially resisted deviance definitions and attempted to "normalize" their husbands' behavior. Some attributed the unusual and troubling behavior to the husband's personality, others saw it as a physical problem, and some denied that anything was wrong. Over time, some of the women (slightly fewer than half) changed their perceptions of their husbands' conduct and eventually defined the problem as one of mental illness. Others (about 20 percent) had different ideas and understandings at different times, but didn't move clearly toward any definition of mental illness. Some specific event or the intervention of a friend or family member seems to have precipitated the decision to seek mental health services. Still others (about 33 percent) had different explanations of their husbands' behaviors, but they continued to deny that mental illness was the problem.

Sampson, Messinger, and Towne (1962:88) also examined patterns of family reaction to disruptive behavior. They began with observations about the process of identification and selection:

> Becoming a mental patient is not a simple and direct outcome of "mental illness;" nor is hospitalization in a mental institution, when it comes, the automatic result of a professional opinion. Persons who are, by clinical standards, grossly disturbed, severely impaired in their functioning, and even overtly psychotic may remain in the community for long periods without being recognized as "mentally ill" and without benefit of psychiatric or other professional attention. It is clear that becoming a mental patient is a socially structured event.

Sampson and his colleagues studied 17 families in which the wife and mother was eventually hospitalized and diagnosed as schizophrenic. The families initially accommodated the disturbed or disturbing behavior by with-drawing from interaction with the wife and mother or by reorganizing around some new maternal figure (such as the wife's mother). These accommodations broke down eventually, and during some ensuing crisis, they decided to seek hospitalization.

In other research, Price and Denner (1973) described events that precip-itated decisions to seek treatment. They argued, as others have, that the troubling or troublesome behaviors have existed for some time before any decision is reached to do something. They suggested that the critical change may have little to do with the behaviors or the individual as such. Rather, there are changes in interpersonal relationships that surround the person. For ex-ample, a divorced mother might accommodate her son's unusual and bother-some behavior for a long time. A change in her life that involves a new relationship, such as becoming engaged to marry, may introduce pressure for action by changing the significance or salience of the problem. These changes make the problem more public or otherwise more salient, and this salience creates a crisis: "Something must be done." Perhaps in that crisis, as Scheff (1966) suggested, "insanity" becomes the "guiding imagery" for those sur-rounding the person and a viable definition for the person.

THE ROLE OF THE MENTAL HEALTH SYSTEM As noted earlier, Thomas Szasz (1974:x–xi) has contended that "mental illness" is a *myth*: "I maintain that mental illness is a metaphorical disease; that bodily illness stands in the same relation to mental illness as a defective television set stands to a bad television show. . . . We call jokes 'sick,' economies 'sick,' sometimes even the whole world 'sick'; but only when we call minds sick do we systematically mistake and strategically misinterpret metaphor for fact—and send for the doctor to 'cure' the 'illness.' " If mental illness is a metaphor—that is, if we treat some kinds of behaviors and events as if they involve some physiological or medical problem even in the absence of convincing evidence—then we must examine the role of physicians and other medical personnel who work in the mental health system to understand the *selection* and *treatment* of the mentally ill.

Mechanic (1962) began his analysis of factors that influence the identifi-cation of mental illness by pointing out that criteria of normalcy or appropri-ateness vary by groups and by situation. He noted further that physicians who are trained in the treatment of mental illness use different criteria than do laymen and these criteria are at times indefinite. Moreover, the criteria are more closely related to the *physician's theory of pathology* than they are a product of the diagnostician's ability to understand the *individual's behavior in context*. Finally, physicians who work in mental health settings (especially in public residential facilities) often must make decisions quickly. As a result, they may tend to *assume* illness and to apply some label that seems to fit the facts provided by those who have brought the person for admission or treatment. Studies by Kutner (1962), Wenger and Fletcher (1969), Haney and Michielutte (1968), Mishler and Waxler (1963) and others provide evidence of the presumption of illness at least in decisions to commit people involuntarily.

Scheff (1964:412) argued that psychiatrists who make recommendations at commitment hearings presume illness because their pay is based on the number of examinations they conduct, and they operate in terms of a specific ideology:

> 3. Unlike surgery, there are no risks involved in involuntary psychiatric treatment: It either helps or is neutral, but it can't hurt.
>
> 4. Exposing a prospective mental patient to questioning, cross-examination, and other screening procedures exposes him to the unnecessary stigma of trial-like procedures and may do further damage to his mental condition.
>
> 5. There is an element of danger to self and others in most mental illnesses. It is better to risk unnecessary hospitalization than the harm the patient might do to himself or others.

Scheff countered each of the points in this ideology and concludes that involuntary commitment on the basis of a presumption of illness puts the prospective patient at greater and unjustifiable risk.

The treatment of certain forms of unwanted behavior as "illness" dates at least from the 1600s (Foucault, 1965; Szasz, 1970). This "medicalization" involves "defining behavior as a medical problem or illness and mandating or licensing the medical profession to provide some type of treatment for it" (Conrad, 1975:12). Social control through medical intervention is potent for at least two reasons. First, the profession of medicine has very high prestige in our society and, by tradition, physicians' decisions, diagnoses, and treatments are above question and reproach. Further, the role of the sick person involves a measure of passivity and dependency (see Parsons, 1951:436–437; Loeb, 1956; Scott, 1969). In addition, treating behaviors as medical problems has the effect of "depoliticizing" the deviance and those involved. If something is an illness or a symptom of an illness, there is no purpose in debating or discussing its character (right or wrong) or its value (good or bad). As Szasz (1974) has argued, we have transformed moral and political judgments into diagnoses and treatment—"for the good of the patient" (or prisoner?).

Erving Goffman (1987:108) described becoming a *patient* as moving along a betrayal funnel: "the prepatient starts out with at least a portion of the rights, liberties, and satisfactions of the civilian and ends up on a psychiatric ward stripped of almost everything." This passage involves stages in which rights and privileges decrease while the various agents, including family and hospital staff, maintain the fiction that no further decreases will occur and that the whole process is benign. The mental hospital is a social niche with very special relevance for understanding the socially negotiated reality of mental illness. The following description highlights the characteristics of this niche through a composite sketch that is generally typical of public mental institutions in our contemporary society. (This description is drawn from research reported in the literature, as noted, and from my files.)

Physical and Social Setting: The campus consists of 18 buildings: 14 residential units, an admissions suite with one wing for diagnosis and a second for short-term "crisis intervention," an administrative office complex, and a hospital. There is also a large building at the westernmost edge of the campus that houses the furnace and various maintenance operations. The main buildings were built mostly after 1930 and look like medium-sized hospitals or college dormitories clustered around three major squares. The buildings are linked by concrete sidewalks and separated by expanses of neatly trimmed grass. They are one to three stories high and have flat roofs and undersized windows that are never opened. The buildings have shiny, clean tile floors and cinder block walls painted in subdued tones.

The residential units are organized by building, floor, and wing. Some of the buildings are reserved for patients with diagnoses that involve mild disorders and good prognoses (for example, situational stress disorders and neuroses) while others are "back wards," places to keep those who are chronically ill and have little chance of returning to the community. Other buildings house "special" patients: alcohol and substance abusers, geriatric residents, or adolescents. Within the buildings, there are separate wings or separate floors for male and female patients, for those with different levels of privileges, and for those who represent problems of control ("locked" wards). Nurses' stations occupy central positions on each floor and are mostly glass-enclosed rooms that separate patients from staff, yet allow staff members to see everything and everyone who is in any public, or shared, space (hallways, day rooms). There are single and double patient rooms, day rooms, and reception rooms on most floors.

Roles: At the most general level are the roles of "staff" and "patient." Staff roles are further divided among patient care, administration, and maintenance. Patients are grouped formally by diagnosis and building location, length of stay in the hospital, admittance (first time, returning, or recidivist) and potential for harm to self and others. Informally, patients group by personal traits (gender, age) and interests.

Treatment Staff: Psychiatrists traditionally have occupied the top of the power structure in mental hospitals. Until recently, psychiatrists were legally required to make diagnostic and treatment decisions. Virtually all therapeutic activities were done, ostensibly, under the direction of a medically trained psychiatrist. Further, psychiatrists held virtually all the key administrative positions. Doctoral level psychologists, social workers, and sociologists are recognized now as professionals of equal status for most therapeutic purposes, except, of course, for those that require medical training.

Psychiatrists in state mental hospitals often are foreign born and trained. A large portion of their time is spent prescribing and monitoring antipsychotic medicine. Most maintain a small counseling case load and spend the balance of their time overseeing treatment activities conducted by other members of treatment teams or the treatment staff. Most have relatively little actual contact with patients (Gallagher, 1980:299–300).

Psychologists with doctoral degrees are likely to occupy administrative positions or have primary responsibility for diagnostic testing. Many maintain a counseling case load, and some spend most of their time providing patient treatment services ranging from traditional counseling to behavior modification.

Social workers have a college degree or at least some college education. Some will have had an undergraduate major in social work; others may have majored in sociology, psychology, or other social sciences. Those with master's or doctoral degrees are most likely to be involved primarily in administration. Those who are involved in patient care most likely will be responsible for conducting background studies of newly admitted patients or for making arrangements to facilitate patient's return to their communities.

Nurses carry out much of the medical treatment prescribed by psychiatrists and other staff physicians. They administer medications, do routine physical examinations, maintain ward records (medical charts), and provide personal care services. They often exercise the greatest practical authority on the ward, enforcing "doctor's orders" and managing the activities of the other staff (Wilkinson, 1973).

Psychiatric attendants or aides spend the most time with patients (Perrucci, 1974). They directly supervise patient activities of all types and manage day-to-day affairs on the wards and elsewhere on the campus. Aides often have other, "regular" jobs and work in the hospital for extra money. Others work only at the hospital but may take on extra shifts to supplement typically low wages. Aides usually are among those with the least formal education, though college students sometimes work part-time as attendants while going to school.

Patients: The sick role encompasses conflicting expectations. On the one hand, people who are sick are expected to be passive, relatively dependent, and compliant (Parsons, 1951): Follow doctor's orders, take your medicine, and you'll get well. On the other hand, prevailing beliefs about mental illness suggest that people must help themselves in order to be cured. There are some basic differences in physical and mental problems, but these are not necessarily made clear or resolved within various mental illness niches—especially in mental hospitals. Patients may be told to demonstrate that they are well by acting in certain ways, by being cooperative and doing what they are told, or by admitting that they are sick! "Good" mental patients (1) believe that recovery is possible, (2) recognize the need for treatment, (3) trust the therapist, (4) conform to the hospital rules, and (5) cooperate in the treatment (see Denzin, 1968).

The institutionalized patients have accepted fully and enact, sometimes to the extreme, the expectations of the sick role. They become apathetic and almost completely dependent. They accept their place in the hospital and think of themselves and their future in terms of the hospital (Goffman, 1961; Wing, 1967; Townsend, 1976; Gallagher, 1980:312–313).

Relationships: Among staff, relationships are shaped largely by professional and occupational identities. Physicians continue to occupy positions of power and prestige. They relate to other staff in ways that parallel traditional hospital staff relationships. The physician–patient relationship is regarded as the most compelling and central by nearly all participants. Physicians resist efforts of patients to participate in treatment decision making, and most continue to see the essential problems and solutions as medical—that is, people are mentally *ill*; they can be treated with medicine or other medical devices.

The physician–nurse relationship reflects the traditional medical approach. Nurses carry out physicians' directives and remind other staff of the physician's primacy in the hospital and in the care of patients. Psychologists and other nonmedical professionals often encourage the use of the term *client* or *resident* in place of *patient*. However, they have had little success in changing the basic ideas and relationships. Those who operate from behavioral perspectives struggle against the mainstream medical approach.

Patients are in dependent relationships with almost all other roles within the hospital. Their dependence is enforced in part by the requirements of collective living within a bureaucratically organized setting. Patients must eat, sleep, work, and pursue leisure activities within the constraints imposed by the organization that has responsibility for their care and custody. Aides have the least education but the greatest amount of contact with patients. They have primary responsibility for patients' daily activities. Even those with the best intentions and the most humane orientations find themselves treating patients in impersonal and depersonalizing ways in order to meet the necessities of collective living.

Rationales: The *metaphor* of "mental illness" is not understood or treated as metaphor within mental hospitals. Most staff members take for granted that the people they deal with are *sick* in some sense. There is a strong organic bias among staff and this results in unquestioning acceptance of the medical model. The approach is sufficiently ingrained into the organization of the institution that organic diagnoses are rendered without the use of available diagnostic techniques and facilities that could establish objectively the presence or absence of the condition. An example is the diagnosis of "organic brain syndrome." The shared understandings are expressed below:

> People who are mentally ill must be treated within an appropriate medical facility by those with proper medical training.

> If they weren't sick, they wouldn't be here.

> Watch the way they act. Normal people wouldn't do that.

> Everybody thinks they got here by mistake.

> Fortunately, medicine has come a long way recently. The antipsychotic drugs allow us to treat mentally ill people effectively. Unfortunately, there are too many other so-called professionals mucking up things now.

Among patients, the following rationales may be heard:

> "I was going to night school to get an M.A. degree and holding down a job in addition, and the load got too much for me."

"I got here by mistake because of a diabetes diagnosis, and I'll leave in a couple of days." [The patient had been in seven weeks.]

"The others here are sick mentally but I'm suffering from a bad nervous system and that is what is giving me these phobias." [These first three quotes are from Goffman, 1961:152–153.]

"I'm okay but my family is really messed up. They didn't want me around, and they finally convinced the doctors that I needed to come here."

"My mother was very high strung. She was smart, but she got upset easily. I guess I'm like her. I could do anything I want if people would just try harder to understand me."

Note the taken-for-granted character of mental illness as it is represented in this niche. Illness is *not* a metaphor within this organization, which includes a hospital that is staffed by physicians and nurses and that cares for people called patients. The organization and distribution of power within the hospital, with physicians on top and patients at the bottom, operate to support and sustain the arrangement and to resist alternative definitions and changes. Moreover, the continued existence of mental hospitals reinforces the culturally shared ideas about insanity and, for most people, confirms the medical conception. And the ongoing activities (social actions) within the hospital and other mental health settings reflect and reinforce these cultural images as well.

Social Action: Interpersonal Negotiations

Popular images suggest that mental illness involves behaviors that are idiosyncratic, bizarre, and unpredictable. Accordingly, dealing with the mentally ill requires behavior that is responsive to the unique features of each person and event. Despite these popular beliefs, there are clearly identifiable patterns that characterize the behaviors of those who participate in the selection, identification, and management of mental illness—both as actors (mental illness candidates) and as reactors (family members, mental health workers).

Research on families and mental illness provides a beginning point for understanding the patterning of selection and management of mental illness. These studies (Yarrow and others, 1955; Sampson, Messinger, and Towne, 1962) suggest that families tend to react fairly predictably and to change their reactions in predictable ways over time. Accommodation is the first reaction of most who experience a family member's behavior as troubling. Families next reorganize to minimize the disruptive effects of the person and his or her behavior. Intervention by some outside agency (often a psychiatrist or other physician) often moves the family toward an explicit definition of mental illness (which family members typically understand as a *recognition* of mental illness).

Reactions to residual rule violations may take a number of forms. Lemert (1951), Schur (1971), Becker (1973), and Rubington and Weinberg (1987), among others, have identified patterns. As noted earlier, Scheff (1966) maintained that the usual reaction to such violations is to disregard them. Data on the selection of behaviors and people as mentally ill tend to support that allegation. However, an entire literature has developed to describe and explain reactions that go the other way. Most of the relevant research reflects a labeling perspective. Rubington and Weinberg (1987:24) have contended that reactions to alleged deviance (*violation*) can take any of several *general* forms:

> Optimize: The reactor sees the deviance as temporary and does not react directly to the incident(s) or event(s).
>
> Neutralize: The reactor disregards the deviance and treats it as insignificant.
>
> Normalize: The reactor takes note of the behavior, but treats it as a normal variation of acceptable conduct.
>
> Pessimize: The reactor reacts against the behavior and treats it as threatening, bothersome, and at least potentially permanent.

More specific patterns can be described by focusing on particular types of interactions. The following concepts and definitions point to some of these patterns.

> Ascribing status: A personal trait is defined negatively and the person is treated differently as a result. For example, a person's habit of staring (real or alleged) is identified as a symptom of mental illness.
>
> Stereotyping: Shared understandings of a particular type are created, applied, and sustained. These understandings highlight and exaggerate certain features of reality (groups or behaviors, for example) and ignore or diminish the significance of other features. A mental illness stereotype suggests that those affected tend to be glassy-eyed and to twitch and move in other unconventional ways.
>
> Retrospective interpreting: Understandings and recollections are reconstructed on the basis of new information, especially information that defines something or someone as deviant. For example, after learning of someone's hospitalization, a friend may think or say: "I always thought he was a little strange; I remember one day. . . . "

Status degrading: "The public identity of the actor is transformed into something looked on as lower in the local scheme of social types" (Garfinkel, 1956:420). Competency hearings are one example of this.

Deviance amplifying: The deviance is treated as an important or central feature of the person and conventional people reject the person. Events, behaviors, or traits are accepted as evidence of the person's mental illness and interactions with the person change accordingly.

Note that the outcome of any incident, event, or behavior *is not determined* by the reaction of those around the candidate. Rather, it remains a matter of *negotiation*. In simple terms, any *r*eaction can have either of two logically possible results: collusion or control. *Collusion* refers to reactions that, regardless of intention, tend to encourage, support, or sustain the object of concern (behavior, event, trait). *Control* refers to reactions that, again without regard to intent, tend to diminish, discourage, or eliminate the object of concern. For example, optimizing involves *collusion* when the person is not discouraged by reactions that essentially disregard or legitimize the conduct. It involves *control* when the person discontinues the conduct because it does not provoke a reaction or because of any other reason. The other forms of reaction can be examined in the same way. The key point here is that reactions do not produce determined results.

Consider a topic and point of view that has created considerable controversy among scholars, politicians, and others interested in social policy. *Labeling* has been a dominant concern of researchers and agencies of social control for more than two decades. A central theme of the labeling point of view has been that many of our social control efforts fail because there is more harm than good in selectively identifying and punishing those who violate norms, rules, and laws. Labeling often encourages or increases the undesirable conduct. A closer examination of the relevant issues and processes provides some insight. Labeling involves the creation and application of a definition that points to the object of concern (behavior, event, trait) as something undesirable and negative. Labeling definitions tend to generalize from the object to the person. Rosenberg (1979:10) noted that labeling involves a transformation of descriptions from *verbs* that describe behaviors to *nouns* that describe types of people. The person who was drinking becomes a drunk. The person who was acting crazy becomes a mentally ill person. The collusion versus control argument suggests that labeling will not determine consequences; it is neither collusion or control. A major challenge for social planners, policymakers, and enforcement agents (not to mention parents and other concerned family members) is to discover under what circumstances labeling will produce particular results.

A key point here is that the activities of those who are the subject of deviance-defining reactions also are important and consequential. And they are patterned and predictable to a certain extent. The patterns mirror those of the reactors as they were just described. Actors may *optimize, neutralize, normalize,* or *pessimize.* Optimizing involves denial by the actor. She or he either denies that anything of relevance was done or denies that what was done has any significance for definitions of deviance. In like fashion, the actor may engage in any of the other patterns of reaction—in this case, reaction to the reactions of others. These complex negotiations may produce a number of possible outcomes, some of which are illustrated below:

> Denial/transitory deviance: The actor and others deny the deviance (optimize, neutralize, or normalize); the deviance (*violation*—real or alleged) does not continue (control).

> Denial/hidden deviance: The actor and others deny the deviance (*violation;* optimize, neutralize, or normalize); the deviance continues, with the actor making some effort at concealment (collusion).

> Label/transitory deviance: Others define the behavior as deviant; status ascribing, stereotyping, and other processes of labeling develop. The actor is effectively constrained and discontinues deviance (real or alleged—control).

> Label/secondary deviance: Others define the behavior as deviant; status ascribing, stereotyping, deviance amplifying, and other labeling processes result in continued and increasing deviance (collusion).

Some patterns of interaction reinforce deviance and encourage adjustments and adaptations that, in turn, encourage subsequent and increasing deviance. Researchers have identified key processes that make some deviance persist. The following examples illustrate the processes:

> Master status: A deviance definition becomes the most salient quality of the person. For example, he or she becomes a "mental patient" and adopts the behaviors and attitudes of other patients.

> Role engulfment: As the deviant is treated as "nothing but" a certain kind of deviant, he or she increasingly defines himself or herself in those terms and acts accordingly. For example, a mental patient "accepts" his illness and participates cooperatively in "treatment."

> Secondary deviance: Following rejection by conventional people and groups, the actor adapts using his deviant status and acts in terms of the deviant definition—for example, "institutionalization."

Toward a General Theory of Mental Illness as Deviance

The things that count as mental illness are impressively diverse. The selection of residual rule violations as instances of mental illness is not arbitrary, but it cannot be explained by the characteristics of the chosen incidents. Mental illness is not an *objective* property or trait of any person or behavior. Accordingly, we cannot explain how some people come to "have it" and others do not. Instead, our task is to explain how mental illness is created through selection— that is, how it is negotiated.

Explaining Rates and Patterns of Mental Illness

As noted in Chapters 3 and 4, the explanation of deviance requires attention to the dialectics of *violation* and *sanction* and to the related matters of epidemiology and causation. The following presentation proceeds through the outline of the convergence theory of deviance. Recall that the central variable in the epidemiological theory is *integration*: As *integration* decreases, both *violation* and *social control* increase.

Rubington and Weinberg (1987:5–9) argued that certain conditions, or characteristics of roles and role relationships, facilitate the application of deviant definitions. They described the process as "typing" (or labeling) and identified variables that influence outcomes. Here typing refers to the selection of behavior and people as mentally ill. They offered the following observations: (1) Typing is most effective when the typer and the person typed share and understand the deviant definition, and (2) typing is most likely when people who have power and prestige do it, the alleged deviant is violating important norms or the deviance (*violation*) is extreme, it is negative rather than positive, and the audience benefits from the labeling.

Rubington and Weinberg also contended that there are differences in typing within formal and informal settings. Intimate groups are slower to type one of their own than are outsiders. Further, "experts" and other "third parties" (for example, psychiatrists) are charged with the responsibility and authority of identifying and treating most types of deviants. These third parties often facilitate or even force the typing. Rubington and Weinberg (1987) noted further that typing occurs within a cultural context.

These observations illustrate the selectivity of social control and suggest some of the variables that influence selection. The first postulate and the observations by Rubington and Weinberg suggest that rates of mental illness vary depending on characteristics of actors, typers, and the relationships between actors and typers.

Rubington and Weinberg's observations suggest the relevance of the *commonality* dimension of integration. The first observation points to the *effectiveness* of typing when understandings are shared. The remaining observations deal more with the probability or rate of typing when actors and typers are different. They focus on actor–typer interaction at a microscopic level, but the relationships may hold at broader levels as well. If commonality (shared understandings within a community or society) decreases, then the probability of typing increases. In the language of convergence theory, as integration decreases, social control increases.

The relevance of the "dynamic balance" dimension of integration is suggested in Rubington and Weinberg's observations about power, prestige, "values" ("important norms"), and benefits. Recall that integration has a special meaning from the Marxian point of view. It involves a delicate (perhaps even precarious) balance among parts of the system. Some tension among the parts is normal and a built-in feature of social systems. A decrease in integration means that tensions increase among the parts. Typing (social control) increases as tensions increase (integration decreases).

The demographics of mental illness in the United States suggest the relevance of the solidarity dimension of integration in the epidemiology of mental illness. With few exceptions, people who are most likely to be identified as mentally ill are those who are most different from the conventional majority: the poor, the marginally educated, those with low-status jobs, and those who are single or divorced. Rushing's (1978) research supporting the "status resources hypothesis" provides a partial summary of the effects of low solidarity on rates of mental illness. Taken together, the data suggest that mental illness rates will increase when solidarity decreases, because more instances will be selected for social control.

As noted earlier, mental illness is not a distinct class of behaviors or events. Empirically, mental illness does not exist until it has been "identified" or *selected*. As a result, it is difficult to examine rates of violation separately from rates of social control. The alternative understandings of mental illness as residual rule violations, problems of living, or troublesome behaviors (as described earlier in this chapter) provide a partial solution. Proposition *E2* suggests that such incidents or behaviors will increase as integration decreases. To date, no research documents rates of residual rule violations, problems of living, or troublesome behaviors. But for decades observers have predicted and described the effects of declining integration on the "quality of life." Most agree that the increasing size, complexity, and differentiation of modern Western societies produce increased rates of problems of living. At least in this general sense, integration and rates of violation are related in the ways suggested by the convergence theory.

Thomas Scheff (1963) has provided an excellent example of the application of Postulate 2 to questions of mental illness. Recall that Scheff proposed to understand mental illness as "residual rule violation." He contended that most instances of such violations are denied, disregarded, and transitory. However, when incidents are selected for social control, the stereotyped images of mental illness shape, stabilize, and sustain the behavior of concern. This shaping and sustaining happen as stereotypes are applied to the person and to his or her behavior by those who provide services (doctors, nurses) and, in many cases, by the actor. Thus, while residual rule violations are by nature diverse and highly variable, mental illness becomes patterned through the reactions of others and through the acceptance of stereotyped understandings by the patient.

The enormous and expensive field of mental health has not been able to reduce or eliminate mental illness. Those who accept the illness metaphor and others who have some stake in the system of services argue that the problem is simply too large to manage. They defend their limited success by pointing out that many suffer and few are identified and treated properly. This may be a correct assessment. Or perhaps the illness metaphor is neither accurate nor very useful. In that case, the mental health services system can be little more than a network of social control activities and agencies that select instances of violations (or problems of living or troublesome behaviors) and transform them into mental illness.

Explaining Causes of Mental Illness

Recall that the central variables in the causal theory are *integration, attachment,* and *learning violations:* as *integration* decreases, *attachment* decreases, and *learning* of *violations* increases.

Those who have proposed alternatives to the illness metaphor agree that the sources or causes of residual rule violations, problems of living, and troublesome behaviors are many and diverse. If the variety of things identified as mental illness do not belong to any single or identifiable class, as has been suggested, we will not have much success in finding common causes. With reservations and caution, I suggest a general characterization of the behaviors and events of concern. The proposed description draws most directly from Scheff's view:

> The behaviors and events that are most likely to be treated as instances of mental illness are violations of rules that are implicit, vague, and not otherwise labeled; these behaviors and instances represent a "residue" of concern among generally conventional people; the behaviors are seen as not so much wrong or evil as inappropriate and out of synchronism.

Edwin Lemert's (1967) study of paranoia provides an illustration of the causal process proposed by the convergence theory. People who are diagnosed as paranoid are believed to suffer from delusions, especially false beliefs that people are organized in some way against them. Cameron (1943), for example, asserted that the paranoid individual "organizes" real and imaginary others into a "pseudocommunity" that explains the person's problems and concerns—for example, "I feel afraid because people are trying to kill me." A primary ingredient in the psychiatric understanding of paranoia is that the fears and the pseudocommunity are totally or mostly imagined (they are *delusions*). To the contrary, Lemert found evidence that the concerns expressed by the "paranoics" in his study were based on *real* experiences. Those around them were acting differently and were engaging in suspicious, hostile, and even conspiratorial activities.

Perhaps most importantly, Lemert found that interactions in fact had changed in the direction of excluding those who were eventually diagnosed as paranoid. This *process of exclusion* provides a dramatic illustration of the relevance of *attachment* or, more accurately in this case, the effects of decreasing attachment. In the current analysis, attachment is examined at a microscopic, interpersonal level. The proposed theory focuses more at the macroscopic level of social organization and social niche. However, there is no reason to think that the process or structural characteristic of attachment is fundamentally different at different levels.

Can people *learn* the kinds of violations that may be selected as instances of mental illness? My proposed theory asserts that they can. Such learning may take different forms. For example, learning may occur within a context of limited resources and genetic vulnerability (Kohn, 1973). The result may be strategies for coping that solve some problems but create others. Or they could involve behaviors that are appropriate to the peculiar characteristics of the context but out of step with the larger community. In either case, the learning reflects the lack of attachment between the individual's most immediate niche(s) and the conventional order—those niches that are most closely connected to the norms and laws that are most likely to be enforced.

Learning may also occur during the process in which the individual becomes suspected, identified, or treated as mentally ill. Akers (1985:334–335) noted that therapists and other mental health professionals reinforce (usually inadvertently) patients' comments about being sick and other mental illness "symptoms." And people may learn coping strategies that fit the demands of a treatment situation but involve behaviors that are regarded as evidence of illness. For example, the bureaucracies of public mental hospitals appear to encourage passive, dependent, and even childlike behavior as part of efficient management of large numbers of people. It is possible also that "psychotic episodes" represent reactions to dependency, depersonalization, and other features of institutional life. Perhaps, ironically, these episodes are likely to be taken as further evidence or even confirmation of the original diagnosis—and the concept of mental illness.

More evidence of the learned quality of behaviors and events that may be identified as mental illness involves a measure of "backward" reasoning. Social learning programs have proved remarkably effective in dealing with people who have been diagnosed as mentally ill, including those who have been regarded as the most chronic and hopeless. These programs include behavior modification and "token economy" strategies in which desirable behaviors are systematically rewarded and undesirable behaviors are either punished or at least not rewarded. Inappropriate behaviors, including those described as psychotic and schizophrenic, have been substantially reduced through these programs (see Bandura, 1969; Lloyd and Abel, 1970; Curran, Monti, and Corrivean, 1982; and Akers, 1985, among others). Unfortunately, it is not yet clear whether the results can be sustained in a "real-life" setting in which rewards and punishments cannot be administered (manipulated) systematically. At any rate, the results of these programs suggest that the behaviors are responsive to learning—*perhaps because they were learned in the first place.*

Beyond Myth and Metaphor: Social Policy and Problems of Living

If "mental illness" is *at best* a metaphor, and certainly if the metaphor is inaccurate or just plain wrong, our current efforts at social control (treatment) cannot be effective. Consider, for example, the implications if the concept of problems of living is a better description of the behaviors and events of concern. Problems of living cannot be solved in a hospital where the individual is almost certainly removed from the context and the locus of the problem. Further, such problems probably cannot be solved by medication. In short, the entire medical establishment that encompasses efforts to deal with these problems could turn out to be a misguided and futile (even if well-intentioned) effort.

Should we abandon the entire medically oriented system? Certainly many would argue against that strategy. And such a move is probably at least premature. Still, the costs of continuing the current course are high. It is important that we continue at least to ask questions about the nature of the things we are trying to control. And programs based on the alternative understandings should be attempted experimentally. Efforts to enhance integration and attachment are implicated most specifically. If the issue is problems of living, relevant resources could be identified to improve people's abilities to find solutions.

Consider the example of schizophrenia. As described earlier, Kohn (1973) identified a combination of causal factors: the "conditions of life" of those in the lower social class, a resulting impairment in ability to deal with problems and stresses, and some genetic vulnerability. At least part of what Kohn described refers to the *marginality* (lack of attachment) of those who are at the bottom of the social organization. They receive few of the benefits (rewards and resources) of the extant organization. From the Marxian point of view, increased integration would mean increased participation in that organization, including a larger share of the benefits.

Those who are marginal in our society often share in the good life in a piecemeal fashion. For example, some pursue the dream of a happy and stable family life, but they do so without the necessary means of a job or income. Others find that they can buy a color television set with "nothing down" and a "small monthly payment," but they cannot get food or a place to live as easily. It is easy to criticize these lives, but recall the point: piecemeal participation in the American dream. It is not hard to imagine how such participation would stretch the resources and ability to cope of those involved. The marginality is in itself a problem that many Americans find too taxing. Real change requires access to the means for participating meaningfully and effectively. Sociologists long have known that social integration and various problems of living are related. Nearly 100 years ago, Durkheim's study revealed a clear link between levels of integration and suicide rates. We have yet to develop any program that builds directly on that knowledge.

Deterrence theory (especially as described in Chapter 6; see Silberman, 1976) suggests that "moral support" for rules and laws must be increased to reduce violations. In this case, the rules are residual in character and mostly unstated. How do you increase the moral support for rules that prescribe in a general way how long one can stare into space or what kinds of imaginings are acceptable? The answer is far from clear. Still, the general strategy is promising.

Consider the history of mental health as a policy. Less than a century ago, the idea of mental illness was novel or even radical. Those who promoted the idea and its implications got little support and often encountered stiff opposition. The people and behaviors of concern were regarded as evil and sinful— or worse. Gradually, the ideas of mental illness and health have caught on and have become more or less accepted and even supported financially and morally. Increased moral support *could* mean support for a particular way of understanding the problem. In contemporary American society, that could mean treating the issues as *problems of living* and working cooperatively to find solutions and provide the resources necessary to prevent or resolve the problems.

The Need for Research

Two general theories make up convergence theory. Each needs testing relative to the explanations of mental illness. The epidemiological theory asserts a relationship between levels of integration and types and rates of mental illness.

The causal theory asserts that mental illness types of behavior and definition are learned through social niches that are not closely attached to the conventional order.

RESEARCHING RATES AND PATTERNS OF PROBLEMS OF LIVING My proposed theory points to one area that desperately needs research: the rates and distributions of the behaviors and events that are likely to be identified as instances of mental illness. Studies of the epidemiology of mental illness, *which assume that certain kinds of illnesses exist and that they have recognizable symptoms*, have been done, with increasing sophistication over the years. What would we learn if we could somehow count the instances of residual rule violations or problems of living? That research is really no more difficult than other epidemiological studies. However, counting residual rule violations would allow a better estimate of the *selectivity* of mental illness. Moreover, with those data as the foundation, we could begin to identify systematically the variables that influence selection.

The proposed research would require careful and precise identification and description of the behaviors and events of concern. The list of things to be counted would include those symptoms that are recognized within current mental health diagnostic schemes (for example, the American Psychiatric Association's *Diagnostic and Statistical Manual of Mental Disorders*, or *DSM-III*). Obviously, however, we would need to include other kinds of behaviors and problems as well. These might be identified by cataloging the array of presenting problems that are included when mental health clinicians engage in diagnosing. The list probably would be enormous and diverse, and that finding, in itself, would provide empirical evidence for a major assertion of the proposed theories (social control is selective). The resulting collection might be reduced by some careful sampling so that a more manageable list of rule violating behaviors could be used. Data could be collected on a representative sample of the American population using either a survey questionnaire (anonymous self-report) or interviews.

This is, of course, only one of many studies that the proposed epidemiological theory suggests. Other studies are needed to test the relationships between levels of integration (with the different dimensions) and rates of mental illness.

RESEARCHING CAUSES OF MENTAL ILLNESS The concept of "attachment" here refers to linkages between social niches and the larger society and between individuals and the conventional order. People who are relatively unattached are at greater risk of developing patterns of violating behavior (especially those that may be identified as mental illness), because they experience various problems and they have few resources for managing the problems. Indeed, because of their lack of attachment, or marginality, low-income people and others who are less attached may have even more problems than others have.

Researchers could collect data to describe a representative sample of Americans beginning when the respondents are young (perhaps at age six or eight) and continuing at intervals over time (perhaps as long as 10 to 15 years). A British documentary describing similar research is ongoing (see "From Seven Up to Twenty-Eight," 1964).

Parents or guardians of the subjects would answer the first wave of questions. The questions would ask for information describing family composition, the location of the family within the general community (occupation, education, political and religious affiliations), and relationships to other groups and organizations within the community and society. Information of this sort would be used to characterize the nature and type of "attachment" of the family and its members. Other questions would concern experiences, especially of the subjects, including successes and failures in school, patterns of friendships, participation in sports and other leisure activities, hopes and aspirations, and events or incidents that involve some trouble or problem (an accident or injury or referral to a principal or the juvenile court, for example). Data would be collected subsequently every two or three years. The questions would be substantially the same in an effort to document events, experiences, and changes over time. The respondents would be able to answer the questions themselves in the survey's later stages.

Such a study could identify variations in types and levels of attachment and relate those to experiences that involve problems and violations of residual rules. The research would follow a familiar pattern called the "panel" design. Further description of the method can be found in Bachman, O'Malley, and Johnston, 1978.

Violence

A man in his mid-thirties describes himself and his assaultive behavior:

> I was a good provider for my family and a hard worker. My boss considered me a much better than average employee. He thought that I was a reliable, loyal, and honest worker. Many customers even called and said how nice and polite a driver that I was. I got along good with everybody. My boss knew that I was a very reserved individual and never said anything out of the way to people.
>
> My wife thought that I was boring and a narrow man because my interests and time were completely monopolized by sports and t.v. It disgusted her that all I wanted to do was come home, take my shirt off, sip on a beer, eat, and watch t.v. and then go to different sports events on the weekends with my kids. . . .
>
> She said that I was too rigid and bossy. She felt that I forced her to accept all my decisions with threats about what I would do

if she didn't. I know I sure frightened her when I got mad because
I did let her know that she better damn well accept my decisions
and not complain about it too much. I was a hardworking man,
a good provider, and generous to my family, so there shouldn't
have been any complaints from her about who gave the orders,
what I did, and the rest. But I still had to let her know from time
to time that she better not take her crap too far.

I was out of town, and I called my wife one night to check on
what was going on at home. She told me that she had seen an
attorney and was filing papers to divorce me. I asked her to hold
off until I got back home and could sit down and talk it over with
her, but she said, "No, this time I really mean it." After she told
me that, I blew up and said, "You better not do that to me; if you
do, you'll be sorry for it." She said, "I had a restraining order
placed on you, so if you come around here bothering me, the
police will get you." I said, "If I really want to get you, the police
can't save you." I thought that telling her that would scare her,
but it didn't. She just acted calm and confident like she had
everything all planned out. That got me madder. . . . I figured
that I had to get home and confront her face to face. I just felt
plain mad. I hung up the phone and headed straight for
home. . . .

When I did get home three hours later, she was in bed asleep.
I woke her up and told her to get up, that I wanted to talk. I told
her if she stopped with the divorce, and that I would promise to
act better and . . . but she wouldn't buy any of it. I got angrier
and angrier. Then she came out and said, "Look, please do me
this favor and give me a divorce." At that moment I felt cold
hatred for her inside me. I told myself that I better leave before
I exploded on her, but then I decided to hell with it, and I looked
at her straight in the face and said, "Well, X, you better start
thinking about those poor kids of ours." She said, "I don't care
about them; I just want a divorce."

My hate for her exploded then, and I said, "You dirty, no-
good bitch," and started pounding her in the face with my fist.
She put her arms up and covered her face, so I ran and got my
rifle and pointed it at her. I said, "Bitch, you better change your
mind fast or I'm going to kill you." She looked up and said in a
smart-ass way, "Go ahead then, shoot me." I got so mad and felt
so much hate for her, that I just started shooting her again and
again [Athens, 1980:46–48].

A Sociological Conception of Violence

Most people would agree that the preceding description involves violence. Yet the exact meaning of violence is elusive. *Webster's* defines *violence* as "exertion of physical force so as to injure or abuse" (Mish, 1983). Some violent acts are prohibited by criminal law, including those of murder, manslaughter, rape, and aggravated assault. Others are prohibited by law, but have been overlooked for the most part until recently. Child abuse and wife battering would be examples. Still other behaviors are (or have been) regarded as violent at some times but not at others. Swaddling, for example, is a practice that most contemporary Americans would find abusive. It involves wrapping infants in layers of cloth to form tight and constraining bundles. The wrapping restricts virtually all movement and encourages sleep and lethargy. It tends to be unsanitary because the wrappings are changed infrequently. Nonetheless, physicians and other "experts" recommended it in eighteenth- and nineteenth-century America.

As always, we need to be clear and precise in specifying the acts and events of interest—as we have seen in previous discussions of prostitution and mental illness. The conception of violence must be as generic and as empirically specific as possible. And the definition needs to recognize the probabilistic character of violence. That is, whether or not something is violent must remain an empirical question.

Let's begin by distinguishing between general violence and deviant social violence. *Violence* can be defined as the exertion of force that results in physical damage, harm, injury, or pain. *Social violence* is the use of force in social relationships that results in personal harm, injury, or pain, or in socially defined discomfort or pain. It includes fist-fights, acts of intimidation and oppression, and wife battering, for example—depending upon prevailing social definitions. *Deviant social violence*, then, is social violence that is coupled with some kind of social control. Consider the matter of "wife abuse." Traditional American values endorse male dominance in marital relationships. Some evidence (described in the discussion of "rule of thumb" in "Explaining Rates and Patterns of Violence") suggests that courts of law supported husbands' use of physical "punishment." Within some limits, such punishment was regarded as neither violent nor deviant, yet laws prohibited wife beating. And contemporary standards condemn the use of physical force by husbands or wives. Today, punching is likely to be regarded as both violent and deviant and, more specifically, as spouse abuse. What is or is not violent or deviant is a matter of negotiation.

In the discussions that follow, we will consider two major types of violent acts and events: (1) murder and aggravated assault (excluding those that occur as parts of other crimes) and (2) family violence. Each will be described through the use of the conceptual framework (social organization, social niche, and social action). Then I will present theories (epidemiological and causal—convergence theory) and examine relevant research to evaluate the explanations.

Murder and Aggravated Assault

Officially, the offenses of murder and aggravated assault are closely related. In fact, the difference between them often is a matter of degree. The Federal Bureau of Investigation defines *murder* as "nonnegligent killing of one human being by another." *Aggravated assault* is defined as "an unlawful attack by one person upon another person for the purpose of inflicting severe or aggravated bodily injury." The definitions are elaborated in an effort to distinguish murder, aggravated assault, assault to murder, and attempted murder. The point is that even official government agencies find it necessary to make subjective judgments in distinguishing these categories of crimes (see Flanagan and Jamieson, 1988:562–563).

The Social Organization of Murder and Aggravated Assault

The descriptions that follow draw heavily from *Uniform Crime Report* data, collected by local police departments and collated for the Federal Bureau of Investigation. The data are summarized and published annually in the *Sourcebook of Criminal Justice Statistics* and *Crime in the United States*. These data reflect crimes known to the police for selected years. There are at least two kinds of problems with using these "official" data. First, not all offenses are reported to or discovered by the police, not all reported offenses are recorded, and the recording may not always be done carefully, consistently, or accurately. However, police data on homicides and, to a lesser extent, on aggravated assaults, appear to be reasonably representative of the total of such offenses. Second, some of the data describe only specific years. These data must be used carefully in the effort to describe patterns that seem to have persisted over years.

SOCIAL CHARACTERISTICS OF ASSAILANTS AND THEIR VICTIMS The victims of murder are disproportionately male (75 percent), young (33 percent are between age 20 and 29), and black (41 percent). Keep in mind that only about 12 percent of the U.S. population are black. Likewise, murderers are disproportionately male (87 percent), young (69 percent are between age 15 and 34), and black (45 percent). The proportion of offenders who are black is nearly four times their proportion of the population (Flanagan and McGarrell,

1986:386–387, 417–418, 420; see also the National Center for Health Statistics on youth homicides in Needham, 1988).

Murder usually involves victims and offenders of the same sex and race. In 1985, for example, 83 percent of all murdered males were killed by other males. There is an interesting exception: Men also kill women. Males murdered 90 percent of all females killed. This underscores the fact that males are disproportionately represented as offenders. Ninety-four percent of all black victims were killed by blacks, and 88 percent of all white victims were killed by whites. Approximately 59 percent of all murders were committed with guns (43 percent with handguns). Murder often involves people who are related or at least acquainted. Approximately 59 percent of murders involved victims and offenders who were relatives, friends, or acquaintances. In addition, 39 percent followed arguments, with the focus of the disagreement typically described as "trivial" by witnesses and police (see U.S. Department of Justice, 1986:8–12, 181–182).

An early study by Marvin Wolfgang (1958) and later work by Mulvihill and Tumin (1969) suggest that alcohol and other drugs are routinely a part of homicides. Wolfgang (1958:136) reports that alcohol was present in the victim, offender, or both in 64 percent of the homicide cases in his study. Mulvihill, Tumin (1969:648–649) report the presence of alcohol in as many as 83 percent of the cases.

The national homicide rate in 1985 was 7.9 per 100,000 population and the South led geographic regions with a rate of 10.0. In contrast, New England states had a rate of only 3.2 (U.S. Department of Justice, 1986:7–8, 52–62). This regional variation will be considered further in the following section on subcultures of violence.

There are striking similarities between aggravated assault and homicide patterns. Offenders and victims in both are disproportionately young, black, male, and of low socioeconomic status. Some research suggests that alcohol is present in a high proportion of both types of offenses (Thum, Wechsler, and Demone, 1973). However, although the majority of homicides involve acquaintances, most assault cases, at least as reported to the police, involve strangers. And unlike homicides, most aggravated assaults do not involve firearms (see Bureau of Justice Statistics, 1985). Finally, William Wilbanks (1985) has suggested that blacks are slightly more likely to assault whites than are whites to assault black victims.

SOCIAL CLASS AND THE SUBCULTURE OF VIOLENCE Research to date suggests that offenders and victims are disproportionately lower class, with relatively low education and occupational prestige. Note, however, that official data tend not to provide information on social class. The apparent concentration of murders among the poor has led researchers to pursue hypotheses about poverty and income inequality as causes or explanations of homicide. The research here is solid but difficult to summarize and inconclusive. The major studies are described briefly in the following paragraphs.

Judith and Peter Blau (1982) examined murder and assault rates for the 125 largest metropolitan areas in the United States in 1970. They found that the South had the highest violence rates and that violence rates were positively correlated with both the proportion of blacks and with levels of absolute poverty in the metropolitan areas. But there is an important qualification. When the researchers introduced controls for income inequality across the communities, the relationships among "southernness," poverty, proportion of black residents, and homicide rates disappeared or were reduced substantially. Blau and Blau were convinced by their analyses that the critical variable for understanding homicide rates is *income inequality.*

Steven Messner (1982) studied homicide rates in 204 standard metropolitan statistical areas. He found that racial composition and regional location were related to homicide. His data did *not* support the conclusion that income inequality is related to homicide rates. Instead, he found that poverty and homicide rates were related—but not positively. Those communities with less poverty had the *highest* rates of homicide. In a subsequent study, Messner (1983) again found that income inequality was *not* related to homicide rates, but poverty was—inversely: High poverty areas had low murder rates. William Bailey (1984) replicated Messner's work, but focused on data from central cities rather than metropolitan areas generally. Bailey found that poverty is positively related to homicide rates. Like Messner, he found no significant relationship between homicide rates and income inequality.

What is the relationship among poverty, income inequality, and homicide rates? It is not possible to say on the basis of this research. However, the question is raised again later in the presentation of the general theories of violence. Perhaps poverty is a partial measure of levels of integration. In that case, integration would be a key variable and might provide a basis for interpreting these apparently contradictory findings.

Some suspect that violence is a part of our American tradition (see Graham and Gurr, 1969; Wolfgang and Ferracuti, 1967). Our nation was born in war and has grown up with a frontier tradition, which includes the gun as an essential tool for survival. Our national history also includes witch hunts and lynch mobs. And vigilante groups and movements have been and continue to be a part of our cultural heritage and contemporary experience. The Ku Klux Klan, "survivalists," "Posse Comitatus" (involving mostly Midwestern farmers with strong commitments to resist various government actions), and other citizen protest and resistance groups frequently have used violence or threats of violence to express their point of view or pursue their aims. And violence has an obvious and apparently secure place in movies, novels, and other forms of entertainment and leisure activity in modern America.

Wolfgang (1958; Wolfgang and Ferracuti, 1967) argued that violence is an integral part of our culture and describes a "subculture of violence," defined in part as follows:

> Violence can become a part of the life style, the theme of solving difficult problems or problem situations. It should be stressed that the problems and situations to which we refer arise mostly within the subculture, for violence is used mostly between persons and groups who themselves rely upon the same supportive values and norms. A carrier and user of violence will not be burdened by conscious guilt, then, because generally he is not attacking representatives of the nonviolent culture, and because the recipient of this violence may be described by similar class status, occupational, residential, age, and other attribute categories which characterize . . . the subculture of violence [Wolfgang and Ferracuti, 1967:161].

There is an interesting complexity here. Wolfgang and Ferracuti appear to provide an explanation of violence as a characteristic of lower class, young adult males (as described above). In fact, Wolfgang (1958) provided a compelling case in his earlier work, linking attitudes and behavior, on the one hand, and social control, on the other. He contrasted the subculture of violence with value systems that are the source of official social control: "The upper-middle and upper social class value system defines and codifies behavioral norms into legal rules that often transcend subcultural mores, and considers any of the social and personal stimuli that evoke a combative reaction in the lower classes as 'trivial' " (Wolfgang, 1958:188–189).

However, there are several problems with this thesis. First, empirical evidence of the described subculture is mixed to weak at best (Ball-Rokeach, 1973; Erlanger, 1974, 1975; Magura, 1975; Huff-Corzine, Corzine, and Moore, 1986). Second, some research suggests that violent attitudes and behaviors are not peculiar to lower social classes. Stark and McEvoy (1970:52–53) noted that "Physical violence is reported as equally common among all income groups and education levels. This finding is also true for frequency of physical violence. The middle class is not only as likely as others ever to have engaged in physical aggression, but has done so as often. If anything, the middle class is more prone toward physical assault (punching, beating, slapping) than the poor." And third, there is no reason to believe that the violence of murder and assault are different in any significant way from the violence of lynch mobs, professional crimes (such as contract murder and assassination), or war. Violence may be a subtle but pervasive feature of the social organization and culture of our society—or, perhaps, of all societies.

At least one other dimension of social organization reflects the "normalcy" or routine character of violence in American life: gun ownership and the dedicated efforts to protect the "right" of such ownership. James Wright and his colleagues (1983:xiii; 26–35) estimated that 100 million firearms are in private hands in the United States. They estimated further that guns are owned in something approaching 50 percent of American households and that as many as 7 percent of American adults carry a handgun while outside their homes. And they noted that the annual death toll from firearms is approximately 30,000. They summarized: "Directly or indirectly, firearms violence threatens the quality of life in the society as a whole" (Wright, Rossi, and Daly, 1983:xiv).

Wright and his colleagues examined research on the reasons for owning guns, and focused especially on "fear of crime." They challenged earlier claims that report evidence that "fear of crime" has produced an epidemic of gun ownership (Wright, Rossi, and Daly, 1983; Newton and Zimring, 1969; Spiegler and Sweeney, 1975). Although systematic evidence of this motive clearly is problematic, many people continue to believe that others are arming themselves for self-protection. An interesting, if frightening, irony is suggested by data from a survey of some 2,000 convicted felons in various state prisons (see Wright and Rossi, 1986). Fifty-eight percent reported that they acquired hand-guns for *self-protection,* and 28 percent reported that they had guns to use in the commission of crimes. These findings encourage speculation about the nature of gun ownership. Could we find ourselves in a spiral in which more criminals carry guns to protect themselves from victims who they assume will be armed—to protect themselves? Whatever the outcome may be, gun ownership and some idea that guns are good and necessary for the purpose of protection are a part of modern America.

Violence *is patterned* and not simply a collection of random events—at least within our contemporary society. It is tempting to describe violence as essentially a lower-class, minority activity and to seek explanations in terms of the characteristics of the offenders and their victims. However, we should remember that violence comes in a variety of forms, many of which do not involve significant numbers of poor, young, black men. For example, only one in five mass murderers is black (see Levin and Fox, 1985:51). Likewise, blacks historically have been underrepresented in violence related to organized crime, professional murder (that is, "murder for hire"), and industrial violence (for example, labor union strikes and efforts to break strikes).

Violence is a part of the social organization of our society. We see it in the demographic patterns of offenders and victims, in the relationship (complex as it is) between social class and homicide and assault, in the general norms and subculture of violence, and in our love-hate relationship with guns and their ownership. In addition, violence is reflected in the diverse social niches of American society. The following discussions describe these patterns.

The Social Niches and Social Actions of Violent Crimes

It was a crazy summer. The summer of '68. We fought the cops in the streets.
I mean sure nuff punch-out fighting like in them Wild West movies and
do. . . . We fought that whole summer. Cop cars all over the place and
they'd come jumping out with night sticks and fists balled up. They wore
leather jackets and gloves and sometimes they be wearing them football
helmets so you couldn't go upside they heads without hurting your
hand. . . . All you need be doing was walking down the avenue and here
they come. Screeching the brakes. Pull up behind you and three or four
cops come busting out the squad car ready to rumble. . . .

That's the way it was. Seem like we was fighting cops every day. Funny
thing was, it was just fighting. Wasn't no shooting or nothing like that.
Somebody musta put word out from Downtown. You can whip the niggers'
heads but don't be shooting none of em. Yeah. Cause the cops would get
out there and fight but they never used no guns. Might bust you skull with
a nightstick but they wasn't gon shoot you. So the word must have been
out. Cause you know if it was left to the cops they would have blowed us
all away [Wideman, 1984:112].

This brief description of race riots in the late 1960s illustrates a context
in which violence is a salient and integral feature of group and interpersonal
relationships. Scenes such as these became familiar to residents of urban
America, and to others across the country and around the world, courtesy of
television news reports. Collectively, they represent a significant chapter in the
history of violence in the United States. But even in their entirety, they represent
a small portion of social niches in which violence is endemic. The following
would be among the more obvious examples of "violence-salient" niches: urban
youth gangs and their territories; motorcycle gangs and the assorted places that
they enter and occupy; certain bars, taverns, and pool halls; professional hockey
matches and, to some extent, other professional sports events; high school
football games.

We could examine each of these niches, and others as well, to describe in
detail their physical contexts and the social roles, relationships, and rationales
that give them their distinctive character. The analyses, undoubtedly, would
provide insight into the social realities of violence and deviant violence. However, research to date does not provide sufficient detail to allow a description
of the specific settings, or of any general "violence-prone" setting. Instead,
there is research describing violence as it develops within interaction. One
author, whose research is described in the following paragraphs, refers to
violence as a "situated transaction." This concept collapses the distinction
between *social niches* and *social actions*, as those have been discussed in
previous chapters. Given the limits of available data, it seems useful to follow

that lead. Accordingly, the research on "situated transactions" and "victim precipitation" form the foundation for the current descriptions of the niches and social action of violent crime. Following that, I will introduce research on "subcultures of violence" and "definitions of situations" to describe the kinds of *rationales* that appear to operate within the settings and to organize the activities that produce "violent" outcomes.

SETTINGS, ROLES, AND RELATIONSHIPS David Luckenbill (1977:179–185) described six stages of interpersonal activities through which murder is "produced" as an *outcome*:

> An offensive remark is made or a challenge is issued in some fashion.
>
> The actions are interpreted as personally offensive or threatening by the "offender."
>
> The offender retaliates with some action designed to "save face"; sometimes death or injury occurs at this stage.
>
> The victim retaliates, the violence escalates; sometimes others in or near the situation become involved.
>
> Both offender and victim are now committed to a violent resolution of the conflict; it is at this stage that weapons often are produced.
>
> The police or other social control agents become involved; the victim is dead or dying; the offender may flee, be restrained by others, or call the police himself, among other possibilities.

These "transactions" are only illustrative and suggest the roles and relationships that surround many murder and assault situations (see Felson and Steadman, 1983). Transactions take different forms in different settings and the content of the activities vary greatly (for example, what weapons are produced and the character of the offending remarks). Still, the description captures some of the social and relational realities and patterns of social action that are relevant. The events typically involve *interactions* that include threats and face-saving gestures and activities. Two key processes occur: Tensions escalate and nonviolent options are reduced. And the transactions clearly are *interactive*. The victim plays an active role in his or her own demise.

The idea that victims contribute to their victimization is not new, and empirical evidence increasingly supports it (Bullock, 1955; Curtis, 1975; Luckenbill, 1977). Wolfgang (1958:252) has offered the following definition:

> The term victim-precipitated is applied to those criminal homicides in which the victim is a direct, positive precipitator in the crime. The role of the victim is characterized by his having been the first in the homicide

drama to use physical force directed against his subsequent slayer. The victim-precipitated cases are those in which the victim was the first to show and use a deadly weapon, to strike a blow in an altercation—in short, the first to commence the interplay of resort to physical violence.

Wolfgang restricted victim-precipitation to those instances when the victim starts the violence. It may be useful to include other kinds of victim behavior (for example, verbal taunts or gestures that are interpreted as provocative whether or not the victim intended that). In any case, the concept highlights again the importance of settings, roles, relationships, and patterned social action. Other variables operate within situations and with some regularity to increase the likelihood of violence. For example, values and attitudes that are parts of cultural and subcultural arrangements appear to be important. These can be understood as *rationales*, shared understandings that organize the activities within the settings.

RATIONALES THAT SUPPORT OR PROMOTE VIOLENCE There may or may not be an identifiable "subculture of violence." (This issue was raised and considered earlier in this chapter.) In any case, certain persisting social attitudes and values favor, encourage, and endorse violent reactions and "solutions" to some kinds of "problems." Lynn A. Curtis (1975:62) described one cluster or *niche* that illustrates the point:

> The economic marginality of [black] street corner men commonly results in quick changing and undefined relationships with women. As a result, there is considerable disagreement and distrust about sexual faithfulness. Jealousy quickly can be turned against male competitors. Simultaneously, the contraculture encourages a strong sense of honor, a very brittle sensitivity that can easily be cracked in the course of street rap, drinking, and verbal abuse. "He's a man and I'm a man, and don't take no shit like that."

Ronald Akers (1985:268) has identified other "attitudes": "There is a generalized norm against physical attack, maiming, or killing others, but at the same time there are familiar excuses for doing just that. Thus violence is justified if it is 'unavoidable,' 'in time of war against the enemy,' or 'in self-defense,' or if 'legitimate channels are closed off,' 'that is the only way to get things done,' 'the other person deserves it,' 'you are forced into it'." Lonnie Athens (1980) identified a special group of attitudes or definitions, which he called "violent interpretations of situations." Athens's work on violence and the symbolic interactionist perspective on which it is based (see Blumer 1962) remind us of the importance of meaning in human behavior. (Recall discussions of Weber's contributions to the proposed theories of deviance, as discussed in Chapters 2 and 3.)

Athens has contended that violence occurs when there is a convergence between particular kinds of "*self*-definitions" and particular kinds of *violent interpretations of situations*. He has defined and illustrated types of self-definitions, which he calls *self-images:* violent, incipient violent, and nonviolent (1980:39–44). He also has described kinds of violent interpretations of situations: physically defensive, frustrative, malefic, and frustrative-malefic. His description focuses on the person who becomes violent, called "the actor" in the following accounts (19–27).

> Physically defensive: the actor defines the situation as one in which either the victim will soon physically attack him or someone about whom he cares, or as one in which the victim already is attacking.

> Frustrative: the actor sees the situation as one in which either the victim is resisting or will resist a specific line of action that the actor wants to pursue, or as one in which the victim is indicating that the actor should cooperate in a line of action that the actor does not desire.

> Malefic: the actor sees the situation as one in which the victim is deriding or belittling him and he defines the victim as an extremely malicious or evil person.

> Frustrative-malefic: combines ingredients of the two preceding categories; the actor sees the situation as one in which his efforts are or will be blocked by the victim, or one in which the victim is indicating that the actor should cooperate with a line of action that is not desired by the actor, *and* the actor sees the victim as extremely malicious or evil [Athens, 1980:19–27].

Each of the preceding interpretations includes a definition that indicates to the actor that a violent response is required from him. According to Athens, violence occurs when self-images are linked in particular ways to violent interpretations of situations. Actors who held nonviolent self-images committed violent acts only when they held "physically defensive" definitions of situations. Those with incipient violent self-definitions committed acts of violence only when they held "physically defensive" or "frustrative-malefic" definitions. Finally, actors with violent self-definitions committed acts of violence in situations defined in terms of any of the violent interpretations.

The effort to understand violence can benefit from expanding the description to include a second major type. I will describe family violence using the conceptual framework. Following that, I will introduce and discuss epidemiological and causal theories of violence.

Family Violence

People in our society seem to believe that child abuse, wife abuse, and other forms of family violence are new to human experience. In fact, they are new only in the sense that they have just recently come to be regarded as matters of public concern. And even that conclusion is subject to challenge. For example, Davidson (1977:4) has reported on early American laws and observed that "It is a shock to read laws from the 1800s which regulated wife beating: not criminalized it, but permitted it. Expected it. Accepted it." In contrast, Elizabeth Pleck (1979) reported that most states during that time *did* have laws prohibiting wife beating; states without such prohibitions were the exception. As I will describe later in this chapter, it seems clear that laws did prohibit wife beating. However, they were not the source of meaningful efforts of social control.

In a sense, child abuse was invented—or at least discovered. Historical records reveal that children have been vulnerable to violence, including infanticide, abandonment, swaddling, and selling into slavery, for much of recorded history (Mause, 1974). Americans were sufficiently concerned about abuse and exploitation of children that organizations such as the New York Society for the Prevention of Cruelty to Children developed as a part of a "child-saving" movement in the late 1800s (Platt, 1969). Compulsory public education and the juvenile court emerged at about the same time. These developments signaled the formal and official recognition of childhood as a special time.

From one point of view, this recognition of the special needs of children represented a humane development and was an effort to reduce victimization (Pickett, 1969). From a different vantage point, it represented manipulation and, potentially, exploitation of a different type (Platt, 1969). Legislation was enacted to protect children from neglect. That same legislation was used to remove children from immigrant families and place them in settings where they could learn the value of work and other traditional American values. Compulsory education created the opportunity to learn, and it effectively removed children from competition in the job market. By the middle of the twentieth century, most Americans believed that we had come a long way in humanizing the treatment of children. They saw around them a nation benefiting from social progress, dedicated to the care and education of its children, and prospering in an era that emphasized individual achievement and success.

The discovery of the "battered child syndrome" in the 1950s was undoubtedly unsettling to those who learned of it. The discovery was made by pediatric radiologists who found abnormal patterns of bone fractures and scar tissue in children—patterns that accidents could not explain (McCaghy, 1985:173). In less than 20 years, all 50 states had child abuse laws, and by the early 1970s, procedures had developed to increase the likelihood of identifying and treating abused children and abusing families. Most of those who have researched the topic agree that physical abuse of children is not new. Instead, changing social circumstances created a context in which two things happened: (1) People publicly acknowledged that children are sometimes subjected to physical violence, and (2) elected officials and other authorities (for example, physicians and teachers) decided that privacy in the home is *not* sacred and can be violated for higher purposes—in this case, the protection of children.

Most people in our society regard spouse abuse fundamentally as a problem of husbands mistreating and beating their wives. American society and Western cultures in general have a history of exploitation of women: Cultural values that emphasize dependency and domestic responsibilities have limited opportunities and supported the use of physical punishment of wives by their husbands, laws and legal precedents have implied or asserted that women are the property of their husbands, and traditions have favored privacy in the home over protection of rights and safety. As with child abuse, recognition of the problem of wife abuse came quickly once it started. But little attention has been given to husband abuse. Straus, Gelles, and Steinmetz (1980) reported research results that suggest that husbands are about as likely as wives to be victims of spouse abuse. We know almost nothing about this kind of family violence. Thus, some thirty years after discovering family violence, we remain uncertain how to define or measure it. In practice, abuse is whatever is so recognized by those who have authority.

This practical definition is at least close to the definition of deviance that I have proposed and discussed throughout this book. The general topic has been identified as "family violence." My proposed definition of family violence will make some distinctions that are not obvious in the practical definition. First, abuse of or violence against family members could include sexual activities (incest) and moral subversion (teaching values that differ from or conflict with those of the general society). The discussion here will be limited to acts, episodes, and patterns of physical violence, with violence defined as it was at the beginning of this chapter. More specifically, attention will focus on patterns of physical violence involving people who are members of a common family (broadly defined). Second, the fundamental distinction between *violation* and *deviance* will apply here, as it has elsewhere throughout this work. Thus, *deviant* family violence is physical violence that is connected in some fashion to some act or acts of social control. With these distinctions in mind, we can see that whether or not something is abuse will vary from time to time and place to place. As with other kinds of deviance, family violence is a matter of probability and must be determined empirically.

Social Organization and Family Violence

Straus, Gelles, and Steinmetz (1980) used a very encompassing definition of abuse in a survey of 1,146 parents and found that 63 percent had engaged in at least one violent act against their children. The definition of *violence* included slapping and all other acts that did or were intended to cause pain or injury. It is impossible to know what proportion of those actions resulted in any social control response or to estimate what proportion would be likely to produce such a response. More specifically, these researchers report that approximately 58 percent of the parents slapped or spanked their children, nearly 41 percent were involved in pushing, grabbing, or shoving, and slightly more than 13 percent hit their children with something. There is almost certainly disagreement about the classification of these acts as violent or abusive. These researchers also found that approximately 3 percent of their respondents kicked, bit, or hit with a fist, nearly 1.5 percent reported beating up their children, and approximately .2 percent threatened to use or in fact used a knife or gun against their children.

What is the rate of child abuse in the United States? It is very hard to say on the basis of these data. The researchers estimate that between one and one-half and two million children were vulnerable to injury during the survey year, 1976. However, the estimate must be treated with caution for a variety of reasons: The definition of violence is very broad, the research involved self-reported behavior, and the sample did not include single-parent families. The National Crime Survey (NCS) provides some additional data for considering rates of child abuse. The Bureau of Justice Statistics sponsors this annual survey. Each year, approximately 132,000 people representing 60,000 households are interviewed and asked to recount their experiences as victims of various types of crime. Through that method, some information is created to describe incidents of child victimization that the respondents regard as criminal and are able and willing to report. Recognizing the *severe* limits of this methodology, Klaus and Rand (1984:3) estimated an annual average of 19,000 child victimizations between 1973 and 1981.

In a separate survey, Straus, Gelles, and Steinmetz (1980) questioned 2,143 couples about violence within their homes. Their data suggest that there is at least one beating during the course of marriage for approximately 13 percent of couples in the United States. Sixteen percent of the couples experienced at least one act of violence each year. (Violence is defined here as kicking or punching, hitting or trying to hit with some object, beating, threatening with a knife or gun, using a knife or gun against a spouse.) Langan and Innes (1986) reported data suggesting that more than 450,000 incidents of spouse abuse were reported to interviewers by victims in 1984. However, the researchers do not make clear whether or not this number includes violence by wives against husbands.

It is not currently possible to describe the epidemiology of family violence. Existing evidence is not adequate to support conclusions about the relationships between such violence and social class, race, and assorted other demographic variables. McCaghy (1985:176–177) reviewed research by Zigler (1980), Straus and associates (1980), and Berger (1980a, 1980b) and suggested that there is some relationship between child abuse and gender, marital status, social class, and sociogeographic location. Specifically, such violence may be concentrated among women, and especially women who are single parents, in low-income families, and in families that are isolated physically or socially from neighbors and the community.

Social organization may affect child abuse and spouse abuse in a somewhat more subtle way. Gelles (1973) and Straus and associates (1980) reported on *stress* as a contributor to family violence. Gelles identified several types of stress, but what he calls "structural stress" is of greatest interest here. Structural stress results from social isolation, unemployment, and other social experiences. Straus, Gelles, and Steinmetz (1980) created a "stress index" composed of 18 items (including work-related setbacks and money troubles) believed to be stressful. The research suggests a complex relationship between stress thus measured and child abuse: Stress has a significant effect on child abuse among middle-income families but not among the very poor or the rich.

The Social Niches and Social Actions of Family Violence

We had just finished supper and my stepfather told my brother to wash the dishes, but he refused. My stepfather was drunk, and he started throwing dishes off the table. My mother tried to clear the table before he broke all the dishes, and he smacked her in the face. My brother got up and ran for the back door, but my stepfather cut him off and told him not to leave the kitchen. My mind was on getting out of there as fast as I could before he got me. I got up from the table, but he pushed me back down in the chair and said, "You better not move from that chair until I tell you or I'll beat your ass good just like I did on your birthday." My mother and brother cleared the dishes left on the table and started washing them. He just stood there glaring at us until the dishes were done. Then he told us all to go into the living room. He bolted the front door shut, and my brother turned on the t.v. My stepfather then turned it off so hard that it broke the knob clean off, and he began yelling at my brother again about the dishes [Athens, 1980:56].

The description above illustrates some episodes of family violence, to the extent that they have been described in the research literature. It highlights what some researchers see as kinds of *relationships* that may encourage, support, or allow violent actions and reactions (Berger, 1980a, 1980b). Dailey (1979) contends that the authority structure of the family contains the potential for violence against children. Since the emergence of the idea of childhood, American beliefs have increasingly represented children as incompetent and dependent. Parents are responsible for raising children, teaching them necessary skills and values, and controlling their conduct. However, our culture has never provided much guidance or training in the skills, approaches, or strategies for accomplishing those tasks. Dailey maintains that, given these circumstances, violence fulfills at least two functions for parents: (1) Pain and fear promote compliance among children, who have few alternatives, and (2) the authority of parents is highlighted and reinforced. Family violence, then, is not an aberration of family relationships, but an integral and routine feature of such relationships in our society. For Dailey, the question becomes "Why isn't there more family violence?"

Dailey's thesis helps account for the prevalence of violent acts in American families, but it does not explain why that violence is sometimes frequent and extreme. (Recall the finding from Straus, Gelles, and Steinmetz, 1980, that 63 percent of their sample had engaged in at least one violent act against their children in the preceding year.) Perhaps frequency and severity of abuse are related to the power imbalance in the relationships. If so, we will need to describe family patterns in order to identify the specific character of the relevant roles and relationships.

Many believe that those who are abused as children grow up to become abusive parents, and there is some support for that suspicion (Gelles, 1974). Though somewhat indirect, Garbarino and Gilliam's (1980) research provides some evidence that abuse is learned. These researchers found that one-third of those who had been reported as victims of abuse later were referred to juvenile court. Those who were referred to court for violent offenses were even more likely to have been referred earlier as victims of abuse. And a substantial proportion of "aggressive delinquents" had been subjected to "severe parental discipline."

Violent behavior between husbands and wives is also widespread. Moreover, Laner and Thompson (1982) reported that courting couples abuse one another: 60 percent reported abusive or aggressive behavior within their relationships. Straus (1976) pointed to power relationships as important in this type of family violence as well. Specifically, he sees traditional sexual inequalities and sexist male-female relationships as a source of support for wife abuse. It is not clear how power or other characteristics of "couple relationships" are related to the abuse of husbands or boyfriends. However, women may use violence against their male partners in response to abuse by those men. Gelles (1979:137–142) and Straus (1980:31–33) suggest this interpretation and contend that men are more violent and dangerous than their female partners are.

THE ROLES, RELATIONSHIPS, AND RATIONALES OF FAMILY VIOLENCE
Richard Gelles (1974) has described seven types of violent situations and provided some further description of relevant characteristics of social niches for family violence. The first type is "violence as a threat." In this situation, the actor engages in violence against an inanimate object to threaten, or as if to threaten what might be done. The second, "normal violence," is focused on achieving some acceptable end. The victim typically agrees that she or he deserved it or needed it. An example would be a slap in the face to interrupt some hysterical reaction. Gelles described "secondary violence" and "protective reaction" as actions that are essentially defensive. The violent actor in these cases has been or anticipates that she or he will be a victim of violence or is acting in response to violence directed against another person. For example, a woman might strike her husband to stop him from attacking their child. "Volcanic violence" is essentially stress-related action. The stress may originate inside or outside of the interpersonal relationship, but the violence mostly represents an explosion of tensions. "Alcohol-related" violence occurs when the actor is drinking or drunk. It is interesting to wonder whether such episodes involve violence as a result of intoxication or whether drinking is an excuse to abuse. Finally, "sex-related attacks," Gelles's seventh type of violent situations, occur during arguments and other interactions in which jealousy and accusations of infidelity are central.

This listing does not represent an exhaustive description of situational characteristics surrounding family violence or spouse abuse. However, Gelles's seven types provide a beginning for describing relevant characteristics of social niches that accommodate and encourage family violence.

Toward a General Theory of Violence as Deviance

As noted in Chapters 3 and 4 (and throughout), the explanation of deviance requires attention to the dialectics of *violation* and *sanction* and to the related matters of epidemiology and causation. The following presentation proceeds through the outline of the convergence theory of deviance.

Explaining Rates and Patterns of Deviant Violence

Recall that the central variable in the epidemiological theory is *integration:* As *integration* decreases, both *violation* and *social control* increase.

American society has changed fairly rapidly and unevenly during its history, and the general direction has been toward decreasing integration. (See earlier discussions of this point in Chapter 2 and 6.) This observation and the epidemiological theory suggest two hypotheses: (1) Rates of violence (violations of norms and laws that are likely to be enforced) have increased, and (2) rates of enforcement of norms and rules concerning violence have increased (that is, social control has increased).

Traditional American values provide a foundation of broadly shared understandings about the roles of adults and children. These beliefs also shape and support arrangements such as family structures (parents, children, husbands, wives), gender structures (for example, different expectations for men and women in families, jobs, and careers), and social class. Historically, these values and arrangements have allowed or encouraged certain kinds of violent behavior. Men have been expected to fight to maintain honor, to win respect and admiration, to rescue "damsels in distress," to defend "God and mother country," and to aid many other socially defined purposes. Similarly, various traditions have supported family violence. For example, Martin (1981:192) reported a custom that appears to be the source of the expression "rule of thumb": "In our own country a husband was permitted to beat his wife so long as he didn't use a switch any bigger around than his thumb." Likewise, corporal punishment of children by parents, teachers, and religious leaders is a well-recorded part of American history.

Has nonfamily, interpersonal violence increased over the past three hundred years in our society? The question is very hard to answer empirically. In a report to the National Commission on the Causes and Prevention of Violence, Brown (1979) distinguished between "negative" violence (that which has no direct connection to constructive social or historical development) and "positive" violence—presumably the opposite. He identified the following types of violence as negative: crimes, feuds, lynch mobs, racial, ethnic, and religious prejudice, urban riots, free-lance multiple murder, and political assassination. His list of types of positive violence strongly suggests that the distinctions are matters of value judgment: police actions, revolutions, civil war, Indian wars, vigilantism, agrarian uprisings, and labor conflicts (Brown, 1969: 45–84). Although the distinction between negative and positive violence probably has little analytical value, Brown's work clearly underscores the diversity and pervasiveness of relevant behaviors in our past and present. How can we measure the changes? In a separate part of the commission report, Sheldon Levy (1969:84–100) studied political violence in America over 150 years. His focus was relatively narrow, and he reached the rather surprising conclusion that political violence has not increased by most measures.

More recent data, which describe the crimes of violence of rape, robbery, and assault, suggest that violence may be decreasing, at least in the short run.

National Crime Survey data indicate that rates of violent crime have decreased by nearly 8 percent (from 1973 to 1985, the most inclusive dates for which NCS data currently are available). Greenberg and associates (1987), however, note that there is at least one important counter trend. Rates of violent death clearly are increasing for Americans between the ages 15 and 24. (This research is discussed in some detail later.) It may be that rates of violation, rates of social control, or both have changed in ways that cannot be specified with currently available data.

Research by Blau and Blau (1982) and Bailey (1984), among others, suggests that rates of violence may be related to levels of poverty or inequality or both. And some evidence suggests that both inequality and poverty have increased in recent years. Data from the U.S. Bureau of the Census (1984) suggest that inequality, as measured by income distribution, has remained fairly constant for the past half century. Blonston (1988) reviews recent data that suggest a different picture: In 1977, those households with incomes in the top 10 percent received 30.6 percent of all pretax income earned; for 1988, the figure is projected to be 34.9 percent. Moreover, the percent of people below the federally established poverty line has increased fairly steadily since 1970. It declined slightly in 1984 and 1985, but it remains well above the level of 1970 (12.6 percent in 1970 compared to 14 percent in 1985; U.S. Bureau of the Census, 1986: 442). At the same time, the concentration of poverty among blacks has increased (U.S. Bureau of the Census, 1984:44), and black employment has decreased. In a disturbing analysis, Hacker (1987) estimated that in 1986 only 40 percent of all black men were employed full time in year-round jobs.

As noted earlier, it is not possible today to decipher the relationships among violence, poverty, and inequality. One possibility is that all three factors are related to integration, especially declining integration, and that the key relationship is between integration and violence. That, of course, is the explanation my proposed theory sponsors. Inequality and poverty probably are only two of many factors that are part of or related to declining integration. Recall the multiple dimensions of integration discussed in Chapter 3. Increasing levels of poverty and inequality undercut integration as *commonality* because people live increasingly different styles of life (Durkheim and Weber). And more poverty and inequality mean more tension among parts of communities and societies that are held together in *dynamic equilibrium* (Marx). This proposed explanation is described in more detail and illustrated through recent research on violence among youths.

Greenberg and others (1987) have contended that rates of violent death have been declining during the past two decades for Americans of all ages except those between 15 and 24. They have offered an unusually encompassing definition of "death by violence," including victims of homicide, suicide, motor vehicle accidents, and miscellaneous accidents (such as from boating, falls, fires, and drowning). Although this conception of violence raises some questions, their reasoning seems to be that many accidents involve aggression, self-destruction, or carelessness that has violent implications. Moreover, they noted that rates of violence have increased sharply for this age group even if you limit the definition to homicide and suicide. The researchers limited their study to the white population, presumably to enhance cross-national comparisons. They compared death rates for five periods (1939–1941, 1949–1951, 1959–1961, 1969–1971, 1977–1979) and across geographic regions of the United States. Among other interesting findings, they observed that the Western states of Arizona, Idaho, Montana, Nevada, New Mexico, and Wyoming consistently have had the highest rates of violent death among youth. In contrast, four Northeastern states (Connecticut, Massachusetts, New Jersey, and Rhode Island) consistently have had the lowest rates of violent death for this age group. The differences do not seem to result from the inclusive definition of violence. Indeed, "*suicide* is the cause of youthful violent death that most distinguishes the six Western states from the rest of the country" (Greenberg and others, 1987:41; emphasis added).

Greenberg and his colleagues attempted to refine the analyses by looking at death rates county by county within the four Western states of Nevada, Utah, Arizona, and New Mexico. You may be surprised to find that the highest rates of violent death were found in the *rural* counties. In fact, they observed that "the rural areas of our four Western states typically have higher death rates among their white population than the six high-crime cities show for inner-city blacks" (Greenberg and others, 1987:43; this comparison includes Atlanta, Baltimore, Dayton, Fort Worth, St. Louis, and Washington, D.C., as the high-crime cities).

To this point, analyses have tended to associate low integration with urbanism and population diversity. How, then, can we understand high rates of violence in rural areas through the concept of integration? Recall that integration is conceived as multidimensional. One dimension has to do with what Durkheim called *solidarity*: the "cohesiveness" of social units based on relationships among people in different social positions (see Chapter 3). These relationships are defined and sustained by norms, rules, or laws that establish and enforce common expectations. Groups or communities with low levels of integration are those in which the norms and relationships are relatively ineffective in constraining and shaping behavior. Greenberg and associates contend that *these rural Western communities are low on integration*. Compared to the Northeastern states, divorces rates, geographic mobility, and unemployment are high and the proportion of Catholics is low. These are among the standard correlates and indicators of integration. For example, Catholics typically have low rates of suicide and divorce, presumably because the Roman Catholic

Church's position is unambiguous and its teachings on these matters are relatively insistent—both of which are integrating forces.

Do rates of murder and assault generally predict or parallel rates of family violence? As with violence generally, it is difficult to trace changes in rates of family violence because of the lack of relevant and adequate data. Some American customs support violence within families. At the same time, American efforts to prevent and control family violence date to at least the middle 1800s. Pleck (1979:71) asserts that by 1900 most states had passed laws prohibiting wife beating, and many had harsh penalties. The thrust of her argument can be summarized:

> The difference between the past and the present was not a modern intention to prohibit wife beating but a change in the manner of regulation. A century ago the system of formal regulation against wifebeaters was relatively weak and cumbersome whereas the mechanisms for informal regulation were relatively vigorous and extensive; today the opposite is more nearly the case [1979:71].

If Pleck is correct, official data almost certainly would suggest that family violence has increased. These family matters, as they were considered in the past, have become *public problems*, and they are now subject to *formal* social control. The change may or may not enhance the effectiveness of control, but it certainly facilitates *counting*.

Gil (1970), Gelles (1973), Straus (1980a), and others have suggested that stress is an important correlate of such violence. In particular, Straus (1978, 1980a) has contended that stress from economic problems (especially *poverty*) and *social isolation* are among the major causes of family violence. The concept of stress is problematic at best. The relationships among stress, social isolation, and family violence may parallel those among poverty, inequality, and criminal violence. Stress and social isolation may be correlates or indicators of declining integration. If so, we can predict that rates of family violence are increasing in the same way that rates of criminal violence seem to be.

Explaining Causes of Deviant Violence

Recall that the central variables in the causal theory are *integration, attachment,* and *learning violations:* As *integration* decreases, *attachment* decreases, and *learning* of *violations* increases.

We often are bewildered by seemingly senseless brutality. As a result, we tend to see such acts as resulting from insanity or other compelling forces. People "blow up," "explode," or otherwise lose control. Ronald Akers (1985:263–266) considered these compulsion explanations and rejected them. He has argued instead that the evidence supports a *learning* theory. Pointing to research by Gold (1958), Hartung (1965), and Bandura (1973), Akers has contended that violence is a learned response that results from parental socialization, social imitation, and reinforcement within social and cultural contexts. The most suggestive evidence for the learning explanation of violence is found in the work of David Phillips (1983), who demonstrated that media portrayals of violence (including boxing matches) correlate closely with homicide rates. Likewise, Pitcher, Hamlin, and Miller (1978) provided cross-cultural evidence of the spread of collective violence through mass media.

As noted in earlier chapters, learning violations involves learning both behaviors and definitions that support those behaviors—that is, *rationales*. Wolfgang and Ferracuti (1967) contended that the necessary definitions are available for learning within a subculture of violence. Evidence of the existence of such a subculture is unclear at present. It is clear, however, that our culture supports a variety of shared meanings that justify violence. For example, violence is acceptable or excused when the actor is acting in self-defense, in times of war, when the actor is drunk, when he suffers from some postwar trauma, or when he is protecting his home, property, or family. Athens's (1980) research suggests that some people may learn and incorporate such definitions fairly systematically. As a result of such learning, they may have identifiable predispositions to violence. The tendency to define situations as requiring violent responses or solutions may vary, depending largely on individuals' self-definitions and experience with violence within different settings. Consider this brief illustration of "learning violence":

> I came home from school with my knees all skinned up and my trousers ripped. My grandfather asked me what happened. I told him that a big black kid beat me up at recess. He said that he didn't want any nigger beating up his grandson and then began giving me boxing lessons. I jumped the kid the next day at recess, but he downed me again. When I told my grandfather about it, he whipped me and then told me that I better beat the kid's ass the next day or he was going to whip me even harder. I knew that kid couldn't hurt me as much as my grandfather could, so I tried to whip his ass again. I fired on him at recess and hit him as hard as I could in the face and downed him. While he was down, I kicked him in the head and face good and hard and bloodied his mouth and broke his nose. Then I took his place at school after that as cock of the walk [Athens, 1980:55].

Definitions that support violence are part of our common culture, but they may vary in frequency, intensity, and salience (among other possibilities) across diverse social niches. In some, traditions of violence are integral to definitions of self and peer acceptance—for example, Mexican-American machismo, winning and maintaining honor and protecting the colors in urban gangs. The level of integration of the larger society will influence the extent to which such local definitions will prevail in guiding the conduct of participants. When integration is low, the shared experiences and meanings of the social niche will dominate. Opportunities to learn violence will increase (or remain relatively high) and violence will increase (or remain relatively high). Those who grow up in such niches will have greater opportunities for learning violence.

Murray Straus (1980a:14; Gelles and Straus, 1979) has argued that *family* violence also is learned: "Physical punishment is the foundation on which the edifice of family violence rests. . . . It is the way most people first experience physical violence, and it establishes the emotional context and meaning of violence." Straus maintained that physical punishment has a number of un-intended consequences, including learning the association between love and violence, learning the "moral rightness" of hitting, and learning that use of physical force is justified if something is really important. He asserted further that children learn violence by observing it: being a victim does not teach people to reject violence, but to embrace it as a value. Straus (1980a:16–17) summarized: "In general, the rule in the family is that if someone is doing wrong and 'won't listen to reason,' it is ok to hit. In the case of children, it is more than just ok. Many American parents see it as an obligation. Moreover, this principle carries over to the relationship between husbands and wives."

Research that I reviewed earlier (Garbarino and Gilliam, 1980, for example) supports learning explanations of family violence and violence more gen-erally. At the same time, Straus (1980a) and others have pointed out that we are becoming less tolerant of family violence and more willing to violate family privacy values in efforts to control child and spouse abuse. Again, violence apparently will vary depending upon levels of integration. In periods of rela-tively high integration, contemporary values that condemn family violence will limit and constrain the use of physical force in family interactions. In addition, those who grow up in families within social niches that are closely integrated with official norms and rules will have relatively fewer opportunities to learn violent conduct.

Public Policy: Can Violence Be Deterred?

The discovery of family violence as a public problem has led to increased formal and official intervention and social control efforts. People are more aware of things that go on behind the doors in American households. This greater awareness has led some to believe that the problems are increasing. Indeed, some observers describe an epidemic of child and spouse abuse. But it is not clear that we have seen real changes in the rates of family violence (although the proposed theory predicts increases). Neither is it clear that the development of official and formal methods of intervention have solved any problems or produced more effective control. Straus (1980a:28–29) provides a provocative summary:

> I suggest that American society is now in an historical period in which the "abuse" part of the continuum is being gradually enlarged to include acts of violence which were not previously so defined. This creates the misleading impression of an "epidemic" of child abuse and wife abuse. However, unless a wide range of steps are taken to deal with the basic social causes of violence, the results of this changing definition may do more to create a new class of criminals or a new class of patients than to reduce the level of family violence.

My proposed (epidemiological and causal) theories and the empirically based descriptions of family violence suggest that effective control depends on increased integration. Specifically, the new public views and beliefs about violence among family members must be accepted, endorsed, and enforced by people across the diverse social niches of our society. If that happens, official control measures would be largely unnecessary, except to symbolically reinforce our collective agreements. Public education efforts, like the public service announcements sponsored by the Ad Council and the Church of the Latter Day Saints, may be useful in promoting certain shared meanings. However, our primary social control strategy probably will continue to be through the creation and enforcement of laws.

Research on the effectiveness of official efforts to control domestic violence is beginning to accumulate and raises interesting questions about deterrence and social control generally. Contrary to popular opinion, police intervention may reduce the probability of repeated incidents of wife abuse. An early study by the Police Foundation (1977) provided evidence that patterns of family violence can be detected in calls for police service. More recently, Lawrence Sherman and Richard Berk (1984) reported on a field experiment in Minneapolis in which officers were asked to respond to misdemeanor domestic assaults with one of three options: (1) give advice, (2) order the suspect to leave for eight hours, or (3) arrest the suspect. These response options were assigned at random. The victims (314 total) were interviewed over the next six months to determine their subsequent experience. The interviews revealed that 37 percent of the advised suspects and 33 percent of the suspects ordered off the premises committed a new assault or some other crime against the woman. In contrast, only 19 percent of the arrested suspects committed a new assault during that period.

Patrick Langan and Christopher Innes (1986) pursued one step further the evaluation of police intervention into domestic violence incidents. They examined National Crime Survey data for 1978 to 1982 to determine what proportion of those who were victims of domestic assault reported the events to the police.

They found that approximately 1.8 million women could be classified as "callers" or "noncallers" (1.1 million and 700,000, respectively). The researchers next attempted to assess the effect of reporting the violence. They found that 16 percent of the callers and 23 percent of the noncallers were victimized again by domestic violence within six months. They determined further that subsequent acts of violence against those who reported the events to the police were not more serious that those experienced by the women who did not report.

Up to this point, reviews of deterrence research have suggested that formal social control has little deterrent value. Do the studies presented here contradict this interpretation? Maybe. It seems more likely, however, that they suggest a refinement. None of the domestic violence studies involved significant punishment as part of the control response. For example, only 2 percent of the suspects in the Minneapolis study went before a judge to receive court-imposed punishment. It seems reasonable to suggest, then, that the various responses (calling the police, arresting the offender) involved introducing a definition of the situation rather than carrying out some threatened formal sanction. The offenders were told that their conduct was not acceptable.

Gail Goolkasian (1986:1) reviewed research on the role of criminal court judges in domestic violence cases and began with revealing comments from a former battered woman:

> The judge told him, in no uncertain terms, that the law doesn't allow him to assault me just because I'm his wife. He said that he'll send him to jail if he's brought back for another offense. Right there in the courtroom . . . you should have seen the look on his face. I think he knew the judge wasn't kidding, and that's when he decided to do something about it.

Goolkasian (1986:2) concluded that "research suggests that violence is less likely to recur once a clear message is given that battering is inappropriate behavior which will not be tolerated."

Can we reduce assaults and homicides through similar strategies? Violence is a salient feature of our common culture, endorsed and expressed in national pastimes such as professional sports and a dominant theme in our entertainment such as TV dramas. We believe strongly in the rightness of force—even violent force—as a solution to some problems. The tradition was well established before the War of Independence.

Significant reduction of violence will require real changes in the *level* and *focus* of integration in our society. During popular wars, we experience heightened integration, but it is a decidedly militant integration—even if the violence is directed externally. There is no reason to expect less violence in that circumstance. But war is not the only possible unifying theme. We could begin national campaigns that focus on respect for life, tolerance, or other values that diminish the glory of violence and force. "Just say no" does not have to apply only to drugs. (There is mounting evidence that educational programs such as these can reduce drug use among young people. See *The Washington Post*, n.d., 1989.)

The Need for Research

As with the types of deviance discussed in previous chapters, at least two kinds of research need to be pursued further to specify and begin to test my proposed theory of the deviance of violence. One type of study should focus on the relationships between the social conditions of integration and diversity of social niches, on the one hand, and the rates and distribution of violence, on the other. The theory should allow accurate epidemiological predictions. Sociological research to test these predictions will require a longitudinal design so that rates of integration and rates of violation can be described and related as they change over time (for example, a period of several years).

The second type of research should focus on the patterns of attachment and the learning experiences of those who participate in violent conduct. The theory suggests several hypotheses that can be tested at least partially through a strategy of field research. One hypothesis, for example, would assert that physical punishment of children for discipline is distributed unevenly among families of different social classes in contemporary American society. Families of social classes that are closely represented by dominant and officially sanctioned values and norms pertaining to child rearing are least likely to use physical force as a tool of discipline. A second hypothesis would assert a relationship between growing up in families of differing types and the learning of violence as a solution or strategy for certain kinds of problems. Again, a longitudinal design is essential to trace the development of attachments and learning experiences and to identify developing patterns of violent conduct.

The following discussion provides an illustration of the kinds of research that might be pursued. (You may want to review Chapter 5 as you consider the proposals.)

RESEARCHING RATES AND PATTERNS OF VIOLENCE The major national study of family violence to date is that by Straus, Gelles, and Steinmetz (1980). That study needs to be expanded and replicated. The original research was comprehensive and included key variables influencing the rates and distribution of family violence. Respondent families were rated on a checklist of characteristics described as follows by Straus (1980a:27):

> The procedure was to give each of the 2,143 families in the national survey a "Checklist" score. A family got one point for each characteristic associated with a higher than average rate of husband-wife violence. For ex-

ample, if the husband experienced more than the average amount of physical punishment when growing up, one point was assigned. If the balance of power in the family was lopsidedly male-dominant, another point was added. If the couple experienced a high number of stressful events, such as unemployment, we added another point to their score. Altogether, a couple's score could range from zero (for those who had none of these characteristics) to 25, for those who had all 25. The scores ranged from zero (seven couples), to 18 (two couples), with an average of six characteristics per couple.

The survey needs to be expanded to allow measurement of levels of integration within communities and over time, perhaps a decade. A panel design could survey a cohort of respondents at predetermined intervals (perhaps every two and a half years). It would be necessary to treat respondents as informants for certain parts of the study. For example, they would be asked to report on characteristics of their communities. Questions would be asked that would allow inferences about the nature and amount of value consensus and the extent of interdependence among groups and other parts of the community such as segments of the labor force. Respondents (as informants) also would be asked to define and describe *violence* the way they believe that people within their communities understand it. Finally, as respondents, they would be asked to describe the use of physical force within their families, in much the same way that Straus and his associates (1980) did. The collected data could then be analyzed to identify patterns of association between levels of integration and levels of violence and between sociodemographic characteristics and violence.

We need a similar national-level study of the distribution of criminal violence, including assault and homicide. To date, we have depended primarily on arrest data and the identification of samples and populations from official (typically police) files. We know that many assaults are never reported and that many who have engaged in assaultive violence never become known to the police or represented in any official records. A self-report strategy, like that used by Straus, Gelles, and Steinmentz, would allow major progress in describing actual patterns of nonfamily violence. The study should be expanded, as just described, to allow preliminary testing of the relationships between levels of integration and levels of violence.

RESEARCHING CAUSES OF VIOLENCE The national study by Straus and his associates also provides a starting point for testing hypotheses about the causes of family violence. However, again, we need longitudinal studies of families to trace patterns of development and change. Those studies would allow description of the development of patterns of force and violence and the testing of hypotheses about the relationships among integration, attachment, learning, and violent behavior. The necessary data could be provided through a panel design in which data are collected from a sample of individuals and family groups at predetermined intervals over several years. This strategy would involve the use of extended interviews for gathering information.

The interview schedule would include items that ask respondents to describe relationships with family and friends that have included physical punishment and other forms of violence. Respondents also would be asked to report episodes in which they acted violently either toward a family member or toward anyone else. Finally, the respondents would be treated as informants in order to collect descriptions of patterns and levels of integration within their communities.

CHAPTER 9

White-Collar Crime

About a century ago, the [oil] industry developed in Pennsylvania, and within six years after the discovery of oil the industry's development became linked with John D. Rockefeller and later his Standard Oil Company. He built an international empire on oil, serviced by railroad, pipeline, and other interests; indeed, Rockefeller's monopolistic corporation was unique in history. . . .

As politicians and the public became aware of the extent of this monopoly, Rockefeller became the subject of congressional action. . . . Rockefeller, in fact, did more than anyone else to provoke the Sherman Antitrust Act of 1890. . . . Under Theodore Roosevelt a large-scale federal investigation was undertaken that found how Standard Oil had created a monopoly with exorbitant profits of nearly a billion dollars in twenty-five years [Clinard and Yeager, 1980:238–239].

In a fifteen-year span, some 100,000 Americans paid over $70 million for lightbulbs sold under the Torch brand. The sales were made over the phone with the salesperson claiming to be handicapped and often tearfully pleading for a sale. The bulbs were overpriced by 300 percent and were substandard in quality. Moreover, an investigation by New Jersey revealed that some of the salespersons' doctor-certified disabilities included acne, excess weight, nervousness, hernia, hay fever, and dislocated shoulder [Simon and Eitzen, 1986:90–91].

Out of a host of contenders, Robert L. Vesco appears to hold the crown as the nation's biggest embezzler and pillager of corporations. Vesco's exploits as the head of a far-flung financial empire first came to public light after he acquired control of a Swiss-based complex of mutual funds known as Investors Overseas Services (I.O.S.). According to a subsequent complaint filed by the Securities and Exchange Commission, Vesco siphoned off $224 million in cash and securities from various I.O.S. mutual funds. The money was then spirited away to Vesco-controlled banks in Luxembourg and the Bahamas [Coleman, 1989:86].

Karen Silkwood, a plutonium-plant worker, charged that the Kerr-McGee plant in which she worked was unsafe and that she was contaminated by plutonium radiation exposure. After her death in a somewhat questionable car accident, Karen's family sued Kerr-McGee. During the trial, Kerr-McGee employees testified that they were provided little or no training on the health hazards involved in handling plutonium. They were never told that radiation exposure could induce cancer. Attorneys for Kerr-McGee argued in court, however, that there had been no documented case of plutonium cancer in humans. This was countered by the testimony of Dr. John Gofman, one of the first physicists to isolate plutonium, who said that Ms. Silkwood had an instant "guarantee of cancer based on her exposure" [Simon and Eitzen, 1986:110].

A Sociological Conception
of White-Collar Crime

The examples that open this chapter are diverse and may seem to have little in common. Still, some people would recognize them as instances of white-collar crime. Industrial monopolies, commercial fraud, embezzlement, and unsafe work environments reflect a multidimensional array of violations. They involve different victims: the general public, charity-minded customers, the company and its stockholders, and employees. There are different offenders: corporate magnates and their designated representatives; ordinary citizens looking for easy money; trusted and, typically, highly placed company employees; and company supervisors, managers, and executives. Different types of rules and laws are involved: federal administrative and regulatory rules and laws, criminal statutes, and civil statutes. There are different means for enforcing the rules: federal commissions; federal, state, and local law enforcement agencies; and civil law suits. Finally, there are differences in the threatened consequences of violations, including revocations of licenses, fines, payment of civil awards, and imprisonment.

Note that many of the acts and events that are understood as white-collar crimes are very similar to ordinary crime. Fraud and embezzlement, for example, involve taking money by deceit. The same act—taking money—is larceny, burglary, or robbery if it is done through stealth or through the use of force. Monopoly also involves taking money, although the taking is less direct. Price fixing and other noncompetitive forms of price control inflate prices for consumers and inflate profits for producers. In a sense, it is surprising that fraud, embezzlement, and monopoly are understood and treated as different from ordinary crime. Some have suggested that the difference results from the characteristics of the offenders: White-collar violators are not "real" criminals, and often violators are corporations rather than people. Yet no one has been able to define clearly what makes a person a real criminal. And common sense reveals that corporations cannot *do* anything. Instead, *people* do things, albeit perhaps in the name of, or on behalf of, corporations and companies.

Defining white-collar crime is difficult, but not really more difficult than specifying what is meant by most other types of deviance. (Recall discussions of prostitution, mental illness, and violence in Chapters 6, 7, and 8.) Social scientists have been slow to identify things like price-fixing as topics of interest in deviance research. Edwin Sutherland provided the first systematic study, defining the events of concern as "crime in the upper or white-collar class" (1956:46; see also Sutherland, 1940, 1983). More specifically, Sutherland focused on violations committed by "respectable" offenders in the course of their jobs. He noted that his concept "excludes many crimes of the upper class, such as most of their cases of murder, adultery, and intoxication, since these are not customarily a part of their occupational procedures" (Sutherland, 1949:9).

Other researchers have tried different terms, such as "occupational crime" (Quinney, 1964; Akers, 1985), "corporate crime" (Clinard and Yeager, 1980), "corporations as criminals" (Hochstedler, 1984) "crimes violating trust" (McCaghy and Cernkovich, 1987), and "elite deviance" (Simon and Eitzen, 1986). Some definitions highlight the occupational context (Akers, 1985:228), others focus on the presumed quality of the acts (Edelhertz, 1970), and still others stress the privileged position of offenders. Despite the continued diversity of definitions and approaches, Akers (1985:231) has maintained that most of the major conceptual issues have been resolved.

We have had a clear definition of white-collar crime as occupational crime (encompassing both corporate and individual crimes) at least since the mid-1960s. The term "white-collar" has been retained, but the use of this term is meant only to emphasize crimes by those in upper-status and powerful positions. It is not used to define a type of crime, restrict attention to occupational deviance only at that level, or include all economic offenses by the upper class. The socioeconomic status of the offender is only correlative, not definitive, of occupational crime.

Akers (1985:228) provided a definition of white-collar crime that will serve our purposes: "*the violation of legal norms governing lawful occupational endeavors* during the course of practicing the occupation." (Emphasis is in the original.) Recalling the conception of *deviance* proposed in earlier chapters, we must distinguish between white-collar *violations* and white-collar *crime* (*deviance*). Generally, of course, the difference refers to whether or not social control of any sort is applied. More specifically, the things that qualify as white-collar crime illustrate the consequential nature of social control for shaping deviance. Consider these examples:

Executive efforts to increase corporate profits and stabilize prices and other market factors may be either "shrewd business" or criminal restraint of trade.

Effective sales strategies may involve either "creative merchandising" or misrepresentation.

Corporate profits may be increased by "aggressive product research and marketing" or by fraud.

Use of corporate funds by individuals may involve "creative financing" or embezzlement.

The differences between conventionally accepted practices and white-collar violations and between violations and crime often are a matter of timing and luck, although adeptness may figure in as well. Consider the matter of the development and production of the Ford Pinto. In the mid-1960s, Lee Iacocca and other Ford executives promoted the development of a small, fuel-efficient car to compete with foreign imports. When he became president, he implemented a plan to design and build the Pinto in approximately two-thirds the time normally required. Iacocca established "limits of 2,000." The car was to weigh no more than 2,000 pounds and cost no more than $2,000. As a result of this "rule," a "one pound, one dollar piece of metal [that] stopped the puncture of a gas tank . . . was thrown out as extra cost and weight" (Dowie, 1979:28).

Does this event involve a white-collar violation or aggressive and imaginative management? People have and will continue to argue that issue. Accord-

T A B L E   9 . 1

A Typology of White-Collar Crimes

	Crimes Against the Public	Crimes Within Organizations
	(a)	(c)
CORPORATE VIOLATORS (including individuals acting on behalf of corporations)	monopolies price-fixing consumer fraud pollution	unsafe working conditions labor law violations
	(b)	(d)
NONCORPORATE VIOLATORS	professional malfeasance	embezzlement employee theft

ing to the conceptions proposed here, it qualifies as violation. It involves a departure from generally acknowledged standards of product safety and probably from specific federal administrative rules. Yet it also involves a style of management that is widely admired. Is it white-collar crime? In 1978, the Department of Transportation completed tests that revealed the gas tank defects, and 1971 to 1976 Pintos were recalled. The recall cost an estimated $100 million. There were also civil suits against Ford that brought multimillion-dollar judgments. And more than 50 people are believed to have died as a result of the exploding tanks. Iacocca is now the chief executive at Chrysler and one of the most respected business leaders in the United States. He is not serving time in prison. By all accounts, Ford Motor Company continues to thrive and enjoy a reputation as a responsible and reliable manufacturer. ("Quality is job one" is their latest advertising slogan.) It was and is a *violation* and an instance of white-collar crime by the proposed definition. Yet the consequences do not resemble those of "ordinary" crimes.

In the discussions that follow, I will describe different types of white-collar violations. These violating activities are diverse and can be organized or categorized in different ways. For example, Akers (1985:229) suggested a distinction between (1) crimes against the public and (2) crimes within organizations. Coleman (1987:407) has suggested and supported a slightly different distinction or classification based in part on the intended beneficiary of the violating activity—the organization or the individual (Clinard and Quinney, 1973). Table 9.1 presents a four-fold typology of white-collar crimes produced by considering both distinctions. Each of the types identified in the table will be described using the conceptual framework (social organization, social niche, and social action). The description draws heavily from James Coleman's (1989) excellent summary of the relevant research literature. Next, I will present theories of epidemiology and causation and review a range of empirical research that bears on the theories to assess the explanations. The proposed theories, which derive from the general explanation (convergence theory) developed in this book, connect directly with the major white-collar crime theories.

Crimes Against the Public

Violations against the public range from monopolistic restraint of trade to fraud. The public victims are patients, clients, consumers, businesses, the government, and taxpayers, to name a few. The violators include corporations and their executives in fields and businesses as diverse as automobile manufacturing, leisure activities, financial lending and management, and car, home, health, and life insurance. Violators also include governments and government agencies and their representatives and individuals who practice a profession, occupation, or craft that involves deception.

Not surprisingly, it is difficult to trace even the broad outlines of crimes against the public. There are estimates of the annual costs of white-collar crime, but these vary partly as a result of the definition of the terms: What offenses are included and what counts as a "cost"? Meier and Short (1982) examined violations of trust by people using a significant position of power for illegal gain. They divided costs into "financial harm," "physical harm," and "damage to moral climate." These researchers cited estimates of annual losses ranging from $40 billion to $200 billion for the mid-1970s in the United States. (The estimates come from the U.S. Chamber of Commerce and various government committees, agents, and agencies; Meier and Short, 1982:24–25.) Kramer (1984:19) reported a more recent estimate of the cost of *corporate crime* of $174 to $231 billion annually. (This estimate comes from the Subcommittee on Antitrust and Monopoly of the U.S. Senate Judiciary Committee.)

The Bureau of Justice Statistics (1987) reported that U.S. attorneys investigated 24,507 federal white-collar matters from October 1, 1984, to September 30, 1985. The offenses counted include fraud, embezzlement, forgery, and counterfeiting. There were 10,733 convictions during the period; among them were 64 people charged with offenses valued at more than $10 million each.

Meier and Short (1982) noted that physical harm can affect both consumers and the community at large. They provided illustrations of harm: injury from unsafe products (the Ford Pinto) and pollution of air, water, and the environment generally. Braithwaite (1982) has estimated that each year approximately 150,000 people experience serious injuries from product safety violations. As Meier and Short noted, it is difficult to assess the extent of physical and financial harm because risk is built into many features of human experience, and it is often difficult to connect outcomes to antecedent events.

Describing and evaluating damage to the moral climate is even more difficult. White-collar crime is potentially very damaging because it "threatens the trust that is basic to community life—for example, between citizens and government officials [and] businesses and their customers" (Meier and Short, 1982:27–28). The effects of white-collar crime on public trust, as the social glue that holds communities and societies together, may be critical.

Corporate Violators

SOCIAL ORGANIZATION We begin with a recognition that corporate crime is consequential. What, then, can be said of its incidence, distribution, or pervasiveness? In the earliest systematic effort to detail corporate crime, Sutherland (1940) reported research on the 70 largest industrial corporations in the United States—excluding public utilities and petroleum corporations. Sutherland recognized that the data would tend to underrepresent the actual incidence of violations, but he nonetheless identified a total of 980 "adverse decisions." He reported further that each of the 70 corporations had at least one decision against it for some violation of restraint of trade laws, misrepresentation in advertising, unfair labor practices, financial fraud, or violation of war regulations. Moreover, the corporations had an average of 14 such decisions, 98 percent of the corporations were recidivists (at least two adverse decisions), and 90 percent were "habitual criminals"—that is, they had at least four adverse decisions. Criminal courts made 159 of the decisions, civil courts made 425, and commissions made 361.

Some 40 years after Sutherland's research, Marshall Clinard and his colleagues investigated law violations of nearly 600 of the largest U.S. corporations—the 477 largest manufacturing corporations and the 105 largest wholesale, retail and service organizations. (See Clinard and others, 1979; Clinard and Yeager, 1979, 1980.) Clinard and Yeager (1980:xi) reported on the legal actions 25 leading federal agencies took against these companies during 1975 and 1976. They discovered 1,553 federal legal cases initiated against the companies. Sixty percent of the corporations were charged, and 200 of the 477 manufacturing companies had multiple charges.

Using less clearly defined criteria, investigators of *U.S. News and World Report* ("Corporate Crime," 1982) found that nearly 2,700 corporations were convicted of federal criminal offenses during the 1970s. Taken together, the data from various studies and investigations suggest that white-collar crime by corporations is extensive and diverse.

Massive consolidations have occurred since the turn of the century, in spite of legislation intended to curb monopolistic control. The Sherman Act of

1890 made monopoly and other forms of restraint of trade or competition illegal. The law has been used to dissolve monopolistic organizations and to prevent their development. Nonetheless, concentrated control of manufacturing assets has continued and increased. Simon and Eitzen (1986:70–71) reported that in 1960, 450 corporations controlled approximately half of all manufacturing assets in the United States. By the early 1980s, those corporations controlled approximately 70 percent of the assets and 72 percent of the profits. With several large corporations controlling major shares of most industries, it is somewhat surprising that price-fixing persists as a major form of white-collar criminality.

A survey of presidents of the 1,000 largest manufacturing companies revealed that 47 percent of the presidents of the largest 500 firms believe that corporations engage in price fixing (Green and others, 1972). Seventy percent of the presidents of the next largest 500 corporations believe that such activities occur. The most carefully documented case of corporate price-fixing to date involves what has come to be known as the "Electrical Conspiracy." (Federal grand jury inquiries were begun in 1959 and the cases were tried in 1960 and 1961; see Geis, 1967; Smith, 1961.) The conspiracy involved more than 20 companies that, collectively, controlled most of the industry's assets and sales. The conspiracy involved elaborate undercover procedures and clandestine meetings among corporate executives. These company leaders cooperated to determine prices for equipment and to fix bids for major contracts. They agreed in advance who among them would submit the lowest bid for contracts that ultimately totaled billions of dollars.

Price-fixing and other forms of consumer fraud also are pervasive on a smaller scale, involving individual customers more directly as victims. False or deceptive advertising provides numerous examples. Simon and Eitzen (1986:88) documented the following items:

> In 1978, the Federal Trade Commission ruled that Anacin had falsely advertised its product claiming that it (1) relieved nervousness, tension, stress, fatigue, and depression; (2) was stronger than aspirin; (3) brought relief within twenty-two seconds; (4) was highly recommended over aspirin by doctors; and (5) was more effective for relieving pain than any other single analgesic available without prescription.
>
> In 1979, the nation's largest toymaker, CPG Products, a subsidiary of General Mills, was found guilty of two deceptive acts: (1) use of a television commercial that showed a toy horse being able to stand on its own—when in fact it could not—through the use of special camera techniques and film editing; and (2) use of over-sized boxes in model airplane kits that gave a misleading impression of the size of the contents.
>
> Products are advertised at exaggerated sizes. Lumber is uniformly shorter than advertised—a twelve-inch board really is eleven and one-

quarter inches wide. The quarter-pounder advertised by McDonald's is really three and seven-eighths ounces. Nine-inch pies are in truth seven and three-quarters inches in diameter, because the pie industry includes the rim of the pan in determining the size [cf. Preston, 1975].

More recently, the *Washington Post* ("Paying for Price Fixing," 1988:A16) reported nearly 20 separate charges for price-fixing violations during the past year against persons and companies in the beverage industry. Coca-Cola bottlers pleaded guilty or were found guilty in 10 separate cases and paid fines ranging from $2,000 to $2 million. Pepsi-Cola bottlers pleaded guilty or were found guilty in five separate cases and paid fines ranging from $15,000 to $1 million. Seven-Up, Dr. Pepper, and Royal Crown Bottlers also were charged during the period.

The various corporate violations share a major theme: the pursuit of profit in a competitive social environment. In many ways, crimes against the public are decidedly American and reflect some of the major outlines of our common culture: private ownership of means of production, private consumption, success through effective competition, aggressive pursuit of private interests, and a "bigger is better" attitude.

SOCIAL NICHES Recall that the concept of social niche refers to social and physical arrangements that are composed of roles, relationships, and rationales that exist within particular social and physical settings. In his description of subcultures, Coleman (1987) suggested the relevance of niches for the development of motivations for various types of occupational violations. He contended that at least three subcultures are relevant: (1) organizations in which various activities, including white-collar crime, take place; (2) industries that involve relationships between organizations and individuals (clothing manufacturing, entertainment, steel production); and (3) occupations (accountants, managers) shared by those who work in patterned and regular ways within various organizations and industries. These subcultures (or niches) can be examined individually and in terms of important relationships among them and their participants. For example, a particular executive simultaneously is involved in the social niche of his company (Widget Tech), is related to executives of other companies in the same industry (widget manufacturing and sales), and is a member of occupational and professional groups and associations (CEOs of Southcentral USA, Widget Executives Benevolent Society).

Social niches are relevant for understanding white-collar crime because they tend to isolate their members from the wider society and more broadly shared values. Within such niches, employees learn roles that link participants to common ways of acting. For example, company executives learn to be team players, responding to a host of formal, informal, and generally understood expectations within the company. And professionals learn "standards" and "ethics" that govern their work regardless of their corporate or industrial affiliation. These understandings often operate to constrain behavior. However, they also may encourage some kinds of violations. (I will develop this point further in the discussion of rationales later in this chapter.)

Motives and justifications for violation also are learned within the niches. Carey's (1978:384) description of employees' attitudes toward selling a particular drug in spite of tests revealing dangerous side effects provides an example: "No one involved expressed any strong repugnance or even opposition to selling the unsafe drug. Rather, they all seemed to drift into the activity without thinking a great deal about it." Niches also provide the structure and context in which opportunities to violate become available and identifiable.

Opportunities for violations, and their relative attractiveness, vary from industry to industry. And opportunities differ sharply between profit-seeking corporations and government. Illustrating variation by industry, Coleman pointed to the automobile industry and to Leonard and Weber's (1970) finding that this industry essentially forces car dealers into illegal or unethical business practices. Turning to variation at the organizational level, Coleman (1987:431) concluded (with some reservations) that "the attractiveness of illicit opportunities increases as profitability declines"—that is, *within* any organization. Occupational variations in opportunities for white-collar crime have received little attention. Some variations are fairly obvious: Executive administrators have more opportunities to participate in scams to bilk the public than do mail room clerks; financial consultants have more opportunities to participate in insider trading than do commercial truck drivers. (The argument here is that opportunities to participate in *corporate crime against public victims* vary by occupation.) Occupation also is an excellent example of the relevance of roles in composing social niches.

Hagan and Parker (1985) identified somewhat different social niches by examining the structure of the economy, ownership of means of production, and authority within the workplace. They describe structural positions within the "organization of work": employers, managers, petty bourgeoisie, and workers. They contend that there are important differences among the positions in terms of the opportunities to participate in different types of white-collar crime. They argue also that the probability of being caught and the severity of punishment for those who are caught both vary depending on the structural positions of those involved. Hagan and Parker's (1985:312–313) study of securities violations provides examples: "Employers are located in positions of power that allow them to use organizational resources to commit white-collar crimes," but, they are less likely to be charged under the criminal code.

Neither Coleman nor Hagan and Parker paid attention to the *physical* dimension in the concept of social niche as I use it. However, we can infer its relevance from their discussions of opportunity. Access to various resources (including materials, technology, information, and authority) is partly a matter of *social location* and partly a matter of *physical access*. For example, only high-ranking executives of certain electrical companies were invited to attend the conspiratorial meetings. Those who were chosen met in places removed from the everyday business of their companies and industry. These secret meeting places provided concealment and allowed control over participation and information.

Coleman (1987) provides an excellent discussion of *rationales* for corporate crime. Following Sutherland's (1924) lead, Coleman focused on the importance of "symbolic constructions," or justifications, as integral parts of the causal process in white-collar criminality. He suggests a typology of rationales that includes the following: denial of harm, denial of the necessity of some laws, and assertion of the necessity of certain types of illegal behavior to achieve important goals.

Rationales are specific to the prevailing rules, which include professional standards, occupational norms, company policies, and industry-wide regulations. As with other rationales, they neutralize, suspend, or modify the operating rules—even to the point that some of the rationales become rules in their own right. For example, the assertion about the need to violate certain rules "for the good of the company" can become a part of the rules about being a team player.

SOCIAL ACTIONS Considering the variety of industries and their diverse products and services, we can assume that corporate violations are varied in content and form. Still, certain patterns emerge. Consider the case of the Richardson-Merrell Company. (The following description draws primarily from Coleman, 1989:43–47.) This pharmaceutical company developed and marketed a cholesterol inhibitor to be used by heart patients. While management prepared a major marketing effort, research results began to emerge suggesting problems with the new drug. Female rats given high doses of the drug (MER/29) died; monkeys given the drug suffered weight loss, blood changes, and serious visual problems. MER/29 was sold anyway—and with approval by the Food and Drug Administration. How? One laboratory technician testified that she was told to change the reports on some tests and to make up data for other (nonexistent) test animals showing no harmful side effects. Coleman (1989:44) summarized the results: "By the time MER/29 was finally taken off the market, over four hundred thousand people had used the drug, and at least five thousand had suffered serious side effects—usually the 'classic triad' of hair loss, severe skin problems, and cataracts."

Concealing and falsifying test data required by regulatory companies is one patterned way of victimizing the public. Pharmaceutical companies do it:

Richardson-Merrell with MER/29, Eli Lilly with Oraflex, and A. H. Robbins with the Dalkon Shield, to name just a few. Firestone, a major manufacturer of automobile tires, did the same with mounting evidence of flaws in the Firestone 500 steel-belted radial tire. Production and marketing continued in spite of a government survey, complaints from distributors including Chevrolet, Atlas, Ford, and Montgomery Ward, and investigative evidence compiled by company officials, all of which indicated a very high rate of tire failure. The consequences:

> By the time Firestone stopped production of the 500 at the end of 1977, over 23 million of them had been produced. The whole fiasco has been a devastating blow to the Firestone Corporation. Its president has resigned for 'personal reasons,' and the company has been hit with over 250 damage suits that could add $100 million or more to the $234 million cost of the recall the government forced upon it. . . . But once again the public was the real loser. Tens of thousands of 500s failed on the road, contributing to numerous accidents and at least forty-one deaths [Coleman, 1989:42].

In addition to all of these, it seems likely that Ford concealed evidence of the dangers of the Pinto gas tank (as described earlier), that GM knew of the problems with the brakes in their X-cars, and that Olin Corporation falsified reports to the government to conceal its violations of mercury emissions into the Niagara River.

Concealment involves a set of activities and reflects a set of relationships. It usually cannot be done by a single person acting alone. It involves people within different positions, both within and outside of the organization of concern. Moreover, it reflects a set of shared understandings, illustrated perhaps by a comment by Alfred P. Sloan, then president of General Motors, in response to the question of using safety glass in Chevrolet cars:

> I am trying to protect the interests of the stockholders of General Motors and the corporation's operating position. . . . You can perhaps say that I am selfish, but business is selfish. We are not a charitable institution— we are trying to make a profit for our stockholders [Mintz and Cohen, 1976:110].

Other patterns of corporate violation involve deception, fraud, bribery, and tax evasion. For governments, examples include harassment of private citizens, illegal surveillance, violation of civil liberties, and corrupt use of power. The point is this: Corporate violations of public rights and interests are organized, rather than random, and involve routine features of relationships and shared understandings.

Noncorporate Violators

SOCIAL ORGANIZATION People without formal organizational affiliations and outside of the context of the corporation or firm can carry out violations against the public. Medical quackery, for example, often involves only one or a few practitioners who conceal information from patients or customers, deceive them, or engage in other fraudulent activities. Miller (1978:63) defined the medical quack as "any person who deludes the public by selling medical items that are of dubious value for dealing with the purchaser's complaints." Although he does not mention it specifically in this definition, Miller included the sale of either medical supplies or medical services. Roebuck and Hunter (1970) identified a variety of quacks: those who sell illegal devices or treatments; those who are licensed medical practitioners, but who provide services or "remedies" that are not generally accepted either within or outside of mainstream medical practice; and, licensed physicians who engage in unorthodox practices.

Miller (1978) contends that the practice of medical quackery involves either an itinerant single performer or a central actor within a larger scheme. The following illustration suggests that the quack and other patterns of "noncorporate violations against the public" involve social organizational features that are essential to the practices. Consider the activities of Dudley J. LeBlanc, an accomplished medicine show operator. LeBlanc sold a "medical marvel" called Hadacol, which was claimed as a cure for "anemia, arthritis, asthma, diabetes, epilepsy, heart trouble, high and low blood pressure, gallstones, parlytic stroke, tuberculosis, and ulcers" (Young, 1967:320). LeBlanc traveled in a 17-car special train, provided entertainment with clowns and celebrities (such as Jack Dempsey), sponsored a beauty contest for the local talent, and had prizes, band concerts, and circus acts (a midget and a man over nine feet tall).

LeBlanc and other medical hucksters of the past tailored their practices to the character and organization of their intended clients. They provided an opportunity for entertainment, and they offered remedies for real and imagined maladies for those who had few alternatives. They offered authentication of the wonder drugs in terms that their unsophisticated audiences could understand and believe, principally in the form of testimonials. The relevance of social organization for the practice of medical quackery can be seen in the transition of its major forms with the changing times. Concretely, the traveling medicine show gradually disappeared as conventional medical practice became more widely available and as transportation improved, allowing easier access to medical services. But the quack medical clinic has emerged in contemporary cities, almost certainly taking advantage of the anonymity of the setting and the demand for low-cost, special services (abortion, cancer treatment).

Other forms of noncorporate crimes against the public include charity and educational placement schemes. For example, two men organized a charity fraud called HELP. It purported to raise money to help underprivileged children and cost the public several thousands of dollars before it was uncovered. Similarly, one educational placement operator collected fees of $5,000 to $25,000 to help students get into professional schools. This scheme netted an estimated $1 million (See Bequai, 1978:58).

As with their corporate counterparts, noncorporate crimes against the public involve taking advantage of consumers in a distinctly American way: in the pursuit of profit and often in a conspiracy that involves the victim as a partner in some questionable arrangement, swindle or con. There is a widely accepted truism among con artists and among some legitimate business operators: You can't cheat an honest person. This point of view often is referred to as caveat emptor—let the buyer beware.

SOCIAL NICHES AND SOCIAL ACTIONS The violations of concern here happen outside the organizational context of companies and corporations for the most part. They nonetheless involve constellations of roles, relationships, rationales, and a more-or-less specialized physical setting. And they involve organized and recurrent patterns of activity. The relevance of social niches and social actions for understanding noncorporate white-collar deviance is illustrated in the following description of fortune-telling. Brief illustrations from the social niche and social actions of medical quackery conclude this section.

In the spring of 1988, the American public learned that Nancy Reagan consulted astrological charts and a fortune-teller in arranging President Reagan's appointments and calendar. The news brought widespread negative reactions from the press and the general public. Fortune-telling involves activities that violate some widely shared norms and values and, in some cases, civil and criminal laws. The social niches of fortune-telling facilitate the activities and tend to insulate those involved from social control.

According to Tatro (1974), the men and women who are drawn into fortune-telling come disproportionately from low-income and socially marginal families. And as with those who pursue careers in medicine, law, academia, and business, fortune-telling candidates typically require a sponsor or mentor to make the necessary connections and to learn the basics of the profession. Similarly, fortune-tellers often enter the trade by following in the footsteps of relatives or by joining the family business. Fortune-telling roles include the seer, the client, and, often, supportive role players who lend credibility to the setting and to the fortune-teller's performance. Related roles include the receptionist and the associate (or shill). The receptionist manages appointments and checks to see if the advisor is available when a client comes to call. This role and its performance lend respectability to the operation. Those who occupy this position often are, or at least seem to be, unrelated to the fortune-teller. Further, they often present appearances that are very conventional. The associate may be used to gather bits of information about clients, to activate props, or to provide instruction or direction on the proper response to various experiences. (For example, the associate can dramatize an event by feigning surprise, shock, or fear, thus coaching the client on what is to be seen or felt.) Associates or shills may be witting or unwitting decoys for the fortune-teller's performance. Those who are unaware often provide very convincing legitimation.

The client plays a special role as a collaborator in the performance. The role is essentially supportive or conspiratorial in character. (Most clients do not visit the spiritual advisor to expose deception.) Clients participate in the process of deceiving themselves. Those who decide to seek help from a spiritual advisor may be skeptical or even cynical at first, but they are at least considering the possibility that fortune-telling is real and valuable. The interactions that develop and unfold are managed by the seer to capitalize on the client's readiness to believe.

Tatro (1974) identified two key techniques (*social actions*) fortune-tellers use to control the interactions and provide pursuasive information and predictions. The first, "calculated vagueness," involves a series of general statements about the customer and his or her personal circumstances. These statements are likely to be true both because they are very general and because the seer attends to various cues and clues provided by the person's dress, mannerisms, demeanor, and physical, social, and psychological attributes. The person may be told, for example, that he is strong, smart, and friendly, but that he is not comfortable sharing his feelings with others. Few contemporary American men would disagree with that description of themselves!

A second patterned activity involves what Tatro (1974) called "fishing." The fortune-teller must tell the client something that he or she wants or needs to hear. To do that, the advisor offers a series of vaguely stated characterizations and watches for the customer's response. These may be stated either positively or negatively, as long as they are sufficiently general. For example, the seer may say "I see that you are concerned about your health," or "It does not seem that money is a major problem now." Of course, if the customer responds in a way that suggests otherwise, the fortune-teller can always build from there: "No, money is not now a problem, but it may be in the immediate future!" Through fishing the fortune-teller can identify issues that concern the client, discover the direction of concern, and then restate the discovered information in different words (see Tatro, 1974:296).

The *physical setting* varies depending in part on the particular style of the fortune-teller. Tatro identifies three general types: those who work in relatively permanent houses or buildings within a community, those who travel with carnivals or gypsy caravans, and nightclub "entertainers." Some of the seer's activities will be enhanced by darkness and shadows, and special lighting effects often play a part. The advisor may use a crystal ball or other prop that serves as a mystical vessel—and that can be used to focus the client's attention. Religious statues and other artifacts, tarot cards, and tea leaves set the mood and serve various purposes in the fortune-teller's efforts with the client. Not uncommonly, customer parking is arranged strategically so that the fortune-teller or associate can see the customer's car and license plate but, at the same time, so that the car is hidden from view from others who are passing by. For those operating within relatively permanent quarters, a foyer or other anteroom provides concealment for the advisor and current clients, and a place for others to wait and perhaps be "cased" by an associate.

Finally, the *rationales* that operate within fortune-telling, like those found in other "con" schemes, focus on the absence of a victim. Fortune-tellers note that they do not force people to come to them and that they are simply providing a service that is in demand. They also allude to the pervasiveness of deviant or questionable behavior among people generally, drawing examples in part from things told them in confidence by their clients (Tatro, 1974).

The social niche of the medical quack provides an interesting comparison. Carol Whitehurst (1974) provides a detailed description of one such operation in Mexico, where a clinic provided services to patients (most of whom were Americans) with chronic diseases such as arthritis. She described the physical setting and the related roles as follows:

> Upon entering the clinic one is struck by the modernity of the building and the contrast with most buildings in Mexicali. The interior is spacious and clean, well-lighted and airy. Near the entrance is a glassed-in section for the office girls, their filing cabinets, and adding machines. . . .
>
> On one of the long walls there are two doors displaying the names of the doctors and leading to their offices. Between the doors is a large artificial rubber plant. On the walls there are two framed diplomas and two signs which read, in English, "No smoking." . . .
>
> The receptionists, or office girls, all spoke English and were well groomed, young, and attractive. They also seemed to be entirely bored with their jobs and with the patients. . . . They were not actually rude, but their habit of keeping the patients waiting and never mitigating this with a smile or an apology made me feel that they were totally disinterested.
>
> Upon coming to the clinic for the first time, the patient is asked to fill out a form giving his name, address, telephone number, and age. There is no medical history of any kind requested, nor is it necessary to state your complaint. The patient is then given a number and is asked to wait until the number is called. The wait is usually from two to three hours, depending on how busy the doctor is. It appears that the doctor generally sees from sixty to eighty patients each of the five days a week the clinic is open. . . .

When the patient is finally called, he enters one of the two offices and is seated in one of the deep, comfortable, gold vinyl-covered chairs in front of the doctor's huge desk. The office . . . generally gives an appearance of opulence [Whitehurst, 1974:166–167].

Whitehurst describes her medical examination by "Dr. C." as quick, perfunctory, and, apparently, medically incorrect. (He poked hard enough on her right hip to provoke a pained reaction, which seemed pertinent to his diagnosis even though her previous survey had involved her left hip; he did not comment on the bandages that wrapped her right leg from ankle to knee). Whitehurst described the patients who were interviewed as working class and lower-middle-class, middle-aged and older, primarily white Americans, with complaints mostly of arthritis, but including emphysema or asthma, and exczema. (The description of patients comes primarily from interviews with a sample of 15.)

Whitehurst also described the physical setting and emphasized the ways in which the setting is arranged to create the impression of legitimacy: a clean, spacious, apparently "American" office building in the midst of a poor, decidedly Mexican neighborhood and community. The roles in this "medical clinic" niche are parallel to those that would be found in any American clinical setting, but some aspects are modified or exaggerated. For example, according to Whitehurst (1974:174), the doctors are "dealing in hope." To the extent that this is true, the patient's role requires somewhat greater faith than is ordinary, and the physician's role requires a convincing portrayal of sincerity. Without those, questions about the clinic's location (in an out-of-the-way Mexican community) and the legitimacy of the treatment present continuing problems for the participants.

Many of the patients have been told by "conventional" medical authorities that nothing more can be done for them medically. The clinic doctors assert a counterclaim (*rationale*): "I can cure you—no matter what others have said. All I ask is the chance to prove it" (Cobb, 1958). For their part, patients credit the doctors with superior knowledge and superhuman powers: "They can tell just by looking at you what's wrong" (rationale).

Crimes Within Organizations

The second major type of white-collar crime involves violations within organizations. Examples of violations by corporate violators include dangerous working conditions and exploitation of employees (especially labor). Violations by noncorporate violators include employee theft, embezzlement, and other activities through which the organization becomes the victim.

Corporate Violators

SOCIAL ORGANIZATION In the organization of the American economy, labor is a cost, and by traditional and contemporary definitions, successful competition in business requires minimizing that cost. From that point of view, workers' satisfaction, safety, and health are relevant only to the extent that they decrease or increase profits. Not surprisingly, then, American business firms typically have not pursued policies that emphasize the health and welfare of employees. To the contrary, work-related injuries and illnesses in the United States are extensive by most estimates and may be increasing.

For example, an article in *U.S. News and World Report* ("Is Your Job Dangerous to Your Health?," 1979:39) claims that exposure of workers to contaminating synthetic chemicals is increasing as the production of such chemicals increases—from 1.3 billion pounds in 1940, to 96.7 billion pounds in 1960, to 306.6 billion pounds in 1977. Further, more than 20 million Americans work with chemicals that damage the human nervous system. Similarly, it appears that death rates in coal mining are *increasing*, from .04 per 200,000 employee hours in 1983 to .07 in the first quarter of 1984 ("Mine Safety and Health Administration Data," 1984:39; both this and the article on chemical contaminants are discussed in Simon and Eitzen, 1986:109).

Assessing the extent of work-related injuries and disease is difficult for a variety of reasons: (1) Some industrial accidents result from unsafe conditions, while others result from worker neglect or carelessness; (2) many industrial accidents are not reported, either by workers or by company officials, while others are claimed for worker compensation when the accidents were not work related; (3) many industrial diseases develop and are manifested only over many years, so causal linkages are hard to establish; and (4) the effects of exposure spread beyond the work force that is involved in the production process. Consider the example of vinyl chloride and angiosarcoma (a rare cancer of the liver).

Vinyl chloride is the foundation for the enormous plastics industry. More than a thousand workers are employed producing vinyl chloride, while even more are involved in transforming it into polyvinyl chloride (PVC), and still more work in factories that produce finished plastic products. Over time, cases of angiosarcoma began to appear in remarkable concentrations among people who worked with vinyl chloride and PVC. Manufacturers initially denied the connection between the chemical and lung diseases. The link is now firmly established, but those who are at risk because of exposure are scattered across a variety of companies, industries, and occupational categories. Moreover, even those who do not work directly with vinyl chloride are at risk because of exposure in the environment and through the use of various products, including hair spray. (See Coleman, 1989:33–34).

U.S. News and World Report ("Is Your Job Dangerous to Your Health?,"
1979:42) lists suspected hazards for industrial workers, including arsenic,
asbestos, benzene, cotton dust, radiation, and vinyl chloride. The number of
workers exposed exceeds four million, and they are at risk of developing cancer
(of various types), black-lung disease, bronchitis, emphysema, central nervous
system damage, and sterility and of having spontaneous abortions, among other
possibilities.

Competition, success, achievement, progress, and profit—these salient
values organize American business enterprise and the society generally. Individual and collective efforts, directed by these values, have produced a nation
unequalled in material wealth, and a style of life that is the envy of most around
the world. At the same time, the values imply an ordering of priorities that
encourages, or at least allows, trade-offs. If profit is the first concern, then
moral, social, and civic responsibility are no more than secondary in importance. As the former General Motors president said, "Business is selfish."
Those who regard themselves as business leaders (and who, typically, are so
regarded by others) pride themselves on being hard-nosed realists, implying
that there is no room for sentiment in the cutthroat world of competition. That
point of view can be both callous to health and safety issues and short sighted.

A frequent corporate response to allegations of dangerous working conditions has been denial and resistance. For example, mining companies that were
fined for safety violations not only refused to comply but also declined to pay
the fines: In 1974, there were some 91,000 unpaid fines worth some $20 million
("West Virginia," 1976). Similarly, Coleman (1989:33) has offered the following
summary:

> This pattern of irresponsibility goes far beyond merely ignoring safety
> warnings. Corporations have attempted to suppress evidence that these
> substances were dangerous, funded biased research to "prove" false con-
> clusions, lied to their workers and to the public, battled against adequate
> safety standards, and obstructed enforcement efforts.

SOCIAL NICHES AND SOCIAL ACTIONS The roles, relationships, rationales,
settings, and patterned activities (social actions) of concern here are largely
the same as those described earlier in the section on *corporate violations* against
the public. The victims are different—company employees rather than the
community or society generally. Accordingly, I will focus here on employee
victims.

The asbestos industry provides an example of the relevance of the organization of corporate niches for understanding white-collar violations within
organizations. Prior to the mid-1950s, doctors employed by large asbestos
producing companies were prohibited by company policy from telling patients

(workers) about abnormal chest X rays and from recommending treatment outside of the company facilities. A study published in 1955 established a clear link between asbestos and lung cancer. The asbestos industry responded by hiring researchers to "prove" that asbestos was harmless. "By 1960, sixty-three scientific papers had been published on the problems of asbestos exposure. The eleven studies funded by the asbestos industry all rejected the connection between asbestos and lung cancer and minimized the dangers of asbestiosis. All fifty-two indpendent studies, on the other hand, found asbestos to pose a major threat to human health" (Coleman, 1989:35; Berman, 1978).

Edward Gross (1980:71) contended that the position (role) of top management encourages resistance to efforts that could reduce the production of profits of the organization: "Their ambition will not be merely personal, for they will have discovered that their own goals are best pursued through assisting the organization to attain its goals." Stock options, salaries tied to production figures, bonuses, and other arrangements ensure that top executives will have strong interests in a company's profits. As Clinard (1983:134) observed: "The internal corporate master of the executive is the 'bottom line'; often it is corporate profits, not morality, that provide the test of the effectiveness of top management."

Those in middle management and lower positions typically have little to gain from corporate profits. And workers in the lowest positions within the hierarchy usually have the greatest risk of exposure to dangerous conditions. Thus, the organization of roles and relationships within the niche supports profit as the priority at the expense of concerns about the safety and health of workers. Rationales that support unsafe conditions parallel those discussed in the earlier section on corporate violations against the public, especially those suggested by Coleman (1987). More specifically, major justifications take the form of denying harm, denying the necessity of regulations, and asserting the need to take certain risks.

Noncorporate Violators

SOCIAL ORGANIZATION Some of the cost that labor represents in our private enterprise system comes not from the amount paid in salaries and benefits but from white-collar crime. The violations of concern here include employee theft and embezzlement or, more generally, the illegal use of a job to obtain money, goods, services, or other benefits. Many people think of embezzlement as the major form of white-collar crime. Estimates of losses from theft by employees at all levels suggest that it is extensive and costly. For example, a Chamber of Commerce report estimated the cost of embezzlement and pilferage at $7 billion per year. The report also asserted that some 30 percent of all business failures are the result of employees' dishonesty and that approximately half of all plant and office employees steal (Chamber of Commerce of the United States, 1974).

A more thorough study was conducted and reported by Hollinger and Clark in 1983. These researchers found that 35 percent of retail employees, 33 percent of hospital employees, and 28 percent of manufacturing employees reported some theft. Theft by employees is pervasive, and some now suggest that it is expected by employers and managers who see it as a trade-off for low wages (Mars, 1982; Liebow, 1967). However, violations of performance rules and expectations may be even more extensive. Hollinger and Clark found that from 65 percent to 82 percent of employees violate one or more performance norm or rule: They take long lunch breaks, goldbrick, and abuse sick-leave privileges, for example.

Gerald Mars (1982) contended that employee violations vary depending on the organization of the work and the work setting. Opportunity is one important factor. Those who are unemployed have trouble embezzling funds; embezzling requires at a minimum a position of trust with access to company funds. Most employees have limited access to money, goods, or services and, as a consequence, most employee theft involves small items of little value (Coleman, 1989:81; Altheide and others, 1978:90). Yet evidence indicates that the major share of losses results from violations by those in supervisory positions (Jaspan, 1974).

Some amount of occupational crime is built into the structure of work in our contemporary society. (The following discussion draws heavily from Altheide and others; 1978:90–124.) Consider, for example, early research by Melville Dalton (1959). Dalton observed patterns of inappropriate to illegal allocations of time, materials, and labor in chemical plants. His examination of these incidents led him to conclude that the activities were regarded by those involved as a part of a system of unofficial rewards and perquisites. The line between extra benefits as rewards for merit and loyalty, on the one hand, and illegal use of company goods and services, on the other, was blurred and, according to Dalton, necessarily flexible. Gouldner (1954) reported a similar circumstance in his study of a gypsum factory. The change in plant management highlighted patterns of worker violations that the former manager allowed. Violations included use of company equipment and materials for personal purposes, goldbricking, and loose supervision of time sheets. This leniency appeared to be related to workers' satisfaction and high morale.

Further evidence of the ways in which violations are built into the social organization of work is found in research by Donald Horning (1970). This study of a television plant uncovered understandings that parallel those found in the chemical and gypsum plants. Workers shared ideas about ownership that defined some items as "ownerless." As a result, some things could be taken because they did not belong to anyone. Likewise, Horning found that there were fairly clear ideas about the size and quantity of things that could be taken "without harm."

Altheide and his associates (1978) have pointed to four ways in which occupational crime is built into work in our society:

> Patterns of "wages-in-kind" have emerged over time and are institutionalized in many businesses and industries (taking scraps of materials home for personal use; taking small tools that were just lying around)

> The implications of a society-wide belief in the equality of people (employees who are paid less than others whom they regard as no more than their equals sometimes take the difference in unofficial benefits)

> Work group norms in a variety of settings encourage and support theft of various types; these same norms limit theft in its quantity and form (retail clerks accidentally damage merchandise, which then must be disposed of; the damage and the disposing are done in ways that allow the store managers to reclaim their losses)

> Shared understandings about what constitutes real crime (workers assert that taking things that are going to be wasted or thrown away is not the same as stealing merchandise off of the shelf)

Most generally, employee crime is a part of the social organization of work in the sense that it reflects the central relationships of the process—for example, manufacturing or sales. These relationships include ownership, supervision, and production. Ownership separates those who have from those who do not. Those who own can induce others to perform tasks that will yield a benefit for them (the owners). The inducements almost never will be equal to the owners' benefits. And the organization of business in our society encourages owners to maximize their benefits (profit) by minimizing workers' inducements (salaries or the quality of working conditions). This inequality and the tensions it produces can be managed in a variety of ways. The primary strategies in our society have been (1) social control (various methods of management including supervision) and (2) loyalty (identification with the goals and values of the business and its owners). In a sense, owners and managers are relying on supervision and loyalty to avert or resolve tensions that are created by the organization of power, resources, and benefits. Not surprisingly, these forms of social control are not always effective.

The following discussion of social niches and social actions will focus on embezzlement as a major form of noncorporate, organizational deviance.

SOCIAL NICHES AND SOCIAL ACTIONS Estimates from the *Uniform Crime Reports* indicate that there are approximately 8,000 arrests each year for embezzlement. Typical incidents involve thousands of dollars, and sometimes millions, suggesting that the scale of these violations is enormous. Some incidents are particularly spectacular, involving people who are well known and who successfully steal *hundreds of millions* of dollars. Coleman (1989:86) suggested that the record holder among embezzlers is Robert L. Vesco, who diverted $224 million in cash and securities and then purchased protection against extradition from both Costa Rica and the Bahamas.

The relevance of *social niches* for this type of white-collar crime can be seen in Gerald Mars's (1982) discussion of pilferage among employees in four different types of occupations. Using an animal metaphor, Mars characterized types of work as "donkey," "wolf," "vulture," and "hawk." The structure of each type provides different opportunities within different arrangements. Donkey work is done within highly structured settings, involves little freedom or mobility, and is a part of constraining relationships (direct supervision). Examples include sales clerks and supermarket cashiers. Work of the wolf variety is done within teams or crews and involves relatively little supervisory oversight outside of the team. The work may or may not involve mobility. Examples include shift work in factories and trash collection. Vulture work allows considerable autonomy but at the same time involves organizational constraint. Truck driving and waiting tables are examples. Finally, hawk work requires individuality and autonomy. There is little or no supervision and considerable discretion. Examples include independent professionals (lawyers, professors) and quasi-professionals (pool cleaners, interior decorators).

The description suggests ways in which the organization of work presents or limits opportunities of various types. Generally speaking, only those involved in hawk work will have the opportunity and access required to embezzle money. Donkeys, to be sure, can steal money from cash registers, and vultures and wolves can participate in scams to skim money from customers and clients. However, embezzlement refers more specifically to violations in which people use their positions of trust to divert or otherwise misuse significant sums of money from company coffers. *Roles*—what people do in their jobs—and *relationships*—whether or not they are supervised or have authority—are factors that critically shape the prospects for trust violations or embezzlement.

Donald Cressey (1953, 1965) interviewed incarcerated embezzlers and provided an incisive description of the *rationales* that appear to be critical to this pattern of violations. His description of these "verbalized motives" reveals the essence of the concept of rationales as I use it in this book:

> "Verbalized motives" are not something invented by embezzlers (or anyone else) on the spur of the moment. Before they can be taken over by an

individual, these verbalizations exist as group definitions in which the behavior in question, even crime, is in a sense *appropriate*. There are any number of popular ideologies that sanction crime in our culture: "Honesty is the best policy, but business is business." . . . Once these verbalizations have been assimilated and internalized by individuals, they take a form such as: "I'm only going to use the money temporarily, so I am borrowing, not stealing" [Cressey, 1965:14].

Cressey theorized that three factors encourage this pattern of white-collar crime: a "nonshareable" financial problem; the recognition of opportunity; and, vocabularies of adjustment (that is, "verbalized motive," or rationales). These factors can be understood as aspects of one or more of the social niches occupied by the individual violates trust. The financial problem cannot be shared, for example, because it is discrediting to the person's superiors and to his family (a gambling debt, for example). Opportunity reflects both the person's location within the social niche of work and his or her relationship to others within the setting. And the rationales must relate directly to the person's position at work in order to allow him or her to violate rules that are (or have been) regarded as legitimate. (Cressey's explanation and related research will be discussed further later in this chapter.)

Toward a General Theory of White-Collar Crime as Deviance

Throughout this book, we have observed three distinctions in efforts to explain deviance: (1) the need to account for both violation and social control, (2) the distinction between violation and deviance, and the (3) difference between epidemiology and causation. They remain important issues in this discussion of white-collar crime. Additionally, it should be clear by now that white-collar crime encompasses an impressive variety of acts, actors, violations, and victims. Indeed we may need separate explanations for at least the four types of violation distinguished here: corporate and noncorporate violations against the public and corporate and noncorporate violations within organizations. In spite of these diversities, I will argue in the following pages that the variables and relationships identified in the epidemiological and causal theories (convergence theory) provide general explanations of the phenomena. And more specifically, the proposed theory incorporates and, in some cases explicates, basic ideas about white-collar crime from Sutherland (1940), Cressey (1953), Hagan and Parker (1985), and Coleman (1987).

Explaining Rates and Patterns of White-Collar Crime

Recall that the central variable in the epidemiological theory is integration: As *integration* decreases, both *violation* and *social control* increase.

James Coleman (1987) pointed to the social structure of industrial capitalism and the "culture of competition" as critical for understanding white-collar crime. Although he focused his attention primarily on the causes (or origins) of these violations, Coleman clearly appreciated the significance of these factors in the epidemiology of white-collar crime. He asserted that a "decrease in the availability or attractiveness of legitimate opportunities will normally increase the attractiveness of illegal opportunities" (Coleman, 1987:425). It would seem, then, that a central problem is to describe and explain variations in legitimate opportunities—just as Robert Merton (1938) suggested many years ago. (See Chapters 4 and 6 for a description of Merton's anomie theory of deviance and limited opportunities.) Unfortunately, Coleman suggests instead that the next step is to account for the distribution of opportunities for white-collar crime.

The convergence theory asserts that structural changes that reduce integration will be related to increases in both rates of violation and rates of social control. I have suggested throughout this book that the long-term trend in our society is toward changing types and levels of integration. Chapter 2, for example, has a description of the transition from rural, agricultural society to urban, industrial society. The change included transformations in the composition of families, in the organization of work, and in relationships among individuals and groups within communities and the larger society. In broad terms, the transition was from "mechanical" to "organic" solidarity. (See earlier discussions of Durkheim's work, especially in Chapter 2).

The relevance of these structural changes for violation, social control, and deviance are specified further in Chapter 6 in discussions of historical developments and prostitution. I argue that increased differentiation in this society has resulted in the development of increasingly diverse social niches. Further, these diverse niches provide the context in which expectations that diverge from conventional norms can and do develop. (As indicated in previous discussions, "conventional norms" refer to those that are most widely shared and/or those that are most likely to be enforced.) Coleman (1989:13) observes that bureaucratization has had a profound impact on modern social life. One major consequence of huge corporations and government agencies dominating our lives is the segmenting of social experience.

In a separate work, Coleman (1987:420) provided a specific example of *segmentation:* "The economic sphere is usually constructed as a separate realm from the world of home, family, and friendship, and both worlds contain their own values and operative principles." Thus, generally shared norms and values, such as ideas about fairness and the common good, are separate or separable from expectations about business, profit, and financial success. Coleman (1987:423) concluded: "Because of this isolation, work-related sub-cultures are often able to maintain a definition of certain criminal activities as acceptable or even required behavior, when they are clearly condemned by society as a whole."

Has white-collar crime increased over the past several hundred years in American society? It is hard to know for certain because we have not kept systematic data to describe the range of diverse activities that do, or might, count as violations. But changes in the organization of the society generally and of work more specifically virtually guarantee that those activities have increased. For example, most observers agree that American society is now beyond industrialization as the major social and economic force in social organization (Bell, 1976). In this postindustrial state, the distribution of workers' roles has changed sharply, producing at least one critically important consequence: The proportion of the labor force engaged in white-collar work has more than tripled since the turn of the century (U.S. Bureau of the Census, 1984). It is almost certain that the opportunities for white-collar violations have increased, and, if Coleman is correct, there must have been significant increases in the rates of those violations.

The proposed theory also asserts that decreased integration is related to increases in social control. And, again, this pattern (decreasing integration, increasing social control) has been documented in various chapters, especially, Chapters 2, 6, and 7). Matters of occupational and organizational conduct have not been exceptions in this trend. Indeed, the primary direction of change clearly has been toward *increasing* efforts to regulate and control these activities. However, some commonly accepted assumptions are not true—for example, antimonopoly sentiments and rules are not modern inventions. Concerns about the effects of restraint of trade are part of a long Western tradition and have firm roots in English and American common law (see Coleman, 1989:146–148).

In the United States, traditions and informal expectations have given way to law and formal enforcement efforts for virtually all types of white-collar crime. Populist movements promoted early antimonopoly legislation (the Sherman Act of 1890), and continued concerns and agitation produced refinements of interpretation, application, and enforcement (in the Clayton Act of 1914 and the Celler-Kefauver Act of 1950). Early efforts by muckraking journalists encouraged the drafting and passage of the Pure Food and Drug Act and the Meat Inspection Act in the early 1900s, while later consumer movement activities resulted in the Pure Food and Drug Act of 1962. Since that time, consumer protection legislation has increased at a remarkable pace and has included the National Traffic and Motor Vehicle Safety Act of 1966 and the Consumer Product Safety Act of 1972.

Coleman (1989:148) has provided a careful and detailed discussion of the emergence and change of laws concerning white-collar crime. He also summarized a part of the relationship between integration and social control that my theory proposes:

> The consumer's movement was part of an effort to find an effective substitute for the informal controls of the small town. The growth of industrial capitalism brought about fundamental changes in the techniques of production. . . . [For example] the environmental movement stemmed from the desire of people to protect themselves from the new hazards created by industrial technology and to preserve the quality of the environment.
>
> Thus, *conflicts* and *contradictions* in the political economy provided the original impetus for the social movements that agitated for new legislation. The conflicts between producers and consumers, labor and business, farmers and corporations, are inherent in industrial capitalism, and any changes in the delicate balance between those conflicting groups may spur appeals for legislative intervention [emphases added].

Of course, legislation is only a part of the process of social control. Enforcement of rules and laws represents a separate problem and question. In fact, rates of "legislating" and rates of enforcing could vary independently. For now, however, the theory asserts that both are parts of the general process of social control and, thus, they vary together because they are both related to levels of and changes in integration. (I will consider issues related to enforcement more fully in discussions of policy implications later in this chapter.)

Explaining Causes of White-Collar Crime

Recall that the central variables in the causal theory are *integration, attachment,* and *learning violations:* As integration decreases, attachment decreases, and learning of violations increases.

Edwin Sutherland (1940:12) conducted the first systematic study of white-collar crime and introduced the first effort to explain its origins and causes. The "framework" of his arguments is revealing:

> White-collar criminality is real criminality, being in all cases in violation of the criminal law.
>
> White-collar criminality differs from lower-class criminality principally in implementation of the criminal law, which segregates white-collar criminals administratively from other criminals.

A theory of criminal behavior which will explain both white-collar criminality and lower-class criminality is needed.

A hypothesis of this nature is suggested in terms of differential association and social disorganization.

Taken together, the first and second premises recognize the distinction between violation and crime (or deviance). Violation of the law is violation and thus for Sutherland, "real crime." At the same time, all violations are not treated the same and the differences are important. The final assertion provides a summary of a causal theory of white-collar crime and, for Sutherland, *all crime:* "White-collar criminality, just as other systematic criminality, is learned in direct or indirect association with those who already practice the behavior. . . . [And] those who learn this criminal behavior are segregated from frequent and intimate contact with law-abiding behavior" (Sutherland, 1940:11).

Recall the review of Sutherland's theory in Chapter 4. In his later work, Sutherland proposed substituting the term *differential social organization* for *social disorganization* in order to emphasize that crime is "rooted in the social organization and is an expression of that social organization" (Sutherland and Cressey, 1978:83). White-collar crime is not an exception. "Groups and individuals are individuated; they are more concerned with their specialized group or individual interests than with the larger welfare. Consequently, it is not possible for the community to present a solid front in opposition to crime" (Sutherland, 1940:11). Sutherland's ideas about social disorganization and individuation closely parallel what are here called *declining* integration and attachment. Frank Hartung (1950) offered a similar idea in his interpretation of research on the wholesale meat industry. He suggested the alternative term of *social differentiation.*

Donald Cressey (1953) refined Sutherland's "differential association" learning theory of white-collar crime in his study of convicted embezzlers. Both the original ideas and Cressey's refinements are reflected in the causal theory I propose here. As noted earlier in this chapter, Cressey pointed to three factors in the causal process: a nonshareable financial problem, opportunity and the knowledge necessary to act upon the opportunity, and some rationale that adjusts the contradiction between actions and the standards usually observed. Cressey's work is especially important for its discussion of the role of rationales in the development of white-collar crime patterns. Clinard's (1952) study of wartime rationing, Ball's (1960) study of rent control violations, and Mars's (1974) study of pilferage among dockworkers provide some support for Cressey's rationalization hypothesis. these studies also provide concrete examples of what Sutherland (in Sutherland and Cressey, 1978:81) called "definitions favorable to law violation" and Cressey (1953) called rationalizations, or "verbalized motives."

Clinard (1952) disagreed with some aspects of Cressey's proposed causal process. For example, he asserted that personality characteristics are important parts of causation for some violators. However, additional support for differential association variables, as opposed to personality factors, is provided by Robert Lane's (1953) observations of patterns of violation within certain firms—patterns that persisted in spite of several changes in the management of those firms. Clinard also questioned the causal role of the "nonshareable financial problem." Some of the subjects of his wartime black market study did not evidence such problems.

Likewise, Dorothy Zietz's (1981) study of female embezzlers raises questions about the causal significance of the "nonshareable problem." These women clearly experienced financial crises. However, the problems were widely known among the women's families, friends, and supervisors. "Nonshareable problems" probably are not necessary causes of white-collar crime. Rather, they are simply among those definitions or rationales that can promote white-collar crime.

Recall that Cressey's theory focused specifically on embezzlement. Even with the limitation just discussed, it is not clear that the theory can be generalized to other types of white-collar crime. The remaining factors (opportunity and the knowledge to act upon the opportunity and rationales that justify violation) are very general. More importantly, they are stated or implied variables in Sutherland's general theory of crime. It is useful to think of Sutherland's explanation as a "'principle of normative conflict' which proposes that high crime rates occur in societies and groups characterized by conditions that lead to the development of extensive criminalistic subcultures" (Cressey 1978:95). This general thesis clearly is consonant with the arguments developed here concerning declining integration and attachment, the differentiation of social niches, and the consequent increase in opportunities to learn violating conduct.

James Coleman (1987:408) built from the foundations of Sutherland's and Cressey's work. He was concerned with locating the origins of symbolic motivations ("verbalized motives," or rationales) for white-collar crimes. He asserted that "criminal behavior results from the coincidence of appropriate motivation and opportunity." However, Coleman concluded that no theory of motivation can explain the causes of these crimes and turned instead to an examination of structural positions in advanced capitalist nations. He defined opportunity as "a potential course of action, made possible by a particular set of conditions, which has been incorporated into an actor's repertoire of behavioral possibilities" (Coleman, 1987:409).

Opportunities for white-collar crime are distributed unequally in industrial societies. On the one hand, a "culture of competition" provides a set of general values that may encourage aggressive pursuit of success, even to the point of cheating or otherwise going beyond the rules. On the other hand, there are normative restraints that operate through generally shared values and ideals (cooperation, mutual support, and fair play). These general restraints lose effectiveness somewhat in industrial societies because of increasing segmentation. Increasing segmentation and the consequent increase in opportunities to violate, like Sutherland's and Cressey's individuation and normative conflict, appear to be parts of the more general processes that are here called declining integration and attachment and increased opportunities to learn and perform violations.

Coleman has provided an excellent and detailed analysis of the structure of opportunity in the United States as an advanced industrial nation. Perhaps most importantly, he asserted that "law is the most basic of all forces shaping the distribution of opportunities, for it is the law that ultimately determines which behaviors are considered criminal offenses" (Coleman, 1987:425). In addition to recognizing the role of social control in shaping deviance, Coleman described ways in which the social organization shapes both violation and social control: "[The laws] are products of conflicts among many competing social interests, the outcome of which ultimately reflects the structure of power and the internal contradictions of contemporary industrial capitalism" (1987:425). It would be difficult, indeed, to improve upon Coleman's assertion as a statement of the *dialectical* reality of deviance as it has been described and explained in this book.

Hagan and Parker (1985) proposed a structural theory of both white-collar crime and its punishment. They proposed a *relational* measure of class position and identified four structural positions of concern: employers, managers, petty bourgeoisie, and workers. Hagan and Parker's research focused on securities violations and revealed that structural position is related to both the kinds of crimes committed and the kinds of punishment that result. For example, employers commit crimes that are the largest in scope (have the most victims and occur over the largest geopolitical area), but they do not receive sanctions commensurate with that scope. Let's now turn our attention to the issues of social control and the deterrence of white-collar crime.

Policy Implications: Deterrence and White-Collar Crime

It appears that white-collar violations and social control efforts directed against them are increasing. During the past century, there have been increasing opportunities for virtually all types of white-collar crime and increases in rules and laws governing corporate, organizational, and occupational conduct. These changes may be inextricably linked with the processes of industrialization and the development of related technologies. That is, there may have been increases in white-collar crime and social control regardless of changes in levels of integration within communities and the society. However, it appears that changing rates and types of integration typically accompany industrial development. If that is true, we may be observing the simultaneous effects of two major causal variables: increased opportunities (for violation and social control) and declining integration. In addition, public awareness of white-collar crime has increased steadily since the turn of the century and has reached a very high level since the late 1960s. The net result is a widely shared public perception that white-collar crime, business crime, and coporate misconduct are rampant.

Public opinion surveys in the early 1980s (see Harris poll 1983; Gallup, 1983a, 1983b; and Green, 1982) reveal low levels of confidence among respondents who were asked to rate business, business executives, corporations and their leaders, and government. Moreover, research since the early 1950s reveals that the public is concerned about white-collar crime and, under some circumstances, supports serious penalties for violators. For example, Newman (1953) found that respondents favored more severe penalties for food adulteration than were in fact given by administrative agencies. And Peter Rossi and his associates (1974) found that Baltimore respondents rated "manufacturing and selling drugs known to be harmful to users" as more serious than crimes such as armed robbery and assault with a gun.

Formal social control efforts have taken four primary forms: criminal statutes and their enforcement, rules and laws promulgated and enforced by administrative regulatory agencies, civil law and civil law suits, and professional ethics and professional self-regulation. The best evidence to date suggests that all of the various strategies have been used sparingly, the efforts have been underfunded and inefficient, and the deterrence results have been negligible (see Coleman, 1989: 153–198). Beginning as early as Sutherland's research in the 1930s, researchers have observed that white-collar offenders are unlikely to suffer the consequences of criminal justice prosecution.

Clinard and Yeager (1980) have reported that only 4 percent of the penalties levied for corporate crimes involved criminal cases against executives. Of those individuals who were convicted, 62.5 percent received probation, over 21 percent received suspended sentences, and approximately 29 percent received short jail terms, which averaged just over a month. (The total exceeds 100 percent because the categories are not mutually exclusive. For example, offenders could receive both suspended sentences and probation.) McCormick (1977) reported that less than 5 percent of those who were convicted of criminal antitrust charges served any time in jail. Susan Shapiro (1985:182) examined cases of stock fraud: "Out of every 100 suspects investigated by the SEC [Security and Exchange Commission], 93 have committed securities violations that carry criminal penalties. Legal action is taken against 46 of them, but only 11 are selected for criminal treatment. Six of these are indicted; 5 will be convicted and 3 sentenced to prison. . . . Of those found to have engaged in securities fraud, 88 percent never have to contend with the criminal justice system at all."

There is an interesting controversy in the research on sanctions against white-collar criminals. The issue concerns the relationship between the social status of offenders (relative wealth, power, and prestige) and the severity of the penalty following conviction. It generally has been assumed that higher status offenders get less severe penalties. That conclusion has been based on the following reasoning: (1) Prosecutors and judges will be reluctant to incarcerate those with powerful positions in the community, and (2) people who have the most resources will be best able to avoid severe consequences for their actions. It came as some surprise, then, that Wheeler, Weisburd, and Bode (1982) found a positive relationship between social status and sentence severity. These researchers examined violations of eight major white-collar offenses for the fiscal years 1976 to 1978 in seven federal judicial districts. The major finding with regard to social status and sentencing was that the probability of imprisonment rises with the occupational status of the defendant. Hagan and Parker (1985) have since provided an interpretation that appears to clarify the matter. Apparently, there is a complex relationship between structural position (including occupational status) and the kinds of white-collar violations committed. Employers are likely to commit different kinds of crimes than workers do. Further, there is a complex relationship between the kinds of violations committed and the form of social control that results. Hagan and Parker, for example, found that employers were least likely to be subject to the criminal code.

The general explanation of white-collar crime (as proposed in this chapter) suggests that effective social control requires changes in the social organization of society and the organization of work and business within the society. At the present time, the worlds of business and work are relatively insulated from dominant, conventional values that have to do with honesty, fair play, equality, and humanity. Work and business activities are organized around values of competition, achievement, and notions about reality that emphasize cutthroat, selfish pursuit of interests. It is possible that a new "business ethos" could emerge that would lessen the gap between business ethics and general values. There is no evidence that "dog-eat-dog" competition or selfish individual aggression are necessary to the success of work and business enterprises— although we clearly *assume* that the two necessarily go together.

Social changes that increase the convergence between "business values" and general social values (changes that increase integration) should reduce the level of violations and the rate of social control. Some would suggest that hard-nosed business leaders would never consider such changes. Their shared values are based on assumptions about human nature that deny sentiments such as altruism and loyalty. There may be a convincing argument, however, from research on employee theft. Evidence increasingly indicates that worker loyalty is a, if not the, critical variable in employee theft. Hollinger and Clark (1983), for example, found that workers with high levels of job satisfaction are unlikely to steal—even when they have the opportunity. They also noted that factors such as family income and economic pressures are not related to employee theft. In addition, good research evidence shows that informal work groups tend to define acceptable types and amounts of employee theft. It seems to follow, then, that one way to reduce employee crime is to increase the level of job satisfaction among workers and within informal work groups.

If leaders within business communities were convinced of the value of employee loyalty and job satisfaction, other changes might follow. Efforts to operate companies as "good citizens" might increase. Programs to enhance worker safety might be expanded. Businesses might pursue humane and philanthropic policies and practices without any tax incentive. Any and all of these practices would tend to reduce the insulation of the world of work from the broader values of the society and, in the process, increase the social control effects of increased integration.

In the short run, however, it seems likely that we will continue on the course of more rules, laws, and regulatory agencies and activities. The most likely result, from historical experience, is that work and business generally will become *more* isolated and insulated from the larger society—at least to the extent necessary to resist and elude social control.

The Need for Research

Research on white-collar crime has accumulated since Sutherland's (1940) pioneer effort. The accumulation of knowledge has been slow, in part because of the diversity of issues and topics the concept covers. I introduced a typology to facilitate systematic thinking about the diverse violations and to encourage comparisons among the types. For example, are fraud and antitrust violations similar in any way? Does it make sense to talk about white-collar crime as including both embezzlement and environmental pollution? In addition to the problem of diverse violations, explaining white-collar crime is difficult because many of the violations involve activities that are complicated and arcane. For example, few social researchers have good working knowledge of the intricacies of securities exchange. Moreover, gaining access to relevant data is difficult. Many of those who would be the subjects of research have the power to deny potentially revealing investigations.

Research is needed to pursue explanation of the separate (but related) matters of epidemiology and causality. It is not currently possible to describe with any precision the distribution of any type of white-collar violation. Neither is it possible to describe the distribution of social control activities or organizations. As has been noted throughout this book, we cannot hope to explain anything until we can at least describe it in some systematic fashion. But some promising theories are consonant with some systematic observational data. Research in the future can build from existing data and from early theoretical efforts. Suggestions for future research follow.

Researching Rates and Patterns of White-Collar Crime

The typology of white-collar violations introduced earlier in the chapter (see Table 9.1) provides a conceptual foundation for basic epidemiological description. At the most fundamental level, research is needed to enumerate and describe the "membership" of the four cells of the typology: (1) corporate crimes against the public, (2) noncorporate crimes against the public; (3) corporate crimes within organizations, and (4) noncorporate crimes within organizations. To date, the composition of the types has only been suggested by examples. It would be useful as a beginning simply to identify instances of white-collar violation and attempt to classify them using the typology. Such an effort undoubtedly would reveal the limits of the typology and should help to refine or revise it as a tool for systematic description.

Hagan and Parker's classification suggests a different way of identifying, describing, and counting white-collar crime events. Their research suggests that violations vary by structural positions. Future research should expand on these observations. Do managers violate antitrust laws? Are employers more likely than managers to engage in fraud or misrepresentation? In addition, Hagan and Parker's classification of structural positions could be combined with my proposed typology of violations to suggest other important questions: Are there relationships between structural positons and types of violations as defined by the typology? Do rates of particular types of white-collar violations increase or decrease with changes in the distribution of types of jobs (managers, workers)?

The epidemiological theory poses two central questions for research: (1) Do rates of white-collar violation increase as integration decreases? (2) Do efforts to control white-collar violations increase as integration decreases? Research should focus on nationally representative samples to avoid problems of generalization that have plagued previous studies. Furthermore, we need comparative research. Do Western societies or those at similar points of industrialization have similar patterns and rates of white-collar crime? Have white-collar violations increased simply because there are more opportunities, or do rates of violation vary consistently with levels of integration (regardless of opportunities)?

Researching Causes of White-Collar Crime

Four related theories of the origins of white-collar crime are reviewed in this chapter and summarized, at least partially, in the proposed convergence theory. Sutherland (1940) proposed that white-collar crime is caused by differential social organization and learning within different associations. He argued that the social organization becomes incapable of preventing business and corporate crime because of the individuation of interests and values. When that happens, some people have increased opportunities to learn both the techniques of violating and the necessary motives or definitions that favor violation. Cressey's (1953) theory of embezzlement builds from Sutherland's theory and asserts that embezzling occurs when people experience three necessary conditions: unshareable financial problems, opportunities to solve those problems through violation of trust, and learned motives or rationalizations that justify the prospective behavior.

Hagan and Parker (1985) have proposed that the structural organization of work influences the opportunity for white-collar violations. They have argued further that this organization determines the likelihood of any punishment and, for those sanctioned, the type of punishment. Coleman (1987) proposed an integrated theory that asserts that the structure of modern capitalism (and, presumably, the structure of any economy) determines the distribution of opportunities and the nature and types of motivations for white-collar crime.

The convergence theory proposed here is generally consonant with all four theories, specifies some of the proposed concepts, and asserts relationships among the causal variables. For example, Sutherland's concepts of "individuation" and "differential social organization" are understood as issues of integration. (Recall that I define *integration* specifically in terms of the classical sociological theories of Durkheim, Marx, and Weber.) His concept of learning, which Cressey and Coleman include, is specified as learning violations and is related to the concept of integration through the idea of attachment. A test of hypotheses from the convergence theory would provide partial tests of one or more of the four specific theories.

Future research requires a careful and precise identification of the behaviors and events that count as instances of white-collar violation (perhaps using the proposed typology for identification and classification). The current proposal focuses on corporate crimes against the public, especially misrepresentation of products. Future research also requires a careful and precise identification of the activities that count as social control. In this proposal, the following types of social control are to be examined: civil suits, criminal prosecutions, regulatory agency investigations and penalties, and professional sanctions (for example, censure of a pharmaceutical company). The research will use a three-stage sampling procedure. First, industrial countries will be sampled. From the population of industrialized nations, a sample of three countries will be selected. The industries that are common to those countries will be identified and listed. At stage two, a representative sample of industries will be selected. For the example, imagine that the number of industries selected is six. At stage three, the largest companies in the industries in each country will be identified.

In the United States, most industries are dominated by no more than three or four companies. If other industrial nations have similar patterns of concentration, we should be able to represent the industries with no more than six to eight companies—and still reflect variation in the size of companies. In that case, the final sample would consist of slightly less than 150 companies (three countries, six industries, eight companies per industry = 144 companies). A sample of that size is not uncommon in research on corporate crime (see the review of earlier research throughout this chapter). From here, however, the research problem becomes more difficult. For example, there is the problem of language, plus issues of law and custom and their variations from nation to nation and society to society.

In addition, counting violations presents a formidable problem. The proposed theory and virtually all of the previous research support the conclusion that social control is selective. We should expect to find instances of violation that have not been detected by social control agencies. The simplest way to identify violations is by examining the activities and records of social control agencies. But we need to know about violations that *have not been subjected* to social control. One strategy is to question those who may be violators. Hollinger and Clark (1983) apparently were successful in doing that, but their research was on employee theft. They asked employees of various industries to report their violations. The proposed research would require self-report data from those who are in a position to encourage, require, commit, and/or conceal misrepresentations.

At the same time, the proposed research must provide for the collection of data to describe variations in integration. By borrowing from Hansmann and Quigley's (1982), study of societal heterogeneity and homicide (see Chapter 5), integration would be measured in terms of differences in income, language, ethnicity, and religion among groups within each country. Heterogeneity thus becomes a measure of levels of integration. Income heterogeneity would be measured (observed) using the Gini coefficient. If all incomes are equal in a nation, the Gini coefficient is zero. As income differences increase, the coefficient approaches a value of one. Language, ethnic, and religious heterogeneity would be measured using a coefficient that calculates the number of different languages, ethnic groups, and religions in a nation, as well as the proportion of people who speak or belong to each.

The basic hypothesis asserts that higher levels of heterogeneity (thus, *lower* levels of integration) are associated with higher rates of corporate misrepresentation of products (higher rates of white-collar crime).

Some Final Thoughts
on Social Policy

A recent article in the *New Republic* (Kondracke, 1988:16) argues against the legalization of drugs. The argument is well reasoned and appears to be compelling—partly because it fits contemporary, conventional biases. The author begins with an assertion that seems unassailable: "The next time you hear that a drunk driver slammed into a school bus full of children or that a stoned railroad engineer has killed 16 people in a train wreck, think about this: if the advocates of legalized drugs have their way, there will be more of this, a lot more." Clearly, we do not want more of this. But does the argument stand on its merits? If criminal penalties for the possession of heroin are eliminated, will more people drink alcohol, drive drunk, and slam into school buses? Turn the question around. If penalties for the possession or sale of heroin are increased, will fewer drunk people crash into school buses? The relationships between rules and penalties and between penalties and compliance are complex. And the relationships between types of penalties and types of drug use are complex.

Kondracke is concerned about the consequences of removing legal sanctions for the possession and use of a variety of drugs. Like many others, he assumes that legalization or decriminalization is a form of approval: If it's not against the law, it must be okay. I have denied that point of view in this book. Moreover, the literature of research on crime and deviance provides strong evidence that law and its enforcement are *not effective* in preventing, reducing, or otherwise controlling most kinds of human behavior. Still more, law does not determine individual beliefs or social orientations to most matters. Do people in American society practice religion because it is required by law? Would more Americans go to church if criminal statutes required attendance? Would children stop eating and craving chocolate if it were made illegal? Would adults stop drinking and craving coffee if criminal statutes prohibited its possession and use? We may choose to have laws because we want to punish people who act or fail to act in certain ways. But preventing and encouraging social actions of various sorts probably can be done more effectively through other devices.

The comparison of heroin, church attendance, chocolate, and coffee may seem odd. We often assume that some kinds of behaviors or substances are naturally dangerous and deviant, while others are neutral, harmless, or acceptable. But this reasoning, too, has been questioned systematically throughout this book. Whether or not something is dangerous or deviant is an empirical question. Still, it seems natural to assume the dangerousness of at least some kinds of drugs. Szasz (1985:ix) has offered an interesting point of view in contrast:

> There is probably one thing, and one thing only, on which the leaders of all modern states agree; on which Catholics, Protestants, Jews, Mohammedans, and atheists agree; on which Democrats, Republicans, Socialists, Communists, Liberals, and Conservatives agree; on which medical and scientific authorities throughout the world agree; and on which the views, as expressed through opinion polls and voting records, of the large majority of individuals in all civilized countries agree. That thing is the "scientific fact" that certain substances which people like to ingest or inject are "dangerous" both to those who use them and to others; and that use of such substances constitutes "drug abuse" or "drug addiction"—a disease whose control and eradication are the duty of the combined forces of the medical profession and the state. However, there is little agreement—from people to people, country to country, even decade to decade—on which substances are acceptable and their use therefore considered a popular pastime, and which substances are unacceptable and their use therefore considered "drug abuse" and "drug addiction."

Szasz proceeds to argue that the issues of addictiveness and dangerousness are matters of social judgment and politics. Many chemical substances could be identified as drugs. Some of these are selected and treated as drugs; others are not. In our own society, for example, we have been reluctant to characterize alcohol, tobacco, and caffeine as drugs and to recognize the chemical dependency that they create. Yet we have been enthusiastic about selecting other drugs for condemnation and control. We have invented laws, agencies, and practices to deal with the drugs that are selected as harmful to individuals and society. *A critical question concerns the consequences of efforts to control.* Szasz (1985:12) offered this assessment: "Our drug abuse experts, legislators, psychiatrists, and other professional guardians of our medical morals have been operating chicken hatcheries: they continue—partly by means of certain characteristic, tactical abuses of our language—to manufacture and maintain the drug problem they ostensibly try to solve."

Szasz has argued that efforts to control drug use result in the creation and maintenance of the drug problem. This is not a new idea. The conception of deviance proposed in this book contends that violation and social control are linked inextricably and that social control shapes and sustains violations—and thus deviance. Neither is it a new idea for scholars of deterrence. Durkheim (1895/1966) recognized the normalcy of both *violation*, which he called crime, and *social control* (punishment); both are regular and necessary features of viable social organization.[1] Mead (1928) described criminal law as a "two-sided sword" that creates a "permanent class of deviants." More recently, Gary Marx (1981) argued that social control agents and agencies contribute to deviance through "escalation, nonenforcement, and covert facilitation."

Efforts to control prostitution through criminal law and its enforcement have given rise to practices that protect participants from the police—and make them vulnerable to exploitation by law enforcers and by pimps and assorted others who live or work at the margins of conventional society. Medicalization is also a method of formal social control. In the case of various problems of living, residual rule violations, or troublesome behaviors, medicalization has given rise to the enormous and profitable industry of mental health/mental illness. Interventions of incredible proportions and at high levels of technical sophistication have not produced declining rates of mental illness or convincing evidence that the problems are medical in nature. Instead, those who are selected or otherwise drawn into the system are *more likely* to remain "mentally ill"—and, the further the person goes into the system, the more likely he or she will be to stay within the system.

In the history of American society, the state, or government, is the agency empowered to exercise force legitimately. There are some exceptions. Government authorities historically have disregarded the use of force—including violence—in families, for example. Only recently have systematic formal efforts emerged to contend with child and spouse abuse. To date, there is some limited evidence that formal intervention may deter spouse abuse. However, it appears that informal definitions are the key to deterring family violence. Formal sanctions threatened or imposed by police officers and criminal courts may not make much difference. (See the discussion of the study by Sherman and Berk, 1984, in Chapter 8.) Likewise, research on white-collar crime suggests that *work group norms* are critical both as causes of violation and as constraints that limit the type and amount of misconduct.

When we look broadly and historically at social organization, violation, social control, and deterrence, an interesting pattern emerges. Our own and other industrial societies have grown in size and complexity and have become more differentiated. Social change generally and differentiation more specifically undermine what Durkheim called "mechanical solidarity": integration founded on similarity among the parts. At the least, the changes that characterize modernizing Western societies seem to produce shifts toward organic solidarity: integration based on interdependence among the parts. As the nature of social organization changes, modes of social control change. Informal social control based on consensus, agreement, or *similarity* of expectations works effectively in simple, mechanically organized societies. Differentiation tends to undermine consensually based social control. Threats to the social order give rise to more formal devices of control as informal efforts fail—or *appear to be* inadequate.

The pattern does not stop here. Instead, a self-perpetuating cycle begins. Formal social control is introduced to supplement or replace informal devices. Formal efforts are less fully grounded in basic shared understandings and agreements and are not as effective as informal methods of control. They nonetheless displace informal practices by making them seem unnecessary or illegitimate. Because the formal efforts are, at best, only marginally effective, it is likely that more and more formal procedures will be introduced. This, in turn, further reduces the informal foundations of agreement, and formal efforts become still less effective.

Obviously, this portrait of social organization, change, and social control is painted with very broad strokes. It nonetheless captures major outlines of change as they were described by the classical theorists whose works provide a foundation for the general convergence theory proposed here. Durkheim's multidimensional conception of social organization (seen in terms of solidarity, equilibrium, and commonality), Marx's conception of dialectical social order in continuous tension, and Weber's descriptions of shared understandings and the consequences of rationalization all point to consequences of differentiation for the maintenance of social order. A central thesis is that formal social control is necessarily less potent and less effective than informal social control.

Imagine a continuum of social control, with the most potent forms of informal control at one end and the most potent forms of formal social control at the other. At the informal pole, we might find religious communities like those at Jonestown. Jim Jones established a religious sect, called "The Peoples Temple," in 1956. In 1974, Jones and his followers established a utopian community in the South American country of Guyana. Four years later, more than 900 members of the community committed suicide en masse because Jones told them that life was no longer worth living and that they should "die with dignity." Mothers watched as infants were given cyanide-laced Kool-Aid and participated in distributing the poison to their older children. With only a few objecting, this community of believers destroyed themselves—because it was the right thing to do.

Federal prisons would be found at the other end of the imaginary continuum. Many of these are modern structures, rationally and intentionally designed to facilitate the management of people who are being held against their will. Most employ management, supervision, and custodial strategies and tactics that reflect the latest technical and scientific knowledge. Most are equipped with sophisticated surveillance and control equipment. And most federal prisons are staffed with officers, clinicians, and administrators who are relatively highly trained and well paid. In spite of all of that, most corrections personnel and assorted experts agree that prison staff govern by *consent of the inmates*. Moreover, rates of crime and rule violation are extremely high *within* the prisons—and illegal drug trafficking is virtually out of control (Bunker, 1979).

It is not necessarily surprising to find crime in prison. After all, a very high proportion of the members of this community are criminals! But federal prisons are supposed to represent our very best efforts to subject people and their conduct to formal control. Neither is it surprising that people will make strong commitments on the basis of religious faith. At the same time, these observations support and refine the thesis about the relative effectiveness of formal and informal methods of social control. Somewhere along the way, the idea developed that law and its enforcement are the necessary and legitimate devices for social control in so-called advanced, modern societies. More than 70 years ago, Weber saw the ascendance of formal rule as the legitimate form and source of authority (Weber, 1978, 1958).

We have come to respond to conflicts and threats of various sorts with the common plea: "There ought to be a law." For the most part, political leaders and policymakers have obliged. The laws may not be enforceable. They may produce undesired or unintended consequences—for example, supporting and sustaining the behaviors or practices of concern. And they may even contribute to overall decreases in the level of effective social control. Nonetheless, formal methods of social control probably will continue to increase. For example, more laws will be passed and more money will be committed in an all-out war against drugs. The military will be enlisted to mount an assault on the "dealers of death." Drug testing will be made mandatory. Arrests, convictions, and imprisonment may increase.

Meanwhile, research evidence continues to accumulate in support of these conclusions: (1) Family and friendship groups critically influence decisions about drug use, (2) value-based drug education programs can work effectively to deter drug use, (3) treatment programs that facilitate changes in addicts' friendship and other social relationships are effective in ending addictive drug use, and (4) the primary result of the most extensive, expensive, and sophisticated law enforcement efforts ever developed has been to make drug trafficking the most lucrative industry in the history of modern nations.

Still, the general explanation developed in this book asserts that increased social control is related to *increased* integration. Does the illustrative analysis contradict this theoretical premise? No. Instead, it reflects the complexity of social integration. Social integration and social control are *dialectically* related, an argument I have developed since the beginning of this work. When integration decreases, social control increases. As social control increases, integration increases—but the nature of the integration may well change in the process. For example, the long-term trend in the United States has been from *mechanical* solidarity with decreasing integration, to increasing formal social control, to increasing *organic* solidarity. Organic solidarity within a society that continues to differentiate may be fragile by nature. That is, social order is maintained, but the organization of parts is essentially pluralist. There is not so much an overall consensus, or dominant conventional order, as there are shifting alliances among diverse social niches, and rules and laws that are highly situational. Increased integration in this context may refer to instances of enforced or reinforced alliances among certain segments of the society. Consider the following illustration.

The launching of a new federal initiative against drug use and drug trafficking is an instance of increased social control. It well may represent a victory for and an increase in a sense of common purpose among the following: local, state, and federal law enforcement agents and agencies; traditional and conservative political groups and individuals; fundamentalist and conservative church groups; and companies that manufacture and sell high-tech surveillance instruments, weapons, and other equipment. At the same time, a change in priorities may mean that other interests are less well served, and the tactics and strategies may alienate other groups. The following groups may experience declining attachment as a result of the social control effort: inner-city residents who experience law enforcement as a kind of "invading force," the military personnel who are asked to take on new responsibilities that are defined as thankless at best and as interfering with primary missions, yacht owners who are harassed by Coast Guard search and seizure tactics; and AIDS victims and their friends and relatives who believe that more money should be spent on research and treatment to save lives.

Issues of social organization and social control are not simple or one dimensional—but they are not indecipherable either. The convergence theory suggests several principles and this analysis of its policy implications:

1. Social control never works exactly as intended. (There are always unintended consequences.)

2. The nature and form of social control are not determined by the object(s) of concern.

3. Informal social control is potentially much more potent than formal social control is.

The last of these principles raises a problem of critical significance. Is informal social control the answer? Many of the discussions throughout this book imply so. However, there are several problems. First, the concept of social control is not well defined, and distinctions between formal and informal methods have not been specified.[2] Second, informal social control strategies apparently are effective only to the extent that they are grounded in consensus. There is evidence of agreement on some controversial issues, and that may surprise many readers. (See the discussion of policy implications in Chapter 6 for a more detailed description of the potential for consensus.) But it is unlikely that such consensus will exist naturally or automatically in a society as complex and differentiated as ours.

The final issue may be the most troubling. The deterrent power of informal social control depends heavily on agreement. Because we value representative democracy, we tend to believe in majority rule—unless, of course, our point of view is in conflict with the dominant position. The awesome power of informal social control and the fact that the power is based in consensus may be especially threatening to people who live in a highly diverse society and who value individuality and individual freedoms. Social control could be very effective. However, the costs and consequences may not be entirely acceptable: rigid conformity, group enforced political and social beliefs, and group-think approaches to decision making. Heresy and treason likely would become the most serious offenses. Shunning and ostracism would be the major penalties.

In the last analysis, violations and social control have consequences that are positive and negative, both from individual points of view and from the point of view of the survival of the society. Prostitution, for example, may provide an outlet for sexual wants or needs that does not directly threaten the institution of the family as we know it. Yet as practiced in our society, prostitution involves and facilitates exploitation. Hookers, tricks, pimps, bar and hotel owners, vice officers, and informants—each of these exploits the others in various combinations. Criminal statutes provide communities with resources for controlling sexual practices and transactions. Still, there is little evidence that law enforcement is efficient in controlling commercial vice. And, on the face of it, there seems little reason to believe that there is any value in transforming someone who is regarded as immoral into someone regarded and treated as criminal.

There is no simple solution for formulating and developing social control policies and practices. However, one theme stands out: The consequences of control should not be worse than those of the behavior of concern. Obviously, this conclusion implies a moral or ethical standard. Such is the nature of social control—and of policy decisions more generally. The proposed explanation of deviance suggests that the relevant standard is social integration. Will control efforts enhance the integration of the community generally, or will they enhance integration in one segment at the cost of further alienating other segments?

No matter how urgent the problem may seem or how compelling the case may be for controlling it, there are limits to our ability to mandate and exact compliance. We have pursued two primary strategies of social control in this century: (1) declaring war (on crime, on poverty, on the "dealers of death") and (2) medicalizing diverse problems of living such as mental illness, alcoholism, and homosexuality. Both approaches involve metaphors that may not be very appropriate. And both deny the political nature of the issues. We have *chosen* to be concerned in particular ways about particular things while we continue to disregard (or even support) remarkably similar things. For example, our national leaders are currently debating the use of military personnel and equipment in the war on drugs. However, nobody is talking seriously about an offensive against Johnny Walker, Jim Beam, or Mogan David, who, as dealers of death, have impressive body counts. The damage, destruction, loss of life, and human misery that can be caused by either cocaine or alcohol certainly justify efforts of the character of a war—if such efforts have any promise of success. We have now tried these tactics on both alcohol and drugs. The results have been remarkably similar and not at all promising.

There is clear and compelling evidence that control through force has limited power in human affairs. The tension between social order and individual freedom may be the ultimate dialectic.

Endnotes

CHAPTER 1

1. This example is taken from conversations between myself and a student in my deviance course some years ago. The student's name, of course, is not Jason.

2. The approaches referred to here are described in ways that oversimplify. These and other points of view will be described more fully in later discussions that introduce convergence theory.

3. The question of harmfulness is more complex than is suggested here. For example, the emergency room data do not indicate how often use of the drugs results in emergency room visits or fatalities. Harm in relation to the frequency of use might be more predictive of deviance.

4. Howard Becker (1963) was among the first to suggest the distinction between "violation," which he called *rule-breaking behavior*, and *deviance*, which he suggested should refer only to those people or behaviors that have been labeled. Becker did not insist on the usage of those terms, but he did caution researchers to recognize the differences. Becker, Kitsuse (1962), Erickson (1962), and others who contributed to the labeling, social definitions, or societal reaction approach argued convincingly that deviance is not inherent in behaviors, persons, or things. Instead, deviance is a property attributed by definition. In making this

important point, these researchers and theorists seem to deny the significance of the referent conduct or event. The major difference between this point of view and the one proposed here is that I see deviance as involving *both* violation and reaction—even though the violation may be accused rather than actual. "Violation" is important even if it involves false allegation because it involves alleged behavior that stands in relationship to some rule or prohibition.

5. Several years ago, I heard a state director of drug law enforcement address a group of prosecuting attorneys. He began by noting that law enforcement efforts had proved virtually useless in managing, let alone slowing or stopping, illegal drug trafficking—despite massive spending programs over several decades. Having begun with that conclusion, he proceeded to advocate more money and more programs for drug law enforcement.

CHAPTER 2

1. The functionalist explanation focuses on punishment rather than the norm violating conduct as such.

2. The following diagram, borrowed from Stinchcombe (1968), captures the logic of functional analysis:

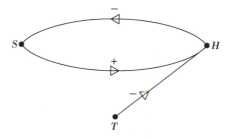

Three variables (elements or components of organization) are identified: S, a structural arrangement; H, homeostasis—a condition of balance; and T, tension produced by forces that tend to undermine or disrupt the homeostasis. When T (for example, violations of norms) threatens the homeostasis (H), punishments in S reinforce the existing order. The example given in the text can be outlined:

> Let S be the structural arrangement of marriage and family, including prohibitions against homosexuality, laws that prohibit various forms of nonmarital sex, and provisions for enforcing the norms and laws.

> Let T be incidents of homosexuality or other real or perceived violations.

> Let H be the contribution of heterosexual marital sex to societal continuity (replacement of members).

The functional circle is completed when the enforcement of norms and rules (S) supports and reinforces the homeostatic condition (H). Note the positive sign and arrow between S and H. See Stinchcombe (1968) and Faia (1986) for excellent and useful discussions of the logic and application of functionalist analysis. Kingsley Davis (1971), provides an example of functionalist explanation in his examination of prostitution.

3. There is considerable controversy surrounding the interpretation of Weber's *verstehen.* Ritzer (1983:125–127) notes that some have interpreted Weber to mean that we must understand the subjective meanings of *individual* human beings. Others insist that Weber's focus was on meanings shared within larger social units (communities or societies). This second interpretation is intended here. My focus is on meanings that are created as *inter*-subjective understandings.

4. We can see Durkheim's appreciation of the multiple dimensions of social reality in his discussions of social facts and collective representations. He contended that social facts are to be considered as *things* (Durkheim, 1966). Nonetheless, he observed that "Social thought . . . by the power which it has over our minds, can make us see things in whatever light it pleases" (Durkheim, 1965:260). And, in spite of his functionalist point of view, he developed a point of view that he called "essential idealism."

Marx emphasized the *material* aspects of social organization, and he clearly was interested in social reality as a force external to individuals. Still, his appreciation of multidimensional social life can be seen in his concepts of the "species being" and the "social mind." Both attend to subjective aspects of human experience (Rossi, 1983:44–45).

5. Many different researchers and theorists have used the concept of "dialectic" in many different ways. (See Rossi, 1983, for an interesting discussion of the variety of meanings attributed to dialectic by Marxist scholars and sociologists.) As used here, the concept encompasses the following ideas about the realities to be observed and explained:

There is an order or organization.

The order consists of parts that stand in a relationship to one another and to the whole that is both complementary and contradictory.

The order is greater than and different from the sum of the parts.

The order or organization has both objective and subjective qualities.

The order is dynamic: temporary and always changing or subject to change as a result of the complementary and contradictory relationships among the parts.

CHAPTER 3

1. I have made this point several times in each chapter. I will develop the issue of social control as a part of social organization here and will consider further the implications of deviance as a part of social organization in subsequent chapters. Social control is a part of social organization. At the same time, the two are related to one another as "part" and "whole," respectively. The idea of dialectic, described in Chapter 2 (especially in end note 5), includes the notion that parts and wholes are related.

2. Social control in its broadest usage refers to social actions or other social phenomena that may be either negative and penalizing *or* positive and rewarding in character. For the purposes of understanding and explaining deviance, however, it seems sufficent to focus on penalties. A case can be made for positive reinforcements that operate to encourage certain lines of behavior and to prevent or discourage other types of activities. As yet, this dimension of social control has not been included in the proposed conception of deviance or the general theories. See Clark and Gibbs (1965) and Gibbs (1977) for particularly thoughtful discussions of social control.

3. The general theory proposed here is called "convergence" theory in part to reflect the idea of deviance as the intersection or convergence of violation and social control. In addition, *convergence* refers to the attempt to find the empirical similarities that are described in previous research and the diverse theories of social organization and deviance.

4. As used here, equilibrium is interchangeable with homeostasis as described in Stinchcombe's model in Chapter 2, end note 2.

5. Integration also refers to the *nature* of organization. The level of integration does not determine the content of the parts. For example, capitalist and socialist societies can be equally integrated in terms of any of the dimensions. And preliterate, hunting societies may operate at about the same level of equilibrium as modern, literate, agricultural societies. The theories proposed here do not include explicit ideas about the relationships among the nature of social organization and violations, social control, and deviance.

6. Note again the "part" to "whole" relationship that is characteristic of the concept of dialectic. Social control is part of integration (I) and part of deviance (D). Both are part of the larger social order or organization. The idea that integration and deviance are dialectically related is the core idea of the proposed theory. Note an important qualification: There undoubtedly are some conditions under which the relationship does not hold or is more complex than suggested by the simple assertion. For now, the theory is stated simply. The relationships will require specification through empirical research.

CHAPTER 4

1. I do not mean to suggest a sharp dichotomy in this discussion of types of concern about deviance and functional organization. The differences are matters of emphasis. Certainly, Parsons and his students attended to the "positive functions" of deviance. And Durkheim was well aware of the potential dysfunctionality of deviance, as noted in Chapter 2.

2. Sykes and Matza (1957) took exception to some efforts to specify the content of Sutherland's proposed "motives, drives, and rationalizations"—especially the counterculture ideas Cohen (1955) proposed.

3. The approach proposed here is *not*, in contrast, a mechanical effort to tie specific theoretical arguments together into some package. A mechanical linking would be inappropriate for several reasons. Most importantly, the earlier theories developed from different initial assumptions and focused on different questions and issues.

4. Recall that the subscripts ($_1$ and $_2$) refer to "system states" (see Chapter 3). Similarly, the order of the terms of the theory refers to system states. At any given point, integration (I) at some level is associated with attachment (A) and the other terms at some level. Changes or differences are then calculated on the basis of that comparison.

5. Hirschi described bonds in terms of *attachments* to parents, friends, and school; *commitments* to aspirations for conventional goals; *involvements* in conventional activities; and *beliefs* in the moral validity of societal rules. These distinctions have been collapsed. I have selected the concept of attachment to emphasize the key point: The relationship of the person to the conventional order through interpersonal relationships (and within social niches) is most important for understanding the negotiation of deviance.

CHAPTER 10

1. An anonymous reviewer of this manuscript has pointed out that Durkheim's reference to "crime" is better translated as *delict*, which means a wrong or an offense, but not a serious crime. Taking that point as a given, the need to distinguish functional deviance from nonfunctional deviance is underscored, but the basic argument about the normalcy of *some* deviance stands.

2. Some significant work has been done toward specifying the meaning of the concept of social control. See, especially, Clark and Gibbs (1965) and Gibbs (1977). The central point here is that the concept needs to be defined more precisely within the context of the proposed conception and explanation of deviance.

Bibliography

CHAPTER 1

Abelson, Herbert I., and Ronald B. Atkinson. 1975. *Public Experience with Psychoactive Substances*. Princeton, N.J.: Response Analysis Corporation.

Aday, David P., Jr. 1977. "The Police and the Juvenile Court: An Interorganizational Relationship and Its Consequences." Ph.D. University of Kansas.

Alcohol, Drug Abuse, and Mental Health Administration. 1981. "New Friendships Help Addicts Give Up Drugs." U.S. Department of Health, Education, and Welfare, *ADAMHA NEWS*, December 24.

Ashley, Richard. 1975. *Cocaine: Its History, Uses, and Effects*. New York: St. Martin's Press.

Ball, John C., and John C. Urbaitis. 1970. "Absence of Major Medical Complications Among Chronic Opiate Addicts." In John C. Ball and Carl D. Chambers, eds., *The Epidemiology of Opiate Addiction in the United States*. Springfield, Ill.: C.C. Thomas.

Becker, Howard S. 1963. *Outsiders: Studies in the Sociology of Deviance*. New York: Free Press.

Berger, Peter L. 1963. *Invitation to Sociology: A Humanistic Perspective*. New York: Doubleday/Anchor Books.

Branch, Taylor. 1988. "Let Koop Do It." *The New Republic*, October 24, pp. 22–26.

Brinkley, Joel. 1986. "Drug Wars Seem to Cause More Trade." In *The Times Herald*, Newport News, Va., Sept. 5, pp. A1, A2.

Bunker, Edward. 1979. "A Junkie View of the Quagmire." In Jerome H. Skolnick and Elliott Currie, eds., *Crisis in American Institutions*, 4th ed. Boston: Little, Brown.

Campbell, Donald T. 1969. "Variation and Selective Retention in Socio-Cultural Revolution." *General Systems* 14:69–85.

Davis, Kingsley. 1959. "The Myth of Functional Analysis as a Special Method in Sociology and Anthropology." *American Sociological Review* 24:757–772.

Drug Abuse Warning Network. 1983. *Data from the Drug Abuse Warning Network (DAWN)*, statistical series, quarterly report, provisional data, series G. no. 12 (July–September). Rockville, Md.: National Institute on Drug Abuse.

Edwards, G. 1980. "Opium and After." *Lancet*, February 16, p. 351.

Eitzen, D. Stanley. 1982. *In Conflict and Order: Understanding Society*, 2nd ed. Boston: Allyn & Bacon.

Erickson, Kai T. 1962. "Notes on the Sociology of Deviance." *Social Problems* 9:307–314.

Faia, Michael A. 1986. *Dynamic Functionalism: Strategy and Tactics*. Cambridge, England: Cambridge University Press.

Gibbs, Jack P. 1966. "Conceptions of Deviant Behavior: The Old and the New." *Pacific Sociological Review* 9:9–14.

Gibbs, Jack P. 1972. "Issues in Defining Deviant Behavior." In Robert A. Scott and Jack D. Douglas, eds., *Theoretical Perspectives on Deviance*. New York: Basic Books.

Goode, Erich. 1984a. *Deviant Behavior*, 2nd ed. Englewood Cliffs, N.J.: Prentice-Hall.

Goode, Erich. 1984b. *Drugs in American Society*, 2nd ed. New York: Alfred A. Knopf.

Grinspoon, Lester, and James B. Bakalar. 1976. *Cocaine: A Drug and Its Social Evolution*. New York: Basic Books.

Kaplan, John. 1983. *The Hardest Drug: Heroin and Public Policy*. Chicago: University of Chicago Press.

Kebler, L. F. 1910. "The Present Status of Drug Addiction in the United States." In *Transactions of the American Therapeutic Society*. Philadelphia: F. A. Davis.

Kitsuse, John I. 1962. "Societal Reaction to Deviant Behavior: Problems of Theory and Method." *Social Problems* 9:247–256.

Lindesmith, Alfred R. 1968. *Addiction and Opiates*. Chicago: Aldine.

Messenger, J. C. 1971. "Sex and Repression in an Irish Folk Community." In Donald S. Marshall and Robert C. Suggs, eds., *Human Sexual Behavior*. New York: Basic Books.

Miller, Judith D. 1983. *National Survey on Drug Abuse: Main Findings, 1982*. Rockville, Md.: National Institute on Drug Abuse.

O'Donnell, John A., Harwin L. Voss, Richard R. Clayton, Gerald T. Slatin, and Robin G. W. Room. 1976. *Young Men and Drugs—A National Survey*, NIDA research monograph no. 5. Washington, D.C.: U.S. Government Printing Office.

Ray, Oakley. 1983. *Drugs, Society, and Human Behavior,* 3rd ed. St. Louis: C. V. Mosby.

U.S. Department of Health, Education, and Welfare. 1981. *Health United States.* Washington, D.C.: U.S. Government Printing Office.

U.S. Department of Justice, Bureau of Justice Statistics. 1981. *Dictionary of Criminal Justice Data Terminology.* Washington, D.C.: U.S. Government Printing Office.

Weinberg, Martin S. 1978. "Becoming a Nudist." In Earl Rubington and Martin S. Weinberg, eds. *Deviance: The Interactionist Perspective,* 3rd ed. New York: Macmillan.

CHAPTER 2

Alexander, Jeffrey C. 1982. *Theoretical Logic in Sociology.* Vol. 1: *Positivism, Presuppositions, and Current Controversies.* Berkeley: University of California Press.

"Campus Gays." 1984. *Virginia Gazette,* November 17, p. 7A.

Cohen, G. A. 1978. *Karl Marx's Theory of History: A Defense.* Princeton, N.J.: Princeton University Press.

Collins, R. 1985. *Three Sociological Traditions.* New York: Oxford University Press.

Durkheim, Emile. 1964. *The Division of Labor in Society.* New York: Free Press. (First published in 1893, trans. George Simpson.)

Durkheim, Emile. 1966. *The Rules of Sociological Method.* New York: Macmillan. (First published in 1895, trans. Sarah A. Solovay and John H. Mueller; ed. George E. Catlin.)

Gans, Herbert J. 1972. "The Positive Functions of Poverty." *American Journal of Sociology* 78 (September): 275–289.

Garfinkel, H. 1967. *Studies in Ethnomethodology.* Englewood Cliffs, N.J.: Prentice-Hall.

Greenia, George D. 1984. "Homosexuality and the Judeo-Christian Tradition: From Tolerance to Fear." Public lecture. Williamsburg, Va., February 6.

Inverarity, J. M., P. Lauderdale, and B. C. Feld. 1983. *Law and Society.* Boston: Little, Brown.

Kreps, Gary A. 1986. "Classical Themes, Structural Sociology, and Disaster Research." In Russell R. Dynes and Carlo Pelanda, eds., *Sociology of Disasters: Contribution of Sociology to Disaster Research.* Gorizia, Italy: Franco Angeli.

Marcus, Ruth. 1986. "Sodomy Ruling's Implications Extend Far Beyond Bedroom." *Washington Post,* July 2, pp. A1, A8.

Marx, Karl. 1967. *Capital,* Vol. 1. New York: International Publishers. (First published in 1873.)

Ritzer, G. 1975. *Sociology: A Multiple Paradigm Science.* Boston: Allyn & Bacon.

Ritzer, G. 1983. *Sociological Theory.* New York: Alfred A. Knopf.

Ruesch, Hans. 1951. *Top of the World.* New York: Harper & Row.

Stinchcombe, Arthur L. 1968. *Constructing Social Theories.* New York: Harcourt Brace Jovanovich.

Tucker, R. C., ed. 1978. *The Marx-Engels Reader.* New York: W. W. Norton.

Warriner, Charles K. 1956. "Groups Are Real: A Reaffirmation." *American Sociological Review* 21:549–554.

Warriner, Charles K. 1970. *The Emergence of Society.* Homewood, Ill.: Dorsey Press.

Weber, Max. 1958. *The Protestant Ethic and the Spirit of Capitalism.* New York: Charles Scribner's. (First published in 1904/1905, trans. Talcott Parsons.)

Weber, Max. 1968. In Guenther Roth and Claus Wittich, eds., *Economy and Society: An Outline of Interpretative Sociology.* New York: Bedminster Press. (First published in 1921.)

Yoder, Edwin M., Jr. 1986. "The Idea of Privacy." *Washington Post, July 6, p.B8.*

CHAPTER 3

Bennett, Linda A., and Genevieve M. Ames. 1985. *The American Experience with Alcohol: Contrasting Cultural Perspectives.* New York: Plenum Press.

Biddle, Bruce J., and Edwin J. Thomas. 1966. *Role Theory: Concepts and Research.* New York: Wiley.

Blumer, H. 1951. "Collective Behavior." In Alfred McClung Lee, ed., *New Outline of the Principles of Sociology.* New York: Barnes & Noble.

Bryant, Clifton D. 1982. *Sexual Deviancy and Social Proscription: The Social Context of Carnal Behavior.* New York: Human Sciences Press.

Chambliss, William J. 1978. "The Saints and the Roughnecks." In Barry Krisberg and James Austin, eds., *The Children of Ishmael: Critical Perspectives on Juvenile Justice.* Mountain View, Calif.: Mayfield.

Dubin, Robert. 1978. *Theory Building,* rev. ed. New York: Free Press.

Gibbs, Jack p. 1977. "Social Control, Deterrence, and the Morally Committed." *Social Forces* 56:408–423.

Gusfield, Joseph R. 1963. *Symbolic Crusade: Status Politics and the American Temperance Movement.* Urbana: University of Illinois Press.

Hofstadter, Richard. 1955. *The Age of Reform.* New York: Vintage Books.

Kotarba, Joseph A. 1984. "One More for the Road: The Subversion of Labeling within the Tavern Subculture." In Jack D. Douglas, ed., *The Sociology of Deviance.* Boston: Allyn & Bacon.

Linton, Ralph. 1936. *The Study of Man.* New York: Appleton-Century-Crofts.

Miller, Gale. 1978. *Odd Jobs: The World of Deviant Work.* Englewood Cliffs, N.J.: Prentice-Hall.

Platt, Anthony M. 1969. *The Child Savers: The Invention of Delinquency.* Chicago: University of Chicago Press.

Ray, Oakley. 1983. *Drugs, Society, and Human Behavior.* St. Louis: C. V. Mosby.

Stryker, Sheldon. 1980. *Symbolic Interaction.* Redwood City, Calif.: Benjamin Cummings.

Sutherland, Edwin H., and Donald R. Cressey. 1978. *Criminology,* 10th ed. Philadelphia: J. B. Lippincott.

Thio, Alex. 1983. *Deviant Behavior,* 2nd ed. Boston: Houghton Mifflin.

Tittle, Charles R. 1983. "Social Class and Criminal Behavior: A Critique of the Theoretical Foundation." *Social Forces* 62 (December):334–358.

Tittle, Charles R., and W. J. Villemez. 1977. "Social Class and Criminality." *Social Forces* 56:474–502.

Tittle, Charles R., W. J. Villemez, and D. Smith. 1978. "The Myth of Social Class and Criminality: An Empirical Assessment of the Empirical Evidence." *American Sociological Review* 43 (October):643–656.

Weber, Max. 1968. In Guenther Roth and Claus Wittich, eds., *Economy and Society: An Outline of Interpretative Sociology.* New York: Bedminister Press. (First published in 1921.)

CHAPTER 4

Akers, Ronald L. 1973. *Deviant Behavior: A Social Learning Approach.* Belmont, Calif.: Wadsworth.

Akers, Ronald L. 1985. *Deviant Behavior: A Social Learning Approach*, 3rd ed. Belmont, Calif.: Wadsworth.

Anderson, Linda S., Theodore S. Chiricos, and Gordon P. Waldo. 1977. "Formal and Informal Sanctions: A Comparison of Effects." *Social Problems* 25:103–114.

Anderson, Nels. 1923. *The Hobo: The Sociology of the Homeless Man.* Chicago: University of Chicago Press.

Becker, Howard S. 1953. "Becoming a Marijuana User." *American Journal of Sociology* 59 (November):235–242.

Burgess, Robert L., and Ronald L. Akers. 1966. "A Differential Association-Reinforcement Theory of Criminal Behavior." *Social Problems* 14:128–147.

Chambliss, William J. 1964. "A Sociological Analysis of the Law of Vagrancy." *Social Problems* 12 (Summer):67–77.

Chambliss, William J., and Robert B. Seidman. 1971. *Law, Order and Power.* Reading, Mass. Addison-Wesley.

Cloward, Richard A. 1959. "Illegitimate Means, Anomie, and Deviant Behavior." *American Sociological Review* 24 (April):164–176.

Cloward, Richard A., and Lloyd E. Ohlin. 1960. *Delinquency and Opportunity: A Theory of Delinquent Gangs.* New York: Free Press.

Conger, R. D. 1976. "Social Control and Social Learning Models of Delinquent Behavior: A Synthesis." *Criminology* 14:17–40.

Cressey, Paul G. 1932. *The Taxi-Dance Hall: A Sociological Study of Commercialized Recreation and City Life.* Chicago: University of Chicago Press.

Davis, Kingsley. 1937. "The Sociology of Prostitution." *American Sociological Review* 2:744–755.

Davis, Kingsley. 1948. *Human Society.* New York: Macmillan.

Davis, Kingsley. 1976. "Sexual Behavior." In Robert K. Merton and Robert Nisbet, eds., *Contemporary Social Problems*, 4th ed. New York: Harcourt Brace Jovanovich.

Dentler, Robert A., and Kai T. Erickson. 1959. "The Functions of Deviance in Groups." *Social Problems* 7:98–107.

Erickson, Kai T. 1966. *Wayward Puritans: A Study in the Sociology of Deviance*. New York: Wiley.

Erickson, Maynard, Jack P. Gibbs, and Gary F. Jensen. 1977. "The Deterrence Doctrine and the Perceived Certainty of Legal Punishments." *American Sociological Review* 42:305–317.

Gibbons, Don C. 1982. *Society, Crime, and Criminal Careers: An Introduction*, 4th ed. Englewood Cliffs, N.J.: Prentice-Hall.

Goode, Erich. 1984. *Drugs in American Society*, 2nd ed. New York: Alfred A. Knopf.

Grasmick, Harold G., and Herman M. Milligan, Jr. 1976. "Deterrence Theory Approach to Socioeconomic/Demographic Correlates to Crime." *Social Science Quarterly* 57:608–617.

Grasmick, Harold G., and George J. Bryjak. 1980. "The Deterrent Effect of Perceived Severity of Punishment." *Social Forces* 59:469–491.

Gusfield, Joseph R. 1963. *Symbolic Crusade: Status Politics and the American Temperance Movement*. Urbana: University of Illinois Press.

Hirschi, Travis. 1969. *Causes of Delinquency*. Berkeley: University of California Press.

Jenson, Gary F., Jack P. Gibbs, and Maynard Erickson. 1978. "Perceived Risk of Punishment and Self-Reported Delinquency." *Social Forces* 57:57–78.

Kavolis, Vytautas. 1977. "A Universal Criterion of Pathology." In Earl Rubington and Martin S. Weinberg, eds., *The Study of Social Problems: Five Perspectives*, 2nd ed. New York: Oxford University Press.

Kitsuse, John I., and Aaron V. Cicourel. 1963. "A Note on the Uses of Official Crime Statistics." *Social Problems* 11:131–138.

Lemert, Edwin M. 1953. "An Isolation and Closure Theory of Naive Check Forgery." *Journal of Criminal Law, Criminology, and Police Science* 44 (September–October):296–307.

Lemert, Edwin M. 1958. "The Behavior of the Systematic Check Forger." *Social Problems* 6 (Fall):141–149.

Marcos, Anastasios, Stephen J. Bahr, and Richard E. Johnson. 1986. "Test of a Bonding/Association Theory of Adolescent Drug Use." *Social Forces* 65 (September):135–161.

Matsueda, R. L. 1982. "Testing Control Theory and Differential Association: A Causal Modeling Approach." *American Sociological Review* 47:489–504.

Meier, Robert F., and Weldon T. Johnson. 1977. "Deterrence as Social Control: The Legal and Extralegal Production of Conformity." *American Sociological Review* 42:292–304.

Merton, Robert K. 1938. "Social Structure and Anomie." *American Sociological Review* 3 (October):672–682.

Merton, Robert K. 1957. *Social Theory and Social Structure*, 2nd ed. New York: Free Press.

Merton, Robert K. 1976. "Introduction: The Sociology of Social Problems." In Robert K. Merton and Robert Nisbet, eds., *Contemporary Social Problems*, 4th ed. New York: Harcourt Brace Jovanovich.

Mills, C. Wright. 1943. "The Professional Ideology of Social Pathologies." *American Journal of Sociology* 49 (September):165–180.

Nye, F. Ivan. 1958. *Family Relationships and Delinquent Behavior.* New York: Wiley.

Parsons, Talcott. 1951. *The Social System.* New York: Free Press.

Quinney, Richard. 1969. *Crime and Justice in America.* Boston: Little, Brown.

Quinney, Richard. 1974. *Critique of Legal Order.* Boston: Little, Brown.

Reckless, Walter R. 1973. *The Crime Problem,* 5th ed. New York: Appleton-Century-Crofts.

Rosenquist, Carl M. 1977. "The Moral Premises of Social Pathology." In Earl Rubington and Martin S. Weinberg, eds., *The Study of Social Problems: Five Perspectives,* 2nd ed. New York: Oxford University Press.

Scheff, Thomas J. 1966. *Being Mentally Ill.* Chicago: Aldine.

Schur, Edwin M. 1965. *Crimes Without Victims: Deviant Behavior and Public Policy.* Englewood Cliffs, N.J.: Prentice-Hall.

Scott, Robert A. 1969. *The Making of Blind Men.* New York: Russell Sage Foundation.

Shaw, Clifford R. 1930. *The Jack-Roller: A Delinquent Boy's Own Story.* Chicago: University of Chicago Press.

Silberman, Matthew. 1976. "Toward a Theory of Criminal Deterrence." *American Sociological Review* 41:442–461.

Sutherland, Edwin H., and Donald R. Cressey. 1955/1978. *Criminology,* 10th ed. Philadelphia: J. B. Lippincott. (First published in 1924 with Sutherland as sole author.)

Sykes, Gresham M., and David Matza. 1957. "Techniques of Neutralization: A Theory of Delinquency." *American Sociological Review* 22:664–670.

Thrasher, Frederick M. 1927. *The Gang.* Chicago: University of Chicago Press.

Tittle, Charles R. 1980. *Sanctions and Social Deviance: The Question of Deterrence.* New York: Praeger.

Turk, Austin T. 1969. *Criminality and the Legal Order.* Skokie, Ill.: Rand McNally.

Zorbaugh, Harvey W. 1929. *The Gold Coast and Slum.* Chicago: University of Chicago Press.

CHAPTER 5

Aday, David P., Jr. 1979. "Further Developments in the Uses of Official Crime Data." Presented at the annual meeting of the Southern Sociological Society, Atlanta, Georgia, April.

American Sociological Association. 1984. "Court Case Establishes Limited Protection for Scholars." *ASA Footnotes,* August, 11.

Bailey, Kenneth D. 1982. *Methods of Social Research,* 2nd ed. New York: Free Press.

Brown, Edward J., Timothy J. Flanagan, and Maureen McLeod, eds. 1984. *Sourcebook of Criminal Justice Statistics—1983.* Washington, D.C.: U.S. Government Printing Office.

Campbell, Donald T. 1957. "Factors Relevant to the Validity of Experiments in Social Settings." *Psychological Bulletin* 54(4):297–311.

Dixon, Donald T. 1968. "Bureaucracy and Morality: An Organizational Perspective on a Moral Crusade." *Social Problems* 16 (Fall): 149–151.

Dubin, Robert. 1978. *Theory Building*, rev. ed. New York: Free Press.

Epstein, Edward J. 1977. *Agency of Fear.* New York: G. P. Putnam's.

Goode, Erich. 1984. *Deviant Behavior*, 2nd ed. Englewood Cliffs, N.J.: Prentice-Hall.

Hansmann, Henry B., and John M. Quigley. 1982. "Population Heterogeneity and Sociogenesis of Homicide." *Social Forces* 61:206–224.

Hanson, Bill, George Beschner, James W. Walters, and Elliott Bovell. 1985. *Life with Heroin: Voices from the Inner City.* Lexington, Mass.: Lexington Books.

Hirschi, Travis, and Hanan Selvin. 1966. "False Criteria of Causality in Delinquency Research." *Social Problems* 13:254–268.

Humphreys, Laud. 1975. *Tearoom Trade: Impersonal Sex in Public Places*, enlarged ed. Chicago: Aldine.

Inciardi, James A. 1986. *The War on Drugs: Heroin, Cocaine, and Public Policy.* Mountain View, Calif.: Mayfield.

Kitsuse, John I., and Aaron V. Cicourel. 1973. "A Note on the Uses of Official Statistics." *Social Problems* 11:131–139.

McGarrell, Edmond F., and Timothy J. Flanagan, eds. 1985. *Sourcebook of Criminal Justice Statistics—1984*. Washington, D.C.: U.S. Government Printing Office.

Merton, Robert K. 1949a. "The Bearing of Empirical Research on Sociological Theory." In Robert K. Merton, *On Theoretical Sociology: Five Essays New and Old.* New York: Free Press.

Merton, Robert K. 1949b. "The Bearing of Sociological Theory on Empirical Research." In Robert K. Merton, *On Theoretical Sociology: Five Essays New and Old.* New York: Free Press.

Musto, David F. 1973. *The American Disease: Origins of Narcotic Control.* New Haven, Conn.: Yale University Press.

Pfuhl, Erdwin H., Jr. 1986. *The Deviance Process*, 2nd ed. Belmont, Calif.: Wadsworth.

Reasons, Charles R. 1974. "The Politics of Drugs: An Inquiry in the Sociology of Social Problems," *Sociological Quarterly* 15 (Fall):393–394.

Stapleton, W. Vaughan, and Lee E. Teitelbaum. 1972. *In Defense of Youth: A Study of the Role of Counsel in American Juvenile Courts.* New York: Russell Sage Foundation.

Singer, Max. 1971. "The Vitality of Mythical Numbers." *The Public Interest* 23 (Spring):3–9.

Steffensmeier, Darrell J., and Robert M. Terry. 1975. *Examining Deviance Experimentally.* Port Washington, N.Y.: Alfred Publishing.

Sutherland, Edwin, H., and Donald R. Cressey. 1978. *Criminology*, 10th ed. Philadelphia: J. B. Lippincott.

Warwick, Donald P. 1975. "Tearoom Trade: Means and Ends in Social Research." In Laud Humphreys, *Tearoom Trade: Impersonal Sex in Public Places*. Chicago: Aldine.

von Hoffman, Nicholas. 1975. "Sociological Snoopers and Journalistic Moralizers." In Laud Humphreys, *Tearoom Trade: Impersonal Sex in Public Places*. Chicago: Aldine.

CHAPTER 6

Akers, Ronald L. 1985. *Deviant Behavior: A Social Learning Approach*, 3rd ed. Belmont, Calif.: Wadsworth.

American Law Institute. 1959. *Model Penal Code and Commentaries*. Philadelphia: American Law Institute.

American Law Institute. 1985. *Model Penal Code and Commentaries*. Philadelphia: American Law Institute.

Anderson, Eric. 1974. "Prostitution and Social Justice: Chicago, 1910–15." *Social Service Review* 48:203–228.

Arnold, William R., and Terrance M. Brungardt. 1983. *Juvenile Misconduct and Delinquency*. Boston: Houghton Mifflin.

Becker, Howard S. 1963. *Outsiders: Studies in the Sociology of Deviance*. New York: Free Press.

Benjamin, Harry, and R.E.L. Masters. 1964. *Prostitution and Morality*. New York: Julian Press.

Bieber, Irving. 1962. *Homosexuality: A Psychoanalytic Study of Male Homosexuals*. New York Basic Books.

Bracey, Dorothy Heid. 1979. *"Baby Pros": Profiles of Juvenile Prostitutes*. New York: John Jay Press.

Bryan, James H. 1965. "Apprenticeships in Prostitution." *Social Problems* 12:287–297.

Calhoun, Arthur W. 1945. *A Social History of the American Family*. New York: Barnes & Noble.

Carmen, Arlene, and Howard Moody. 1985. *Working Women: The Subterranean World of Street Prostitution*. New York: Harper & Row.

Costa, Cheryl. n.d. *Tapestry* 49, n.p.

Davis, Kingsley. 1937. "The Sociology of Prostitution." *American Sociological Review* 2:744–755.

Davis, N. J. 1971. "The Prostitute: Developing a Deviant Identity." In James M. Henslin, ed., *Studies in the Sociology of Sex*. New York: Appleton-Century-Crofts.

DeLamater, J., and P. MacCorquodale. 1979. *Premarital Sexuality: Attitudes: Relationships, Behavior*. Madison: University of Wisconsin Press.

Diana, Lewis. 1985. *The Prostitute and Her Clients*. Springfield, Ill.: C. C. Thomas.

Durkheim, Emile. 1956. *The Division of Labor in Society*. New York: Free Press. (First published in 1893.)

Flanagan, Timothy J., and Edmond F. McGarrell, eds. 1986. *Sourcebook of Criminal Justice Statistics—1985*. U.S. Department of Justice, Bureau of Justice Statistics. Washington, D.C.: U.S. Government Printing Office.

Ford, Clellan, and Frank A. Beach. 1951. *Patterns of Sexual Behavior.* New York: Harper & Row.

Gagnon, John H. 1977. *Human Sexualities.* Chicago: Scott, Foresman.

Gagnon, John H., and William Simon, eds. 1973. *The Social Sources of Human Sexuality.* Chicago: Aldine.

Gallup, Gordon G., Jr. 1986. "Unique Features of Human Sexuality in the Context of Evolution." In Donn Byrne and Kathryn Kelley, eds., *Alternative Approaches to the Study of Sexual Behavior.* Hillsdale, N.J.: Lawrence Erlbaum.

Gray, Diana. 1973. "Turning Out: A Study of Teenage Prostitution." *Urban Life and Culture* 1:401–425.

Greenwald, Harold. 1958. *The Call Girl.* New York: Ballantine Books.

Gregersen, Edgar. 1982. *Sexual Practices: The Story of Human Sexuality.* New York: Franklin Watts.

Hagan, John. 1985. *Crime, Criminal Behavior, and Its Control.* New York: McGraw Hill.

Hanson, Bill, George Beschner, James M. Walters, and Elliott Bovell. 1985. *Life with Heroin: Voices from the Inner City.* Boston: D. C. Heath.

Heyl, Barbara Sherman. 1979. *The Madam as Entrepreneur.* New Brunswick, N.J.: Transaction Books.

Holzman, Harold R., and Sharon Pines. 1982. "Buying Sex: The Phenomenology of Being a John." *Deviant Behavior* 4:89–116.

Hunt, Morton M. 1975. *Sexual Behavior in the 1970s.* New York: Dell.

James, Jennifer. 1977. "Prostitutes and Prostitution." In E. Sagarin and Fred Montanino, eds., *Deviants: Voluntary Actors in a Hostile World.* Morristown, N.J.: General Learning Press.

James, Jennifer, and Jane Meyerding. 1977. "Early Sexual Experiences and Prostitution." *American Journal of Psychiatry.* 134:1381–1385.

Kinsey, A. C., W. B. Pomeroy, and C. E. Martin. 1948. *Sexual Behavior in the Human Male.* Philadelphia: W. B. Saunders.

Kinsey, A. C., W. B. Pomeroy, C. E. Martin, and P. A. Gebhard. 1953. *Sexual Behavior in the Human Female.* Philadelphia: W. B. Saunders.

Lowney, Jeremiah, Robert W. Winslow., and Virginia Winslow. 1981. *Deviant Reality: Alternative World Views*, 2nd ed. Boston: Allyn & Bacon.

McCaghy, Charles H. 1985. *Deviant Behavior: Crime, Conflict, and Interest Groups*, 2nd ed. New York: Macmillan.

McGarrell, Edmond F., and Timothy J. Flanagan, eds. 1985. *Sourcebook of Criminal Justice Statistics—1984*. U.S. Department of Justice, Bureau of Justice Statistics. Washington, D.C.: U.S. Government Printing Office.

Marshall, Donald S. 1971. "Sexual Behavior in Mangaia." In Donald S. Marshall and Robert C. Suggs, eds., *Human Sexual Behavior*. New York: Basic Books.

Maurer, David W. 1974. *The American Confidence Man*. Springfield, Ill.: C. C. Thomas.

Merton, Robert K. 1938. "Social Structure and Anomie." *American Sociological Review* 3:672–682.

Miller, Gale, 1978. *Odd Jobs: The World of Deviant Work*. Englewood Cliffs, N.J.: Prentice-Hall.

Millett, Kate. 1973. *The Prostitution Papers: A Candid Dialogue*. New York: Avon Books.

Milner, Christina, and Richard Milner. 1972. *Black Players*. Boston: Little, Brown.

"Police Arrest 13 in Prostitution Crackdown." 1985. *Daily Press*. Newport News, Va. November 3, p. C3.

Rasmussen, Paul. 1984. "Massage Parlors as a Sex-for-Money-Game." In Jack D. Douglas, ed., *The Sociology of Deviance*. Boston: Allyn & Bacon.

Reiss, Ira. 1973. *Heterosexual Permissiveness Inside and Outside of Marriage*. Morristown, N.J.: General Learning Press.

Reiss, Ira. 1980. *Family Systems in America*, 3rd ed. New York: Holt, Rinehart & Winston.

Reiss, Ira. 1986. *Journey into Sexuality*. Englewood Cliffs, N.J.: Prentice-Hall.

Roby, Pamela A. 1969. "Politics and Criminal Law: Revision of the New York State Penal Law on Prostitution." *Social Problems* 17:83–109.

Roby, Pamela A. 1972. "Politics and Prostitution: A Case Study of the Revision, Enforcement, and Administration of the New York State Penal Laws on Prostitution." *Criminology* 9:425–447.

Roebuck, Julian B., and Robert Bruce Hunter. 1970. "Medical Quackery as Deviant Behavior." *Criminology* 8:46–62.

Sheehy, Gail. 1973. *Hustling: Prostitution in Our Wide Open Society*. New York: Delacorte.

Silberman, Matthew. 1976. "Toward a Theory of Criminal Deterrence." *American Sociological Review* 41:442–461.

Socarides, Charles W. 1975. *Beyond Sexual Freedom*. Chicago: Aldine.

Stewart, George Lee. 1972. "On First Being a John." *Urban Life and Culture* 1:255–274.

Sykes, Gresham M., and David Matza. 1957. "Techniques of Neutralization: A Theory of Delinquency." *American Sociological Review* 22:664–670.

Tatro, Charlotte H. 1974. "Cross My Palm with Silver: Fortune-Telling as an Occupational Way of Life." In Clifton D. Bryant, ed., *Deviant Behavior*. Skokie, Ill.: Rand McNally.

Terman, Lewis M. 1938. *Psychological Factors in Marital Happiness*. New York: McGraw-Hill.

Tittle, Charles R. 1980. *Sanctions and Social Deviance: The Question of Deterrence*. New York: Praeger.

Winick, Charles, and Paul M. Kinsie. 1971. *The Lively Commerce: Prostitution in the United States*. Chicago: Quadrangle Press.

Women Endorsing Decriminalization. 1973. "Prostitution: A Nonvictim Crime?" *Issues in Criminology* 8 (Fall):160.

CHAPTER 7

Akers, Ronald L. 1985. *Deviant Behavior: A Social Learning Approach*, 3rd ed. Belmont, Calif.: Wadsworth.

American College of Neuropsychopharmacology—Food and Drug Administration Task Force. 1973. "Neurologic Syndromes Associated with Antipsychotic Drug Use." *The New England Journal of Medicine* 289:20–23.

American Psychiatric Association. 1978. *Diagnostic and Statistical Manual of Mental Disorders*, 3rd ed. Washington, D.C.: American Psychiatric Association.

Ash, P. 1949. "The Reliability of Psychiatric Diagnoses." *Journal of Abnormal and Social Psychology* 44:271–276.

Bachman, Jerald G., Patrick M. O'Malley, and Jerome Johnston. 1978. *Adolescence to Adulthood: Change and Stability in the Lives of Young Men*. Youth in Transition, vol. 6. Ann Arbor: Institute for Social Research, University of Michigan.

Bandura, A. 1969. *Principles of Behavior Modification*. New York: Holt, Rinehart & Winston.

Becker, Howard S. 1973. *Outsiders: Studies in the Sociology of Deviance*. New York: Free Press.

Blau, Peter M. 1956. "Social Mobility and Interpersonal Relations." *American Sociological Review* 21:290–295.

Blauner, Robert. 1964. *Alienation and Freedom*. Chicago: University of Chicago Press.

Cameron, Norman. 1943. "The Paranoid Pseudo-Community." *The American Journal of Sociology* 9:33–38.

Clausen, John A., and Carol L. Huffine. 1975. "Sociocultural and Social/Psychological Factors Affecting Social Responses to Mental Disorder." *Journal of Health and Social Behavior* 16:405–420.

Clausen, John A., and M. L. Kohn. 1959. "Relation of Schizophrenia to the Social Structure of a Small City." In B. Pasaminick, ed., *Epidemiology of Mental Disorder.* Washington, D.C.: American Association for the Advancement of Science.

Cockerham, William C. 1979. "Labeling Theory in Disorder: A Synthesis of Psychiatric and Social Perspectives." In Norman K. Denzin, ed., *Studies in Symbolic Interaction*, vol. 2. Greenwich, Conn.: JAI Press.

Cockerham, William C. 1981. *Sociology of Mental Disorder.* Englewood Cliffs, N.J.: Prentice-Hall.

Conrad, Peter. 1975. "The Discovery of Hyperkinesis: Notes on the Medicalization of Deviant Behavior." *Social Problems* 23:12–21.

Curran, James P., Peter M. Monti, and Donald Corrivean. 1982. "Treatment of Schizophrenia." In Alan S. Bellack, Michel Hersen, and Alan E. Dazdin, eds., *International Handbook of Behavior Modification and Therapy*. New York: Plenum Press.

Denzin, Norman, K. 1968. "The Self-Fulfilling Prophecy and Patient-Therapist Interaction." In S. Spitzer and Norman K. Denzin, eds., *The Mental Patient: Studies in the Sociology of Deviance*. New York: McGraw-Hill.

Doherty, Edmund G. 1978. "Are Different Discharge Criteria Used for Men and Women Psychiatric Inpatients?" *Journal of Health and Social Behavior* 19:107–116.

Dohrenwend, Barbara S., and Bruce P. Dohrenwend. 1974. *Stressful Life Events: Their Nature and Effects*. New York: Wiley.

Dohrenwend, Bruce P. 1966. "Social Status and Psychological Disorder: An Issue of Substance and an Issue of Method." *American Sociological Review* 31:14–34.

Dohrenwend, Bruce P. 1975. "Sociocultural and Social-Psychological Factors in the Genesis of Mental Disorders." *Journal of Health and Social Behavior* 16:365–392.

Dohrenwend, Bruce P., and Barbara S. Dohrenwend. 1976. "Sex Differences and Psychiatric Disorders." *American Journal of Sociology* 81:1447–1454.

Dohrenwend, Bruce P., Barbara S. Dohrenwend, Madelyn S. Gould, Bruce G. Link, Richard Neugebauer, and Robin Wunsch-Hitzig. 1980. *Mental Illness in the United States: Epidemiological Estimates*. New York: Praeger.

Dunham, H. Warren. 1965. *Community and Schizophrenia: An Epidemiological Analysis*. Detroit, Mich.: Wayne State University Press.

Dunham, H. Warren, P. Phillips, and B. Scinivason. 1966. "A Research Note on Diagnosed Mental Illness and Social Class." *American Sociological Review* 31:223–227.

Eitzen, D. Stanley, and Jeffrey H. Bair. 1972. "Types of Status Inconsistency and Schizophrenia." *The Sociological Quarterly* 13:61–73.

Ellis, Evelyn. 1952. "Social Psychological Correlates of Upward Social Mobility Among Unmarried Career Women." *American Sociological Review* 17:558–563.

Faris, Robert E., and H. Warren Dunham. 1939. *Mental Disorders in Urban Areas*. Chicago: University of Chicago Press.

Foucault, Michael. 1965. *Madness and Civilization: A History of Insanity in the Age of Reason*. New York: Random House.

Freeman, Howard E., and Ozzie G. Simmons. 1961. "Feelings of Stigma Among Relatives of Former Mental Patients." *Social Problems* 8:312–321.

"From Seven Up to Twenty-Eight" [Film]. 1964. Michael Apted, producer/director. London: Granada Television International.

Gallagher, Bernard J., III. 1980. *The Sociology of Mental Illness*. Englewood Cliffs, N.J.: Prentice-Hall.

Garfinkel, H. 1956. "Conditions of Successful Degradation Ceremonies." *American Journal of Sociology* 61:420–424.

Gershan, E. S., S. D. Targum, and L. R. Kessler. 1977. "Genetic Studies and Biologic Strategies in the Affective Disorders." *Progress in Medical Genetics* 2:103–125.

Goffman, Erving. 1961. *Asylums: Essays on the Social Situation of Mental Patients and Other Inmates*. New York: Anchor Books.

Goffman, Erving. 1987. "The Moral Career of the Mental Patient." In Earl Rubington and
Martin S. Weinberg, eds., *Deviance: The Interactionist Perspective*. New York:
Macmillan.

Gove, Walter R. 1970. "Societal Reactions as an Explanation of Mental Illness: An Evaluation." *American Sociological Review* 35:873–884.

Gove, Walter R. 1972. "The Relationship Between Sex Roles, Marital Status, and Mental
Illness." *Social Forces* 51:34–44.

Gove, Walter R. 1982. *Deviance and Mental Illness*. Beverly Hills: Sage.

Gove, Walter R., and Jennifer Tudor. 1973. "Adult Sex Roles and Mental Illness." *American Journal of Sociology* 77:812–835.

Gove, Walter R., and Patrick Howell. 1974. "Individual Resources and Mental Hospitalization: A Comparison and Evaluation of the Societal Reaction and Psychiatric Perspectives." *American Sociological Review* 39:86–100.

Greenley, James R., and David Mechanic. 1976. "Social Selection in Seeking Help for
Psychological Problems." *Journal of Health and Social Behavior* 17:249–262.

Haney, C. Allen, and Robert Michielutte. 1968. "Selective Factors Operating in the Adju-
dication of Incompetency." *Journal of Health and Social Behavior* 9:233–242.

Hollingshead, August B., and Frederick C. Redlich. 1953. "Social Stratification and Psychiatric Disorders." *American Sociological Review* 18:163–169.

Hollingshead, August B., and Frederick C. Redlich. 1958. *Social Class and Mental Illness*. New York: Wiley.

Hollingshead, August B., R. Ellis, and E. Kirby. 1954. "Social Mobility and Mental
Illness." *American Sociological Review* 19:577–584.

Horney, Karen. 1937. *The Neurotic Personality of Our Time*. New York: W. W. Norton.

Horwitz, Alan. 1977. "The Pathways into Psychiatric Treatment: Some Differences Between Men and Women." *Journal of Health and Social Behavior* 18:169–178.

Jaco, E. Gartley. 1960. *The Social Epidemiology of Mental Illness*. New York: Russell Sage
Foundation.

Kallman, F. J. 1953. *Heredity in Health and Mental Disorder*. New York: W. W.
Norton.

Karno, Marvin. 1966. "The Enigma of Ethnicity in a Psychiatric Clinic." *Archives of
General Psychiatry* 14:516–520.

Kendall, R. E., J. E. Cooper, A. J. Gourley, J. R. M. Copeland, L. Sharpe, and B. J.
Gurland. 1971. "Diagnostic Criteria of American and British Psychiatrists." *Archives
of General Psychiatry* 25:123–130.

Kitano, Harry H. L. 1962. "Changing Achievement Patterns of the Japanese in the United
States." *The Journal of Social Psychology* 58:257–264.

Kohn, M. L. 1973. "Social Class and Schizophrenia: A Critical Review and Reformation."
Schizophrenia Bulletin 7:69–79.

Kolb, L. C. 1973. *Noyes' Modern Clinical Psychiatry*. Philadelphia: W. B. Saunders.

Kornhauser, A. 1965. *Mental Health of the Industrial Worker.* New York: Wiley.

Krohn, Marvin D, and Ronald L. Akers. 1977. "An Alternative View of the Labeling Versus Psychiatric Perspectives on Societal Reaction to Mental Illness." *Social Forces* 56:341–361.

Kulka, Richard A., Joseph Veroff, and Elizabeth Douvan. 1979. "Social Class and the Use of Professinal Help for Personal Problems: 1957 and 1976." *Journal of Health and Social Behavior* 20:2–17.

Kutner, Luis. 1962. "The Illusion of Due Process in Commitment Proceedings." *Northwestern University Law Review* 57:383–399.

Lemert, Edwin M. 1951. *Social Pathology.* New York: McGraw-Hill.

Lemert, Edwin M. 1967. "Paranoia and the Dynamics of Exclusion." In Edwin M. Lemert, ed., *Human Deviance, Social Problems, and Social Control.* Englewood Cliffs, N.J.: Prentice-Hall.

Lemkau, P. V., and Guido M. Crocetti. 1962. "An Urban Population's Opinions and Knowledge About Mental Illness." *American Journal of Psychiatry* 118:692–700.

Levy, Leo, and Louis Rowitz. 1973. *The Ecology of Mental Disorder.* New York: Behavioral Publications.

Liem, Ramsay, and Joan Liem. 1978. "Social Class and Mental Illness Reconsidered: The Role of Economic Stress and Social Support." *Journal of Health and Social Behavior* 19:139–156.

Linsky, Arnold S. 1970. "Community Homogeneity and Exclusion of the Mentally Ill: Rejection Versus Consensus About Deviance." *Journal of Health and Social Behavior* 11:304–311.

Lloyd, K. E., and L. Abel. 1970. "Performance on a Token Economy Psychiatry Ward: A Two-Year Summary." *Behavior Research and Therapy* 8:1–9.

Loeb, Martin B. 1956. "Some Dominant Cultural Themes in a Psychiatric Hospital." *Social Problems* 4:17–20.

McMahon, James T. 1964. "The Working Class Psychiatric Patient: A Clinical View." In Frank Riessman, Jerome Cohen, and Arthur Pearl., eds., *Mental Health of the Poor.* New York: Free Press.

Marx, John H., and S. Lee Spray. 1972. "Psychotherapeutic 'Birds of a Feather': Social Class Status and Religio-Cultural Value Homophily in the Mental Health Field." *Journal of Health and Social Behavior* 13:413–428.

Mayer, Herta, and Gerald Schamess. 1969. "Long-Term Treatment for the Disadvantaged." *Social Casework* 50:138–145.

Mechanic, David. 1962. "Some Factors in Identifying and Defining Mental Illness." *Mental Hygiene* 46:66–74.

Meile, Richard L., David Richard Johnson, and Louis St. Peter. 1976. "Marital Role, Education, and Mental Disorder Among Women: Test of an Interaction Hypothesis." *Journal of Health and Social Behavior* 17:295–301.

Mishler, E. G., and N. E. Waxler. 1963. "Decision Processes in Psychiatric Hospitalization: Patients Referred, Accepted, and Admitted to a Psychiatric Hospital." *American Sociological Review* 28:576–587.

Myers, Jerome K., and Leslie Schaffer. 1954. "Social Stratification and Psychiatric Practice: A Study of an Outpatient Clinic." *American Sociological Review* 19:307–310.

National Institute of Mental Health. 1978. "Changes in the Age, Sex, and Diagnostic Composition of the Resident Population of State and County Mental Hospitals, United States 1965–1975." Mental Health and Statistical Note no. 146. Washington, D.C.: Department of Health, Education, and Welfare.

Nunnally, J. C., Jr. 1961. *Popular Conceptions of Mental Health.* New York: Holt, Rinehart & Winston.

Parsons, Talcott. 1951. *The Social System.* New York: Free Press.

Pearlin, Leonard, and Joyce S. Johnson. 1977. "Marital Status, Life-Strains, and Depression." *American Sociological Review* 42:704–715.

Perrucci, Robert. 1974. *Circle of Madness: On Being Insane and Institutionalized in America.* Englewood Cliffs, N.J.: Prentice-Hall.

Phillips, Derek L. 1963. "Rejection: A Possible Consequence of Seeking Help for Mental Disorders." *American Sociological Review* 28:963–972.

Phillips, Derek L., and Bernard E. Segal. 1969. "Sexual Status and Psychiatric Symptoms." *American Sociological Review* 34:58–72.

President's Commission on Mental Health. 1978. *Mental Health in America,* vol. 1. Washington, D.C.: U.S. Government Printing Office.

Price, Richard H., and Bruce Denner, eds. 1973. *The Making of a Mental Patient.* New York: Holt, Rinehart & Winston.

Rieger, Darrel A., Irving D. Goldberg, and Carl A. Taube. 1978. "The De Facto U.S. Mental Health Services System." *Archives of General Psychiatry* 35:685–693.

Rosenberg, Morris. 1979. *Conceiving the Self.* New York: Basic Books.

Rosenthal, David. 1970. *Genetic Theory and Abnormal Behavior.* New York: McGraw-Hill.

Rowden, David W., and others. 1970. "Judgments About Candidates for Psychotherapy: The Influence of Social Class and Insight-Verbal Ability." *Journal of Health and Social Behavior* 11:51–58.

Rubington, Earl, and Martin S. Weinberg, eds. 1987. *Deviance: The Interactionist Perspective.* New York: Macmillan.

Rushing, William A. 1971. "Individual Resources, Societal Reaction, and Hospital Commitment." *American Journal of Sociology* 77:511–526.

Rushing, William A. 1978. "Status Resources, Societal Reactions, and Type of Mental Hospitalization." *American Sociological Review* 43:521–533.

Rushing, William A. 1979a. "The Functional Importance of Sex Roles and Sex-Related Behaviors in Societal Reactions to Residual Deviants." *Journal of Health and Social Behavior* 20:208–217.

Rushing, William A. 1979b. "Marital Status and Mental Disorder: Evidence in Favor of the Behavioral Model." *Social Forces* 58:540–556.

Sampson, Harold, Sheldon Messinger, and Robert D. Towne, 1962. "Family Processes and Becoming a Mental Patient." *American Journal of Sociology* 68:88–96.

Scheff, Thomas J. 1963. "Cultural Stereotypes and Mental Illness." *Sociometry* 26:438–452.

Scheff, Thomas J. 1964. "The Societal Reaction to Deviance: Ascriptive Elements in the Psychiatric Screening of Mental Patients in a Midwestern State." *Social Problems* 11:447–463.

Scheff, Thomas J. 1966. *Being Mentally Ill.* Chicago: Aldine.

Schur, Edwin M. 1971. *Labeling Deviant Behavior: Its Sociological Implications.* New York: Harper & Row.

Schwab, John J., Judith M. Brown, Charles E. Holzer, and Marilyn Sokolof. 1968. "Current Concepts of Depression: The Sociocultural." *International Journal of Social Psychiatry* 14:226–234.

Scott, Robert A. 1969. *The Making of Blind Men.* New York: Russell Sage Foundation.

Silberman, Matthew. 1976. "Toward a Theory of Criminal Deterrence." *American Sociological Review* 41:442–461.

Srole, Leo, Thomas S. Langner, Stanley T. Michael, Marvin K. Opler, and Thomas A. C. Rennie. 1962. *Mental Health in the Metropolis: The Midtown Manhattan Study.* New York: McGraw-Hill.

Szasz, Thomas S. 1970. *The Manufacture of Madness.* New York: Dell.

Szasz, Thomas S. 1974. *The Myth of Mental Illness,* rev. ed. New York: Harper & Row.

Townsend, John M. 1976. "Self-Concept and the Institutionalization of Mental Patients: An Overview and Critique." *Journal of Health and Social Behavior* 17:263–271.

Warheit, George J., Charles E. Holzer, and Sandra A. Avery. 1975. "Race and Mental Illness: An Epidemiological Update." Journal of Health and Social Behavior 16:243–256.

Wenger, D. L., and C. R. Fletcher. 1969. "The Effects of Legal Counsel on Admissions to a State Mental Hospital: A Confrontation of Professions." *Journal of Health and Social Behavior* 10:66–72.

Wilkinson, Gregg S. 1973. "Interaction Patterns and Staff Response to Psychiatric Innovations." *Journal of Health and Social Behavior* 14:323–329.

Wing, J. K. 1967. "Institutionalism in Mental Hospitals." In Thomas J. Scheff, ed., *Mental Illness and Social Process.* New York: Harper & Row.

Yarrow, M., C. Schwartz, H. H. Murphy, and L. Deasy. 1955. "The Psychological Meaning of Mental Illness in the Family." *Journal of Social Issues* 11:12–24.

CHAPTER 8

Akers, Ronald L. 1985. *Deviant Behavior: A Social Learning Approach*, 3rd. ed. Belmont, Calif.: Wadsworth

Athens, L. H. 1980. *Violent Criminal Acts and Actors: A Symbolic Interactionist Study*. New York: Routledge & Kegan Paul.

Bailey, William C. 1984. "Poverty, Inequality and City Homicide Rates: Some Not So Unexpected Findings." *Criminology* 22:531–550.

Ball-Rokeach, S. 1973. "Values and Violence: A Test of the Subculture of Violence Thesis." *American Sociological Review* 38:736–749.

Bandura, A. 1973. *Aggression: A Social Learning Analysis*. Englewood Cliffs, N.J.: Prentice-Hall.

Berger, A. M. 1980a. "The Child-Abusing Family I: Methodological Issues and Parent-Related Characteristics of Abusing Families." *American Journal of Family Therapy* 8(3):53–66.

Berger, A. M. 1980b. "The Child-Abusing Family II: Child and Child-Rearing Variables, Environmental Factors, and Typologies of Abusing Families." *American Journal of Family Therapy* 8(4):52–68.

Blau, Judith R., and Peter M. Blau. 1982. "The Cost of Inequality: Metropolitan Structure and Violent Crime." *American Sociological Review* 47:114–129.

Blonston, Gary. 1988. "America's Income Gap." *Daily Press*, Newport News, Va., February 7, pp. I1,I5.

Blumer, H. 1962. "Society as Symbolic Interaction." In A. Rose, ed., *Human Behavior and Social Processes*. Boston: Houghton-Mifflin.

Brown, R. M. 1969. "The American Vigilante Tradition." In H. D. Graham and T. R. Gurr, eds., *Violence in America*. Washington, D.C.: U.S. Government Printing Office.

Bullock, Henry A. 1955. "Urban Homicide in Theory and Fact." *Journal of Criminal Law, Criminology and Policy Science* 45:567–569.

Bureau of Justice Statistics. 1985. *Criminal Victimization in the United States, 1983*. Washington, D.C.: Department of Justice.

Curtis, L. 1975. *Violence, Rape, and Culture*. Lexington, Mass.: Lexington Books.

Dailey, T. B. 1979. "Parental Power Breeds Violence Against Children." *Sociological Focus* 12:311–322.

Davidson, T. 1977. "Wife Beating: A Recurring Phenomenon Throughout History." In M. Roy, ed., *Battered Women: A Psychosociological Study of Domestic Violence*. New York: Van Nostrand Reinhold.

Erlanger, H. S. 1974. "Social Class Differences in Parents' Use of Physical Punishment." In M. A. Straus and S. Steinmetz, eds., *Violence in the Family*. New York: Dodd, Mead.

Erlanger, H. S. 1975. "Is There a Subculture of Violence in the South?" *Journal of Criminal Law and Criminology* 66:483–490.

Felson, R. B., and H. J. Steadman. 1983. "Situational Factors in Disputes Leading to Criminal Violence." *Criminology* 21:59–74.

Flanagan, Timothy J., and Edmond F. McGarrell, eds. 1986. *Sourcebook of Criminal Justice Statistics—1985.* U.S. Department of Justice, Bureau of Justice Statistics. Washington, D.C.: U.S. Government Printing Office.

Flanagan, Timothy J., and Katherine M. Jamieson, eds. 1988. *Sourcebook of Criminal Justice Statistics—1987.* U.S. Department of Justice, Bureau of Justice Statistics. Washington, D.C.: U.S. Government Printing Office.

Garbarino, James, and Gwen Gilliam. 1980. *Understanding Abusive Families.* Lexington, Mass.: Lexington Books.

Gelles, R. J. 1973. "An Exploratory Study of Intra-Family Violence." Unpublished Ph.D dissertation, Durham, N. H.: University of New Hampshire.

Gelles, R. J. 1974. *The Violent Home: A Study of Physical Aggression Between Husbands and Wives.* Beverly Hills: Sage.

Gelles, R. J. 1979. "The Truth About Husband Abuse." In R. J. Gelles, ed. *Family Violence.* Beverly Hills: Sage.

Gelles, R. J., and M. A. Straus. 1979. "Violence in the American Family." *Journal of Social Issues* 35(2):15–39.

Gil, D. G. 1970. *Violence Against Children.* Cambridge, Mass.: Harvard University Press.

Gold, Martin. 1958. "Suicide, Homicide, and the Socialization of Aggression." *American Journal of Sociology* 43:651–661.

Goolkasian, Gail. 1986. "Confronting Domestic Violence: The Role of Criminal Court Judges." In *U.S. National Institute of Justice.* Washington, D.C.: U.S. Government Printing Office.

Graham, H. D., and T. R. Gurr, eds. 1969. *Violence in America: Historical and Comparative Perspectives,* vols. 1 and 2: *A Report to the National Commission on the Causes and Prevention of Violence.* Washington, D.C.: U.S. Government Printing Office.

Greenberg, Michael R., George W. Carey, and Frank J. Popper. "Violent Death, Violent States, and American Youth." The Public Interest 87:38–48.

Hacker, Andrew. 1987. "American Apartheid." *New York Review of Books.* December 3, 1987.

Hartung, F. 1965. *Crime, Law, and Society.* Detroit, Mich.: Wayne State University Press.

Huff-Corzine, Lin, Jay Corzine, and David C. Moore. 1986. "Southern Exposure: Deciphering the South's Influence on Homicide Rates." *Social Forces* 64:906–924.

Klaus, Patsy A., and Michael R. Rand. 1984. "Family Violence." In *U.S. Bureau of Justice Statistics Special Report.* Washington, D.C.: U.S. Government Printing Office.

Laner, M.R., and J. Thompson. 1982. "Abuse and Aggression in Courting Couples." *Deviant Behavior* 3:229–244.

Langan, Patrick A., and Christopher A. Innes. 1986. "Preventing Domestic Violence Against Women." In *U.S. Bureau of Justice Statistics Special Report.* Washington, D.C.: U.S. Government Printing Office.

Levin, Jack, and James A. Fox. 1985. *Mass Murder.* New York: Plenum Press.

Levy, Sheldon. 1969. "A 150-Year Study of Political Violence in the United States." In H. D. Graham and T. R. Gurr, eds., *Violence in America: Historical and Comparative Perspectives.* New York: Bantam Books.

Luckenbill, D. 1977. "Criminal Homicide as a Situated Transaction." *Social Problems* 25:176–186.

McCaghy, Charles H. 1985. *Deviant Behavior: Crime, Conflict, and Interest Groups*, 2nd ed. New York: Macmillan.

Magura, Stephen. 1975. "Is There a Subculture of Violence?: Comment on Ball-Rokeach." *American Sociological Review* 40:831–835.

Martin, D. 1981. "Battered Women." In B. Galaway and J. Hudson, eds., *Perspective on Crime Victims.* St. Louis: C. V. Mosby.

Mause, Lloyd de, ed. 1974. *The History of Childhood.* New York: Psychohistory Press.

Messner, Steven F. 1982. "Poverty, Inequality, and the Urban Homicide Rate: Some Unexpected Findings." *Criminology* 20:103–114.

Messner, Steven F. 1983. "Regional Differences in the Economic Correlates of the Urban Homicide Rate: Some Evidence on the Importance of Cultural Context." *Criminology* 21:477–488.

Mish, Frederick C., ed. 1983. *Webster's Ninth New Collegiate Dictionary.* Springfield, Mass.: Merriam-Webster.

Mulvihill, D., and M. Tumin. 1969. *Crimes of Violence: A Staff Report to the National Commission on the Causes and Prevention of Violence*, vol. 11. Washington, D.C.: U.S. Government Printing Office.

Needham, Nancy R. 1988. "Kids Who Kill." *NEA Today* February, pp. 10–11.

Newton, G. D., Jr., and F. E. Zimring. 1969. *Firearms and Violence in American Life: Report Submitted to the National Commission on the Causes and Prevention of Violence.* Washington, D.C.: U.S. Government Printing Office.

Phillips, D. 1983. "The Impact of Mass Media Violence on U.S. Homicides." *American Sociological Review* 48:560–568.

Pickett, Robert. 1969. *House of Refuge: Origins of Juvenile Justice Reform in New York, 1815–1857.* Syracuse, N.Y.: Syracuse University Press.

Pitcher, Brian L., Robert L. Hamlin, and Jerry L. Miller. 1978. "The Diffusion of Collective Violence." *American Sociological Review* 43:23–35.

Platt, Anthony M. 1969. *The Child Savers: The Invention of Delinquency.* Chicago: University of Chicago Press.

Pleck, E. 1979. "Wife Beating in Nineteenth Century America." *Victimology* 4:60–74.

Police Foundation. 1977. *Domestic Violence and the Police: Studies in Detroit and Kansas City.* Washington, D.C.: Police Foundation.

Sherman, Lawrence W., and Richard A. Berk. 1984. "The Specific Deterrent Effects of Arrest for Domestic Assault." *American Sociological Review* 49:261–272.

Spiegler, J. H., and J. J. Sweeny. 1975. *Gun Abuse in Ohio*. Cleveland: Governmental Research Institute.

Stark, R., and J. McEvoy, III. 1970. "Middle Class Violence." *Psychology Today* November, pp. 52–65.

Straus, M. A. 1976. "Sexual Inequality, Cultural Norms, and Wife Beating." *Victimology* 1:54–76.

Straus, M. A. 1978. "Stress and Assault in a National Sample of American Families:" Paper presented at the Colloquium on Stress and Crime, National Institute of Law Enforcement and Criminal Justice. Washington, D.C.: MITRE Corporation.

Straus, M. A. 1980. "Wife Beating: How Common and Why?" In M. A. Straus and G. Hotaling, eds., *Husband-Wife Violence*. Minneapolis: University of Minnesota Press.

Straus, M. A., R. J. Gelles, and S. Steinmetz. 1980. *Behind Closed Doors: Violence in the American Family*. New York: Anchor/Doubleday.

Thum, D., H. Wechsler, and H. Demone, Jr. 1973. "Alcohol Levels of Emergency Service Patients Injured in Fights and Assaults." *Criminology* 10:487–497.

U.S. Bureau of the Census. 1984. *Statistical Abstract of the United States*. Washington, D.C.: U.S. Government Printing Office.

U.S. Bureau of the Census. 1986. *Statistical Abstract of the United States*. Washington, D.C.: U.S. Government Printing Office.

U.S. Department of Justice. 1986. *Crime in the United States: Uniform Crime Reports, 1985*. Washington, D.C.: U.S. Government Printing Office.

The Washington Post. 1989. "High School Drug Use at 10-Year Low." In *The Times Herald*, Newport News, Va., n.d., p. A10.

Wideman, John Edgar. 1984. *Brothers and Keepers*. New York: Penguin Books.

Wilbanks, William. 1985. "Is Violent Crime Interracial?" *Crime and Delinquency* 31:117–128.

Wolfgang, M. 1958. *Patterns of Criminal Homicide*. Philadelphia: University of Pennsylvania Press.

Wolfgang, M., and F. Ferracuti. 1967. *The Subculture of Violence*. London: Tavistock.

Wright, James D., Peter H. Rossi, and K. Daly. 1983. *Under the Gun: Weapons, Crime, and Violence in America*. New York: Aldine deGruyter.

Wright, James D., and Peter H. Rossi. 1986. *Armed and Considered Dangerous*. New York: Aldine deGruyter.

Zigler, Edward. 1980. "Controlling Child Abuse: Do We Have the Knowledge and/or the Will?" In George Gerbner, Catherine J. Ross, and Edward Zigler, eds., *Child Abuse: An Agenda for Action*. New York: Oxford University Press.

CHAPTER 9

Akers, Ronald L. 1985. *Deviant Behavior: A Social Learning Approach*, 3rd ed. Belmont, Calif.: Wadsworth.

Altheide, David, Patricia Adler, Peter Adler, and Duane Altheide. 1978. "The Social Means of Employee Theft." In John M. Johnson and Jack D. Douglas, eds., *Crime at the Top*. Philadelphia: J. B. Lippincott.

Ball, Harry V. 1960. "Social Structure and Rent-Control Violations." *American Journal of Sociology* 65:598–604.

Bell, Daniel. 1976. *The Coming of Post-Industrial Society: A Venture in Social Forecasting*. New York: Harper Colophon.

Bequai, August. 1978. *White-Collar Crime: A 20th-Century Crisis*. Boston: D.C. Heath.

Berman, Daniel. 1978. *Death on the Job: Occupational Health and Safety in the United States*. New York: Monthly Review Press.

Braithwaite, J. 1982. "Enforced Self-Regulation: A New Strategy for Corporate Crime Control." *Michigan Law Review* 80:1466–1507.

Bureau of Justice Statistics. 1987. "White-Collar Crime." Washington, D.C.: U.S. Department of Justice.

Carey, J. T. 1978. *Introduction to Criminology*. Englewood Cliffs, N.J.: Prentice-Hall.

Chamber of Commerce of the United States. 1974. *A Handbook on White-Collar Crime: Everyone's Problem, Everyone's Loss*. Washington, D.C.: U.S. Government Printing Office.

Clinard, Marshall B. 1952. *The Black Market: A Study of White-Collar Crime*. New York: Holt, Rinehart & Winston.

Clinard, Marshall B. 1983. *Corporate Ethics and Crime*. Beverly Hills: Sage.

Clinard, Marshall B., and Richard Quinney. 1973. *Criminal Behavior Systems: A Typology*. New York: Holt, Rinehart & Winston.

Clinard, Marshall B., and P. C. Yeager. 1979. "Corporate Crime: Issues in Research." In E. Sagarin, ed., *Criminology: New Concerns*. Beverly Hills: Sage.

Clinard, Marshall B., and P. C. Yeager. 1980. *Corporate Crime*. New York: Free Press.

Clinard, Marshall B., P. C. Yeager, J. M. Brissette, D. Petrashek, and E. Harries. 1979. *Illegal Corporate Behavior*. Washington, D.C.: U.S. Government Printing Office.

Cobb, Beatrix. 1958. "Why Do People Detour to Quacks?" In E. Gartley Jaco, ed., *Patients, Physicians, and Illness*. New York: Free Press.

Coleman, James W. 1987. "Toward an Integrated Theory of White-Collar Crime." *American Journal of Sociology* 93(2):406–439.

Coleman, James W. 1989. *The Criminal Elite: The Sociology of White-Collar Crime*. New York: St. Martins.

"Corporate Crime: The Untold Story." 1982. *U.S. News & World Report*, September 6, pp. 25–30.

Cressey, Donald R. 1953. *Other People's Money*. New York: Free Press.

Cressey, Donald R. 1965. "The Respectable Criminal." *Transaction* 3 (March–April):12–15.

Dalton, Melville. 1959. *Men Who Manage*. New York: Wiley.

Dowie, Mark. 1979. "Pinto Madness." In J. Skolnick and E. Currie, eds., *Crisis in American Institutions*. Boston: Little, Brown.

Edelhertz, Herbert. 1970. *The Nature, Impact, and Prosecution of White-Collar Crime*. Washington, D.C.: U.S. Government Printing Office.

Gallup, George, Jr. 1983a. *The Gallup Report*, July. Wilmington, Del.: Scholarly Resources.

Gallup, George, Jr. 1983b. *The Gallup Report*, October. Wilmington, Del.: Scholarly Resources.

Geis, G. 1967. "White-Collar Crime: The Heavy Electrical Equipment Antitrust Cases of 1961." In Marshall B. Clinard and Richard Quinney, eds., *Criminal Behavior Systems: A Typology*. New York: Holt, Rinehart & Winston.

Gouldner, Alvin. 1954. *Patterns of Industrial Bureaucracy*. New York: Free Press.

Green, Mark J. 1982. *Who Runs Congress?*, 4th ed. New York: Dell.

Green, Mark J., Beverly C. Moore, Jr., and Bruce Wasserstein. 1972. *The Closed Enterprise System*. New York: Bantam Books.

Gross, E. 1980. "Organization Structure and Organizational Crime." In G. Geis and E. Stotland, eds., *White-Collar Crime: Theory and Research*. Beverly Hills: Sage.

Hagan, John, and Patricia Parker. 1985. "White-Collar Crime and Punishment." *American Sociological Review* 50:302–316.

Hansmann, Henry B., and John M. Quigley. 1982. "Population Heterogeneity and Sociogenesis of Homicide." *Social Forces* G1:206–210.

Hartung, Frank E. 1950. "White-Collar Offenses in the Wholesale Meat Industry in Detroit." *American Journal of Sociology* 56:25–34.

Hochstedler, Ellen, ed. 1984. *Corporations as Criminals*. Beverly Hills: Sage.

Hollinger, Richard, and John P. Clark. 1983. *Theft by Employees*. Lexington, Mass.: Lexington Books.

Horning, Donald N. M. 1970. "Blue-Collar Theft: Conceptions of Property Attitudes Toward Pilfering and Work Group Norms in a Modern Industrial Plan." In Edwin O. Smigel and H. Lawrence Ross, eds., *Crime Against Bureaucracy*. New York: Van Nostrand Reinhold.

"Is Your Job Dangerous to Your Health?" 1979. *U.S. News & World Report*, February 5, p. 39.

Jaspan, Norman. 1974. *Mind Your Own Business*. Englewood Cliffs, N.J.: Prentice-Hall.

Kramer, Ronald. 1984. "Corporate Criminality: The Development of an Idea." In Ellen Hochstedler, ed., *Corporations as Criminals*. Beverly Hills: Sage.

Lane, Robert E. 1953. "Why Business Men Violate the Law." *Journal of Criminal Law, Criminology, and Police Science* 44:151–165.

Leonard, W., and M. Weber. 1970. "Automakers and Dealers: A Study of Criminogenic Market Forces." *Law and Society Review* 4:407–424.

Liebow, Elliot. 1967. *Tally's Corner.* Boston: Little, Brown.

McCaghy, Charles H., and Stephen A. Cernkovich. 1987. *Crime in American Society*, 2nd ed. New York: Macmillan.

McCormick, Albert E. 1977. "Rule Enforcement and Moral Indignation: Some Observations of the Effects of Criminal Antitrust Convictions upon Societal Reaction Processes." *Social Problems* 25:30–39.

Mars, Gerald. 1974. "Dock Pilferage: A Case Study in Occupational Theft." In Paul Rock and Mary McIntosh, eds., *Deviance and Social Control*. London: Tavistock.

Mars, Gerald. 1982. *Cheats at Work: An Anthropology of Workplace Crime*. London: Unwin.

Meier, Robert F., and James F. Short. 1982. "The Consequences of White-Collar Crime." In Herbert Edelhertz and Thomas D. Overcast, eds., *White-Collar Crime: An Agenda for Research*. Lexington, Mass.: Lexington Books.

Merton, Robert K. 1938. "Social Structure and Anomie." *American Sociological Review* 3 (October):672–682.

Miller, Gale. 1978. *Odd Jobs: The World of Deviant Work*. Englewood Cliffs, N.J.: Prentice-Hall.

"Mine Safety and Health Administration Data." 1984. In "Behind Gains in On-the-Job Health Safety." *U.S. News & World Report*, June 11, p. 39.

Mintz, Morton, and Jerry Cohen. 1976. *Power Inc.: Public and Private Rulers and How to Make Them Accountable*. New York: Viking Press.

Newman, Donald J. 1953. "Public Attitudes Toward a Form of White-Collar Crime." *Social Problems* 4:228–232.

"Paying for Price Fixing." 1988. *Washington Post*, May 20, p. A16.

Preston, Ivan. 1975. *The Great American Blow Up: Puffery in Advertising and Selling*. Madison: University of Wisconsin Press.

Quinney, Earl R. 1964. "The Study of White-Collar Crime: Toward a Reorientation in Theory and Research." *Journal of Criminal Law, Criminology, and Police Science* 55 (June):208–214.

Roebuck, Julian, and Robert Bruce Hunter. 1970. "Medical Quackery as Deviant Behavior." *Criminology* 8:46–52.

Rossi, Peter H., Emily Waite, Christine E. Bose, and Richard A. Berk, 1974. "The Seriousness of Crimes: Normative Structure and Individual Differences." *American Sociological Review* 39:224–237.

San Francisco Chronicle, "Harris Poll," November 23, 1983, p. A6.

Shapiro, Susan P. 1985. "The Road Not Taken: The Criminal Prosecution for White-Collar Offenders." *Law and Society Review* 19:179–211.

Simon, David R., and D. Stanley Eitzen. 1986. *Elite Deviance*, 2nd ed. Boston: Allyn & Bacon.

Smith, Richard Austin. 1961. "The Incredible Electrical Conspiracy." *Fortune* 63:132–137.

Sutherland, Edwin H. 1924. *Principles of Criminology.* Philadelphia: J. B. Lippincott.

Sutherland, Edwin H. 1940. "White-Collar Criminality." *American Sociological Review* 5 (February):1–12.

Sutherland, Edwin H. 1949. *White-Collar Crime.* New York: Holt, Rinehart & Winston.

Sutherland, Edwin H. 1956. "Crime in Corporations." In Albert K. Cohen, Alfred R. Lindesmith, and Karl Schuessler, eds., *The Sutherland Papers.* Bloomington: Indiana University Press.

Sutherland, Edwin H. 1983. *White-Collar Crime: The Uncut Version.* New Haven, Conn.: Yale University Press.

Sutherland, Edwin H., and Donald R. Cressey. 1978. *Criminology,* 10th ed. Philadelphia: J. B. Lippincott.

Tatro, Charlotte H. 1974. "Cross My Palm with Silver: Fortune-Telling as an Occupational Way of Life." In Clifton D. Bryant, ed., *Deviant Behavior.* Chicago: Rand McNally.

U.S. Bureau of the Census. 1984. *Statistical Abstract of the United States 1984,* 10th ed. Washington, D.C.: U.S. Government Printing Office.

"West Virginia: Life, Liberty, and the Pursuit of Coal." 1976. ABC News Special.

Wheeler, Stanto, David Weisburd, and Nancy Bode. 1982. "Sentencing the White-Collar Offender." *American Sociological Review* 47:641–659.

Whitehurst, Carol. 1974. "The Quack as Healer: A Study in Doctor-Patient Interaction." In Jerry Jacobs, ed., *Deviance: Field Studies and Self-Disclosure.* Palo Alto, Calif.: National Press Books.

Young, James Harvey. 1967. *The Medical Messiahs.* Princeton, N.J.: Princeton University Press.

Zietz, Dorothy. 1981. *Women Who Embezzle or Defraud: A Study of Convicted Felons.* New York: Praeger.

CHAPTER 10

Bunker, Edward. 1979. "A Junkie View of the Quagmire." In Jerome H. Skolnick and Elliott Currie, eds., *Crisis in American Institutions,* 4th ed. Boston: Little, Brown.

Clark, Alexander L., and Jack P. Gibbs. 1965. "Social Control: A Reformulation." *Social Problems* 12:398–415.

Durkheim, Emile. 1966. *The Rules of Sociological Method.* New York: Free Press. (First published in 1895, trans. Sarah A. Solovay and John H. Mueller; ed. George E. Catlin.)

Gibbs, Jack P. 1977. "Social Control, Deterrence, and the Morally Committed." *Social Forces* 56:408–423.

Kondracke, Morton M. 1988. "Don't Legalize Drugs." *The New Republic,* June 27, pp. 16–19.

Marx, Gary T. 1981. "Ironies of Social Control: Authorities as Contributors to Deviance Through Escalation, Nonenforcement, and Covert Facilitation." *Social Problems* 28:221–246.

Mead, G. H. 1928. "The Psychology of Punitive Justice." *American Journal of Sociology* 23:577–602.

Sherman, Lawrence W., and Richard A. Berk. 1984. "The Specific Deterrent Effects of Arrest for Domestic Assault," *American Sociological Review* 49 (April):261–272.

Szasz, Thomas S. 1985. *Ceremonial Chemistry: The Ritual Persecution of Drugs, Addicts, and Pushers*, rev. ed. Holmes Beach, Fla.: Learning Publications.

Weber, Max. 1958. *The Protestant Ethic and the Spirit of Capitalism.* New York: Charles Scribner's. (First published in 1904/1905, trans. Talcott Parsons.)

Weber, Max. 1978. In Guenther Roth and Claus Wittich, eds., *Economy and Society: An Outline of Interpretative Sociology.* Berkeley: University of California Press. (First published in 1921.)

Index

Credits

CHAPTER 2

Campus Gays. 1984. Letter to the Editor. *Virginia Gazette*. November 17. Reprinted with permission of the *Virginia Gazette*. **(p. 27)**

Marcus, Ruth. 1986. "Sodomy Ruling's Implications Extend Far Beyond Bedroom." *The Washington Post*. July 2. Reprinted with permission of *The Washington Post*. **(p. 30)**

Greenia, George D. 1984. "Homosexuality and the Judeo-Christian Tradition." Public lecture. February 6. Reprinted with permission of George D. Greenia. **(p. 34)**

CHAPTER 5

Humphreys, Laud. 1975. *Tearoom Trade*. Hawthorne, N.Y.: Aldine de Gruyter. Copyright © 1970, 1975 by R. A. Laud Humphreys. Reprinted with permission of Aldine de Gruyter, a division of Walter de Gruyter, Inc. **(pp. 76–77, 89)**

Hanson, Bill, George Beschner, James M. Walters, and Elliott Bovelle. Editors. 1985. *Life with Heroin*. Lexington, Mass.: Lexington Books. Copyright 1985 D.C. Heath & Co. Reprinted with permission of Lexington Books, D.C. Heath & Co. **(pp. 78–79)**

Inciardi, James A. 1986. *The War on Drugs*. Palo Alto, Calif.: Mayfield Publishing Company. Reprinted with permission of Mayfield Publishing Company. **(pp. 90–91)**

CHAPTER 6

Daily Press. 1985. November 3. Reprinted with permission of the *Daily Press,*, Newport News, Va. (**p. 103**)

Carmen, Arlene, and Howard Moody. 1985. *Working Women.* New York: Harper & Row. Copyright © 1985 by Judson Memorial Church. Reprinted with permission of Harper & Row, Publishers, Inc. (**pp. 105–111**)

Diana, Lewis. 1985. *The Prostitute and Her Clients.* Springfield, Ill.: Charles C Thomas. Reprinted with permission of Charles C Thomas, Publisher. (**pp. 114–115, 119–120, 121, 122**)

CHAPTER 8

Athens, Lonnie H. 1980. *Violent Criminal Acts and Actors.* Boston: Routledge & Kegan Paul Ltd. (**pp. 161–162, 172, 176, 183**)

Wideman, John Edgar. 1984. *Brothers and Keepers.* New York: Henry Holt. Copyright © 1984 by John Edgar Wideman. Reprinted with permission of Henry Holt and Company, Inc. (**p. 169**)

Straus, Murray A. 1980 "A Sociological Perspective on the Causes of Family Violence." In Maurice R. Green. Editor. *Violence and the Family.* Boulder, Colo.: Westview Press. Reprinted with permission of Maurice R. Green. (**pp. 184, 185, 187–188**)

CHAPTER 9

Coleman, James W. 1989. *The Criminal Elite.* New York: St. Martin's Press. Copyright © 1985. Reprinted with permission of St. Martin's Press, Incorporated. (**pp. 191, 200, 201, 208, 209, 216**)

Simon, David R., and D. Stanley Eitzen. 1986. *Elite Deviance,* 2nd ed. Needham Heights, Mass.: Allyn and Bacon. Reprinted with permission of Allyn and Bacon. (**pp. 190–191, 197–198**)

Whitehurst, Carol. 1974. "The Quack as Healer." In Jerry Jacobs. *Deviance.* Palo Alto, Calif.: Mayfield Publishing Company. Reprinted with permission of Jerry Jacobs. (**pp. 205–206**)

CHAPTER 10

Szasz, Thomas S. 1985. *Ceremonial Chemistry.* Revised Edition. Edsel L. Erickson and Danna Downing. Editors. Holmes Beach, Fla.: Learning Publications. Reprinted with permission of Learning Publications, Inc. (**p. 227**)

ENDNOTES

Stinchcombe, Arthur L. 1968. *Constructing Social Theories.* Orlando, Fla.: Harcourt Brace Jovanovich. Figure 3.7. Copyright © 1968 by Harcourt Brace Jovanovich, Inc. Reprinted with permission of Harcourt Brace Jovanovich, Inc. (**diagram, p. 235**)